THE DRAMA OF SOCIAL LIFE

For Richard Schechner
Friend and Founder

THE DRAMA OF SOCIAL LIFE

JEFFREY C. ALEXANDER

polity

First published in 2017 by Polity Press

Polity Press
65 Bridge Street
Cambridge CB2 1UR, UK

Polity Press
350 Main Street
Malden, MA 02148, USA

ISBN-13: 978-1-5095-1812-8
ISBN-13: 978-1-5095-1813-5(pb)

A catalogue record for this book is available from the British Library.

Typeset in 10.5 on 12 pt Sabon by
Servis Filmsetting Ltd, Stockport, Cheshire
Printed and bound in the UK by CPI Group (UK) Ltd, Croydon, CR0 4YY

The publisher has used its best endeavours to ensure that the URLs for external websites referred to in this book are correct and active at the time of going to press. However, the publisher has no responsibility for the websites and can make no guarantee that a site will remain live or that the content is or will remain appropriate.

Every effort has been made to trace all copyright holders, but if any have been inadvertently overlooked the publisher will be pleased to include any necessary credits in any subsequent reprint or edition.

For further information on Polity, visit our website: politybooks.com

CONTENTS

PREFACE AND ACKNOWLEDGMENTS

In this volume, I bring together, and slightly revise, some recent contributions to cultural pragmatics. These studies of social performance cast a wide empirical net and advance a theoretical framework that is also being ably developed by others. I have been fortunate to receive stimulating feedback from early presentations of these chapters in various milieus. Students and colleagues at Yale were critical for their preparation. I would especially like to express my gratitude to Anne Marie Champagne and Denise Ho (Chapter 1), Mira Debs and Omar Mumallah (Chapter 2), Christine Slaughter and Alex de Branco (Chapter 4), and Christopher Grobe (Chapter 5). Nadine Amalfi, Administrator of Yale's Center for Cultural Sociology, provided invaluable clerical assistance. I thank the following publishers for permission to reprint:

The Paris Review for Ernest Hemingway, "The Art of Fiction," No. 21, interviewed by George Plimpton, Spring 1958, No. 18. (Epigraph)

TDR (*The Drama Review*) for "Seizing the Stage: Mao, MLK, and Black Lives Matter," 61/1, 2016, and "Performance and Politics: President Obama's Dramatic Reelection in 2012," 60/4, 2016. (Chapters 1 and 3)

Bloomsbury Academic for *Performative Revolution in Egypt*, 2011. (Chapter 2)

International Journal of Politics, Culture and Society for "Dramatic Intellectuals: Elements of Performance," 2016. (Chapter 4)

Theory, Culture & Society for "The Fate of the Dramatic in Modern Society: Social Theory and the Theatrical Avant-Garde" 2014: 31(1), 3–24. (Chapter 5)

"Sometimes you know the story. Sometimes you make it up as you go along and have no idea how it will come out. Everything changes as it moves. That is what makes the movements which make the story."

Ernest Hemingway

INTRODUCTION: A NEW THEORY OF MODERNITY FROM RITUAL TO PERFORMANCE

Fictional and factual reports of critical episodes in modern life deploy the metaphor of drama. In his 1985 novel *White Noise*, Don DeLillo described his melancholic hero's thoughts as he witnesses the evacuation of his town in the face of a poisonous chemical cloud: "It was still dark ... Before us lay a scene of panoramic disorder ... It was like the fall of a colonial capital to dedicated rebels. A great *surging drama* with elements of humiliation and guilt."[1] In 2016, the *New York Times* described how the lives of Khizr and Ghazala Khan had become an "an American moment":

> For years, [they] had lived a rather quiet existence of common obscurity in Charlottesville, Va. And then the Khans stepped into a sports arena in Philadelphia and left as household names. In a passionate speech at the DNC [Democratic National Convention], the bespectacled Mr. Khan stingingly criticized Donald J. Trump and his stance on Muslim immigration ... Quickly enough, both Khans felt the verbal lashings of Mr. Trump ... And just like that, they found themselves a pivot point in the *twisting drama* that is American politics.[2]

Identifying an event as dramatic heightens tension and creates anticipation. It turns everyday events into performances, readers into audiences, and ordinary actors into characters, protagonists and antagonists whose struggles drive a churning plot through scene after scene. Everybody knows what drama is. It's what goes on in theaters, movies, and TV. But in order to create critical moments, this aesthetic manner of framing and heightening experience is moved from the world of artifice to social reality. Doing so creates the drama of social life.

Modernity has been critically perceived, from both the left and the right, as the triumph of mechanism over meaning, a process of social

1

and cultural rationalization that produces the disenchantment of the world, a movement from ritual to record. Modern rationalization is supposed to have made myth and ritual impossible, and it is alleged that in art, as well as in life, mechanical reproduction has destroyed the aura of authenticity that makes powerful emotional experience possible. In this discourse of suspicion, such European thinkers as Marx, Nietzsche, Weber, and Benjamin come especially to mind. But one can put a more American and optimistic spin on the same narrative: with modernity, we are all can-do pragmatists, not dreamers and believers.

Yes, it is sometimes acknowledged, symbol and rhetoric can break through into modern life, but the narrative of rationalization claims such extra-rational intrusions are deployed for spectacles whose drama is empty and whose aim is merely mystification. In the spectacle societies of modernity, everything is top-down; nothing comes from the bottom up. We occupy Foucaultian subject positions; we can never be active, drama-producing agents ourselves.

The Idea of a Cultural Sociology

It was to challenge such a desiccated view of modernity that I introduced the idea of a cultural sociology three decades ago, though the contemporary field is much broader than the "strong program" vein I have been mining with students and colleagues in the years since.[3] The fundament of cultural sociology is that individuals and societies remain centrally concerned with meaning. Social dramas and theatrical forms remain at the heart of modern societies themselves. This theoretical effort has involved, in some important part, going back to the later writings of Emile Durkheim, the *fin de siècle* French sociologist who was one of sociology's founding figures. Durkheim's early and middle work, in the 1890s, promoted the standard of rationalized modernity, albeit in a markedly moralistic form. His late work, however, initiated a radical break with the standard view. The *Elementary Forms of Religious Life* conceptualized society as dependent on emotionally intense ritual, the division between sacred and profane symbols, and morally expansive solidaristic ties.[4] The late work applied this suggestive new theory to Australia's Aboriginal society, the earliest and most "primitive" form of human social organization ever recorded. Did Durkheim intend his new ideas to supply the basis for anthropology, regarded in that day as the social science of primitive societies? Or could *The Elementary Forms* be understood, instead, as

2

the first step in creating a new, alternative sociology of modernity? Was Durkheim challenging the standard view of modernity, or subtly reinforcing it?

My own interpretation of late Durkheim pointed to its wider ambition.[5] Erving Goffman's interest in contemporary ritual performances emerges from the intellectual radicalism of late Durkheim.[6] So does the thinking of more macro-oriented sociologists of contemporary ritual and civil religion, such as Edward Shils, Robert Bellah, and Randall Collins.[7] Granting the scope of Durkheim's later intellectual ambition, however, points to another, equally significant question: is his ritual theory of society really modern enough? Can the notion of a society of rituals be reconciled with the pragmatics, conflicts, fragmentations, and competing institutional powers that mark contemporary social life? Can ritual process and experience be conceptually intertwined with such phenomena, or must they be deployed – as, all too often, they were so deployed, not only by Durkheim but also by his successors – to avoid coming to terms with them?

To think clearly about this problem, it is necessary to ask another fundamental question: what is the difference between ritual and performance? This was exactly the question posed by the neo-Durkheimian anthropologist Victor Turner when he met the avant-garde dramaturge Richard Schechner forty some years ago. From this encounter, Schechner moved to theorize social rituals as secular performances, and vice versa.[8] Schechner's idea was that we could capture the worthwhile in late Durkheim, and avoid its pitfalls, by thinking of modern life as resting upon social performances rather than rituals per se.[9] If this is so, then social theory needs to incorporate ideas from the practice and philosophy of drama. That Turner wholeheartedly agreed is reflected in the title of his last book, *From Ritual to Theatre*.[10]

The Cultural Pragmatics of Social Performance

These converging insights have been central to my efforts to theorize the cultural pragmatics of social performance, the fulcrum of which is the continuity and tension between ritual and performance.[11] I have argued that social theorists must use the tools of dramaturgy, drama theory, and theater criticism to develop a cultural sociology of social performance and, with it, a new sociology of modernity. I conceptualize ritual as a particular kind of social performance, a highly "successful" one in which actors, audience, and script become

3

fused. Those watching the performance don't see it as a performance; they identify with the protagonists and experience enmity toward the antagonists on stage; they lose their sense of being an audience, experiencing not artificiality but verisimilitude. The fourth wall of drama, which exists not only inside the theater but outside in society, breaks down, or is broken through.

Rituals become less frequent as societies become more modern. In the course of social and cultural evolution, such fused performances become more difficult to pull off. If we analytically differentiate the elements of social performance, then we can understand how they have slowly but ineluctably become defused over the course of time.[12] For the first 90,000 years of human history, social life was organized inside small face-to-face collectivities, like the bands and tribes of Durkheim's Australian Aborigines. In these simplified and intimate contexts, mounting symbolic performances was not particularly challenging. People understood their social world as anchored by truthful myth and amplified cosmos. Rituals dramatized such legends. The props and stages for such ceremonies were the stuff of everyday social life, and participants and audience members were interchangeable. With the Neolithic revolution some 10,000 years ago, and the movement away from hunting and gathering to domestic cultivation, class societies emerged. Centralized states formed to administer more complex social structures, acting on behalf of tiny elites sequestered from the working masses. In the post-primitive archaic societies of kings, pharaohs, czars, and emperors, collective rituals were not nearly so participatory and inclusive. They seemed more like performances, like spectacles contrived to project ideological meanings to an audience at one remove.

The invention of writing intensified this defusion of the elements of social performance.[13] The narratives and classifications forming the basis for symbolic performance were transformed from primordial myth to humanly created scripts, like the Easter plays of medieval Europe or the Dionysian festivals of the ancient Greeks. The objectification of social meaning into written scripts, whether sacred or secular, separated the background representations that informed the social performances from both actors and audiences. Writing created a new category of specialists, keepers of sacred scrolls whose concern was to ensure correct symbolic interpretation. Were the social figures performing ceremonial scripts doing so in the correct way? Only specialists in textual interpretation had the credibility to say. Such mediation gave birth not only to conservative and dissenting theologians but also to intellectuals; both created heterodoxies and new symbolic forms.[14]

Theologians, religious dissenters, and intellectuals were the first critics.[15] Consider Confucius and Machiavelli. Each emerges amidst the breakdown of fused rituals inside steeply hierarchical societies. Their writings addressed the question of how social authorities could sustain legitimacy in precarious times, not only with elites but with the masses. They advised emperors and princes and aristocrats about presenting themselves to others in order to gain performative effect, how to modulate social representations in such a manner that the rent seams of social order could be sewn back together again. Gentry and mass were audiences that elites made assiduous efforts to persuade. Thus were state ceremonies deployed with dramatic intent on occasions great and small.

The emergence of theaters gave to the growing "artificiality" of social drama an aesthetic form, crystallizing the defusion of the elements of performance. Theater is a conscious and pragmatic effort to create dramatic effect – via art. The metaphysical props of ancient ritual are kicked away, but the performative challenge remains. Theater aims to re-fuse the disparate elements of performance – to overcome the distance between actor and script, performance and audience. In the West, we locate the transition from ritual to theater in the transition from the Dionysian performances of Thespius to Greek drama in the fifth century BCE. Dionysian rituals were proto-performances. On the one hand, they evoked an unquestioned cosmic order; on the other, they acknowledged the contingency of its cosmological status, forming a traveling troupe whose specially formed purpose acted it out. Greek drama went one crucial step further; it was internally agonistic and overtly contrived, and its success was contingent and sharply contested, so much so that prizes were awarded for writing and acting. Greek dramas reference myth. While referencing myth, Greek dramas were not mythical themselves; by this time in Greek history, the elements of such performances had become too defused. Plato longed for re-fusion with archetypical forms, but Aristotle embraced differentiation. His *Poetics* offered a cookbook for creating dramatic effect, providing recipes for plot, for triggering cathartic connections between script and audience, for how playwrights could create sympathy for the suffering on stage.

When this movement toward social and cultural complexity moved backward to simpler and less developed social structure in medieval times, drama as theater disappeared. Cosmological, religious rituals became, once again, the only dramatic forms on offer. Western theater re-emerges in the Renaissance, with Shakespeare and Molière. As Richard McCoy explains, it was because of "the imperfect and tenuous relationship of actor and audience" – performative defusion – that the extraordinary dramatic effect of Shakespeare's plays depended not on religious but on secular, poetic faith.

> Why do his plots seem so compelling, and how do his characters come to seem more real than the people sitting around us in the theater? ... Recent scholarship has tended to sidestep and confuse these questions by conflating religious and theatrical faith and focusing on the plays' theological contexts [but] faith in Shakespeare [is] more theatrical and poetic than spiritual, about our belief in theater's potent but manifest illusions rather than faith in God or miracles.[16]

The newly aesthetic approach to performance, which for the first time fully comprehended drama as theater, emerged during the same historical periods as new social possibilities for inserting collectively organized dramatic action into political life. Theater appears roughly at the same time as the political public sphere – the polis in ancient Greece, the city-state in the Renaissance. If theater contrives to dramatize compulsive emotional conflict, so do publicly organized political movements strive to dramatize urgent social conflicts, to publicly demand political and economic reform. Theater and political movements both project meaning toward distant audiences via more and less artfully constructed symbolic performance.

Such performances – the defused, conflicted, and fragmented social conditions that challenge them, the new forms of cultural and emotional identification they may inspire – are the topics of this book.

The first two chapters focus on social movements that have aimed at radical transformation. I argue that, no matter what the economic and social urgencies fueling their base, and no matter how lucid and rational their policy ambitions, such upheavals in the human spirit must first seize the stage. In the cut and thrust of everyday life, describing Mao Zedong and Martin Luther King, Jr. (MLK) as performers might well seem playful or provocative, merely metaphorical or downright insulting. However, in the framework of a cultural sociology that focuses on the meanings of social life and that theorizes modernity as the transition from ritual to drama, thinking of these massively significant leaders as performers, and the movements they organize as powerful dramas, is simply to assert a deeply relevant social fact (Chapter 1). If Mao and the Chinese Communist Party (CCP) had not been able to dramatize economic exploitation in a manner that arrested and molded the attention of intellectuals and masses, there would have been no revolution in 1949. If MLK and the Southern Christian Leadership Conference had not been able to stage nonviolent protests that projected southern white violence to breathless northern audiences, American Apartheid would not have been legally undermined in the civil rights acts of 1964 and 1965. The same can be said of the radical, insistent, and urgent movement led by Black Lives Matter today. Racial injustice creates enormous frustration and anger, but organized protests must be scripted, acted, directed, and performed vis-à-vis skeptical audiences if justice is to be won. Injustice must be dramatized, and so must the hope for civil repair. Social media certainly facilitated the waves of BLM protests against police killings, but they did not cause them. Internet technologies are a means of symbolic production, devices that allow for the rapid circulation of performance and drama, nothing less, but nothing more.

Similarly reductionist claims about the decisive role of Internet technology were advanced to explain the remarkable uprisings that constituted the Arab Spring. Yet, as I suggest in Chapter 2, in the Egypt of 2011 social media were a double-edged sword. Cell phones and Internet did allow immediate and direct communication among planners and protestors, and presented a platform for disenfranchised citizen-audiences to talk back to political authorities in protected ways. At the same time, repressive state officials possessed the technical power to shut down Internet and cell phone communication if they so chose, and for one critical period late in the seventeen days of protest, that's exactly what they did. But this repression couldn't be sustained. Strongly felt meanings about freedom and solidarity had flowed too freely, the revolutionary script and its performance absorbed too deeply. The elements of the performance that constituted the social drama of the "January 25th Revolution" had been sewn together in an artful manner that created a powerful sense of verisimilitude and authenticity, and the performance could continue without access to social media. The stage of Tahrir Square and messages on landlines and answering machines provided means of symbolic production enough. Mubarak had the means but not the message. His script of top-down modernization couldn't compete with the call for democracy, and he possessed neither the troupe of dedicated actors nor the feeling for the Egyptian citizen-audience that would have allowed him to carry it off.

Who should exercise control over the means of symbolic communication and over whether access was restricted to the wealthy and powerful were also issues in the American presidential contest in 2012 (Chapter 3). Yet, once again, understanding such access in a narrowly material manner misses the boat. In formal democracies, if electoral outsiders mount strong performances, they can redirect discretionary spending among the middling classes, gaining funds sufficient to pay for organizational structure and commercial television time. Seeking re-election, President Obama certainly was not an outsider, but he did begin his campaign against Mitt Romney at a deficit, not only in funding but in legitimation. President Obama had spent the symbolic capital earned by candidate Obama in the historic election of 2008 and, pivoting to his re-election campaign, he was fresh out. Organizationally, the first-term president had gained an extraordinary health care reform, but symbolically he had run out of steam, robotically performing the role of the "last rational man" as newly reimagined Tea Party heroes pushed him harshly off the political stage.

How did Barack Obama pull out a smashing victory from what had appeared likely defeat? He fashioned a fresh narrative, casting himself as a civic-minded but newly sober hero and his Republican opponent as an anti-civil, elitist villain. As Obama proceeded to inhabit this new role with agility and grace, Romney appeared dull and flat-footed, going through the motions, and aloof. As the Democratic president's performance gained momentum, the campaign attracted more than enough funds to meet the practical demands of the day, purchasing sufficient amounts of commercial air time to project the reinvigorated presidential performance far and wide. The wooden facsimile "Romney" came briefly to life during the first presidential debate, as the "Obama" character seemed distracted and stumbled. The presidential persona recovered in the second and third debates, and these later plays within the play saved the day.

In these first three chapters, I note, but do not elaborate on, the element of scripting. In Chapter 4, scripts are singled out for special attention, as I suggest a new way of thinking about intellectuals whose writings inspire mass mobilization and leave massive effects on the organization of social life. Intellectuals are great not because they provide new scientific theories, but because they provide answers for the most urgent and fecund questions of meaning and motivation. Why do we suffer? Why is society arranged in such an iniquitous way? What needs to be done to make social and personal life better again? The theories of Marx, Freud, Keynes, Sartre, Rand, and Fanon powerfully and elegantly address these existential-cum-political concerns. But what made these theories socially, not only intellectually, powerful is quite another thing. The social power of intellectuals depends on their acquisition of performative power. Esoteric theories have to be simplified into action-centered scripts; action plans have to be drawn up, charismatic actors recruited, staff and followers organized and trained, detailed plans for reorganizing social life prepared, and powerful, publicly visible actions have to be put into the scene. Intellectual power is always performative, but the social power of ideas is another thing. It must be organized and displayed outside the academy, to audiences whose interests are less esoteric and more concerned with everyday life things.

In Chapter 5, I return to basic theory. Earlier I suggested that the defusion of the elements of social performances goes hand in hand with social differentiation and cultural complexity. The emergence of classes and distant states demands that performances of elite legitimacy be projected to newly distant others; the appearance of writing allows interpretive debate about the textual bases of performance. Such developments create conditions for the movement from ritual to performance. It is vitally important to recognize, however, that, even after the emergence of theater and the public sphere, the elements of performance continue to defuse. In their effort to create persuasive performances in the political public sphere, for example, US presidents hire speech writers, ministries have bevies of press secretaries, electoral debates are tightly rehearsed, and expert consultants are hired to write the scripts and direct the political *mises-en-scène*.[17]

In this final chapter, I demonstrate that performance has been subject to continuous defusion in theater as well. Once Renaissance theater emerged from ritual, the challenge of performative fusion became the subject of highly reflexive aesthetic innovation. New genres and ways of writing theatrical texts were created and acclaimed; radically different acting techniques were developed and fervently promoted; prop and stage design flourished, becoming specialties; "directors" took over the organization of theatrical production, structuring and coaxing *mises-en-scène*. These and other dramatic innovations are what have preoccupied the theatrical avant-garde. The proverbial "fourth wall" of the theater, the invisible but very real barrier separating audience from performance, must be broken down, by any means necessary, no matter how radical and shocking such innovations first seem.

In art and life, the play's the thing, and every shoulder is bent to the effort of making it succeed.

— 1 —

SEIZING THE STAGE: MAO, MLK, AND BLACK LIVES MATTER TODAY

Social protest should not be conceptualized instrumentally, as a process that depends only upon social networks and material resources. Such factors provide the boundary conditions for symbolic action, but they determine neither its content nor its outcomes. In order to seize power, one must first seize the social stage.[1]

Seizing the stage, producing social dramas, and projecting them successfully to audiences – these are difficult and contingent cultural accomplishments, even for those who possess top-down, authoritarian control. For great power to be perceived as legitimate, equally great performances need be sustained. As producers and directors, dictators try to create ideologically saturated public performances. Massive show trials, such as those produced by Stalin in the 1930s, display orchestrated confessions, which are reported by journalists and distributed in recordings and films. Tightly choreographed, ritual-like, mythopoeic, hero-evoking convocations are aesthetically reconstructed as electrifying and projected by filmmakers to millions of potential audience members beyond the immediate event. The Nazis' 1933 Nuremberg rally, for example, with its tens of thousands of Nazi worshippers in attendance, was reconstructed and ramped up by Leni Riefenstahl in her *Triumph of the Will* (1935).

To the degree that political regimes, authoritarian or democratic, allow power to be more easily challenged, to that same degree does seizing the social stage become still more difficult. In more pluralistic social situations, the elements required for a social protest to project a powerful performance that connects with audiences become separated from one another.[2] To re-fuse these elements, protest performances must be artfully assembled from scratch, from the bottom up. Supplication and inspiration, authentic and heartfelt dramas of

10

sacrifice become central. The mediation of extra-performative conditions – interpretive, material, and demographic resources – becomes significant as well.

Dramatic Radicalism in Twentieth-Century China

Revolutionary social movements tell the world that their eventual triumph is inevitable, and radical theorists conceptualize this necessity as determined by the unstoppable force of material interest. It's a very different story inside revolutionary movements, however. They are dramaturgical engines. Let Marx pretend that the revolution responds merely to objective interest, depicting workers as proto-scientists following rational, instrumental plans. Lenin knew better. Attacking the fallacy of economism, Lenin put ideology at the center of revolutionary mobilization, organizing Bolshevism as an active, pragmatic, top-down party in the service of socialist ideas.[3] Antonio Gramsci dubbed the Communist Party the "modern prince," taking his cue from Machiavelli.[4] In 1917, when Lenin's revolution succeeded, Gramsci created a double entendre banner headline, "Revolution against *Capital*" in *Avanti*, the Italian revolutionary newspaper he edited, ironically suggesting that Marx's scientific theory could never have predicted it. Gramsci knew that the revolution in Russia had succeeded not because of the laws of capital but because of the dramaturgical powers of the Bolshevik Party.[5]

The textual background and its limits

In their radical reinterpretation of Maoist strategy in the decades preceding the Chinese revolution, *Revolutionary Discourse in Mao's Republic*, David Apter and Tony Saich transformed this line of cultural Marxist thinking into a poststructuralist frame. Moving away from a reductionist, ratiocinative conception of ideology toward a Geertzian, thickly semiotic one, they conceptualize the revolutionary organizer as a storyteller, "an agent with a special ability to lift the burden of storytelling from the shoulders of the individual by enabling that person to share it with others [so that] the property of the story becomes the property of the discourse community."[6] The storyteller-in-chief of the Chinese revolution, Mao Zedong, culled "myths, stories, texts, and logical prescriptions" from Chinese and Western traditions, pulling "out of the terrible circumstances and conditions of life prevailing in China" the vision of a "utopic republic." With this vision, Mao "was able to refract and generate a field of force, at the epicenter of which he becomes a teacher."[7]

Apter and Saich are forcefully anti-materialist and anti-"rational actor," but their culturalizing account of the revolutionary process doesn't go nearly far enough. Their political discourse analysis presents the Chinese revolution as an "exegetical creation." But seeing such an extraordinary event merely as an "express embodiment of a structure of ideas" ignores the performative challenges that must be met in real time, the complex process of acting out ideas and getting an audience to believe them. "For stories to be shared with others," Apter and Saich acknowledge, "people must want to listen," but conceptualizing just how to get folks to want to listen is the thing.[8] To suggest simply "words themselves became performatives" keeps us in the dark, inside philosopher J. L. Austin's narrowly linguistic black box, where performativity is achieved by speaking itself. The dramaturgical process that sets the stage, the directing process that organizes *mises-en-scène*, the skillful creativity of actors or the lack thereof, the organizational and symbolic challenge of creating the appearance of seamless fusion between audience, actors, and animating script – all this remains to be conceived. Clearly, Mao had the ability of "communicating to listeners a feeling of privileged access to the interpretive wisdom of a mind in motion,"[9] but the communicating process, the feeling of privileged access, even the attribution of wisdom – all need attention.

Apter and Saich offer a tantalizing glimpse into the black box of dramaturgy when they situate Mao's storytelling inside the caves of Yan'an, where the Chinese Communist movement went into hiding after their "Long March" to escape the ruling Guomindang Party in 1937–38:

> Narrating the stories and writing the texts, [Mao] makes himself part of the process. Everything associated with his person also becomes significant – the long hair, the long fingers, the baggy clothes, the earthy expressions, the fact that he scratches himself with the same fingers that hold the brush. [Mao] was very careful to arrange himself to project just the image he wanted.[10]

In the end, however, Yan'an is portrayed simply as "a semiotic space" and Mao as a leader "in sole possession of an inversionary discourse capable of generating public support," an "interior system of codes, symbols, and icon" that proved "capable [of] unifying a diverse community."[11] But was discourse itself sufficient to unify a fragmented and demoralized community? What actually transpired in the caves of Yan'an? What allowed the ideological revivification process to unfold successfully? "Using metaphors and metonymies Mao creates a code," Apter and Saich argue, "that enables the narrative to endow gestures, acts, dress, dwelling and above all language and literacy with the power of signifiers."[12] But much more must also have been involved – creative, unscripted gestures and movements, props and staging, official and dissenting interpretations, unresponsive and silent audiences, but also cries of delight.

That "an individual has become assimilated into a discursive community"[13] is certainly a useful indicator of cultural-pragmatic success, but what exactly does it measure? What we need to know is how the fusion between speaker and audience is actually accomplished. It is not enough to suggest "a person has absorbed and internalized the ritual."[14] How a contingent and labile performance comes to be *regarded* as an absorptive, repetitive, and solidarizing ritual is what's empirically and heuristically at stake. For texts to be internalized, performance must be felicitous. Apter and Saich note "the revolutionaries' claim that both the [Marxist] dialectic and the system of [Maoist] ideas were always there, an enduring authenticity waiting to be perceived."[15] Claims of authenticity, however, must be dramatically redeemed.

Authenticity is not something already there, waiting to be perceived; it is an attribution made by an inspired audience. Performance is more than a matter of "people poring over the text, interpreting their experiences, and expressing themselves in public utterances that bound addresser and addressee."[16] Binding speaker and audiences is the ambition of performances. Apter and Saich make reference to such terms as "simulacrum" and "spectacle"[17] to identify acts of persuasive ideological speech, but these concepts finesse the detailed texture of social performance; they do not explain them.

Performance in theory and action

Only after performance studies began to open up the black box of discourse theory, conceptualizing the space between signifier and signified, were scholarly investigations into the Chinese revolution able to begin to make things right. "Although the 'cultural turn' in the social sciences has been underway for over a generation," Elizabeth Perry writes in her pathbreaking study *Anyuan*, "it is often conducted as discourse analysis in which writings, speeches, films, festivals, and other communicative materials are treated … as disembodied texts." What such an approach leaves "unanswered," she argues, "is the

13

question of how the revolutionaries managed to introduce such radically new messages and methods in ways that resonated with their target audience." Conceptualizing this process as "cultural positioning," Perry insists that it requires "active effort," that it "hinges as much upon the skills of the messenger as on the substance and syntax of the message itself."[18]

In the early 1920s, the south central Chinese mining town of Anyuan provided the scene of the CCP's first great organizing success. Mao Zedong visited Anyuan shortly after the party's founding. When he arrived "carrying a Hunan umbrella made of oiled paper and dressed in a long blue Mandarin gown of the sort worn by teachers," Perry recounts, it "left a deep impression upon the workers."[19] Still, Mao's wardrobe was out of kilter with his avowedly revolutionary script. The long blue Mandarin gown projected the "sight of a privileged intellectual," a character embodying "the Confucian separation between mental and manual labor" rather than somebody "anxious to interact with lowly coal miners." In contrast with his off-key clothing, the spoken language of the character Mao performed was a much better fit. "Thanks to his rural upbringing and colloquial dialect," Perry records, Mao "was able to converse easily with the workers – most of whom shared his Hunan origins." Regarding the wardrobe malfunction, Mao proved a quick study. After only a week of immersion, he had restructured his character's outfit to fit more seamlessly into the local scene: "By week's end, he had shed his scholar's gown in favor of a pair of trousers, which were more suitable for forays down into the mining pits."[20]

In November 1921, after completing this scouting mission, Mao sent his young communist protégé Li Lisan to Anyuan to begin the hard work of actually organizing a local labor movement. Whereas Mao had draped his character in the modest clothing of revolutionary asceticism, Li saw things differently. He "sashayed ostentatiously around the grimy coal mining town of Anyuan, dressed either in a long Mandarin gown or in stylish Western coat and tie, in a fashion designed to attract attention."[21] Yet, Li's "flamboyant manner" proved as "captivating to ordinary workers" as Mao's more restrained demeanor. One costuming detail of Li's was particularly noted – "the shiny metal badge that (acquired in France) he sported on his chest." The badge "generated persistent rumors of Li Lisan's invulnerability to swords and bullets," Perry tells us, adding that the Communist organizer "did nothing to dispel them."[22] The material accouterment had a performative function, connecting Li's possibly foreign-seeming ideology to a widely beloved Chinese folktale.

The shiny badge seemed to take "a cue from Elder Brother dragon heads whose authority rested upon their reputation for supernatural powers," Perry explains. By deploying this prop, "Li Lisan actively encouraged the belief that he enjoyed the magical protection of 'five foreign countries' bestowed during his travels abroad."[23]

Li did more, however, than just dress the part. He contrived to script his organizing efforts inside the dramatic forms of traditional Hunan ritual:

> To stir up greater interest in the workers' club, Li decided that the night school should host a lion dance at the time of the annual Lantern Festival [,] an occasion when the local elite sponsored exhibitions by martial arts masters, who displayed their skills and thereby attracted new disciplines in the course of performing spirited lion dances. One of Li's new recruits to the workers' club, a highly adept performer by the name of You Congnai, was persuaded to take the lead. You was a low-level chieftain in the Red Gang whose martial arts skills were second to none. He dutifully donned a resplendent lion's costume, tailor-made for this occasion by local artisans, and – to the loud accompaniment of cymbals and firecrackers – gamely pranced from the coal mine to the railway station, stopping along the way at the general headquarters of the company, the chamber of commerce, St. James Episcopal Church, the Hunan and Hubei native-place associations, and the homes of the gang chieftains to pay his respects. As intended, the performance attracted a huge and appreciative crowd, which followed the sprightly dancer back to the workers' club to learn how to enlist as his disciples. Contrary to popular expectation, however, the martial arts master announced to the assembled audience we should no longer study martial arts. Instead, we should all study diligently at the night school. Anyone interested in studying, come with us.[24]

It soon became clear that the communists had something altogether different from traditional pedagogy – whether of the Confucian literary (*wen*) or the martial arts (*wu*) variety. As lion dancer You Congnai put it to the throngs of would-be disciples: "Our teacher's home is in Liling [Li Lisan's native country, just across the provincial border in Hunan], but the ancestral founder of our school lives far, far away. To find him one must cross the seven seas. He's now more than a hundred years old and his name is Teacher Ma [Marx], a bearded grandpa."[25] Li Lisan's imaginative recruitment drive resulted in a large influx of new members to the workers' club.

While the now widely subscribed Anyuan workers' club sponsored courses, Li Lisan quickly realized that "ideologically orthodox articles and lectures ... were not always the best way to capture the workers' attention, especially when it came to the younger workers, who comprised a large percentage of the unskilled labor force at the coal mine." Organizers were "directed toward inventing livelier forms of cultural communication."[26] Six decades later, the head of the CCP's entertainment department in Anyuan during those early years explained its performative ambition:

> We often organized younger workers in the workers' club through singing, dramatic performances, cultural studies, and various recreational activities ... The renovated Anyuan workers' club had just been opened, and every week we held evening gatherings and staged plays there. Our plays had no set scripts but were self-written and self-performed ... The content included opposing the exploitation of workers by capitalists, overcoming imperialism, and defeating warlordism ... These plays drew large audiences, not only workers but also peasants from the surrounding areas.[27]

The department chief's claim that "the propaganda effects" of such performative efforts "were very good" is confirmed by the memories of an elderly worker, who, having witnessed the entertainment as a 10-year-old child, recalled the vivid atmosphere of the live performances"

> The entertainment department [of the Anyuan workers' club] organized the young people to produce and perform "civilized plays" [wen ming xil]. Whenever these were staged, the main hall of the club was packed. Gas lamps were lit. Many of the plays reflected the laboring life of the workers in the mine pits. I remember one night watching a new play inside the club about the terrible treatment of workers under the leather ships of the capitalists. It also showed how the Bearded Marx had engaged in revolutionary activity, and how the Russian working class had taken up arms to struggle against the capitalists. The plot of this drama deeply moved us all. I admired the working class for its fearless spirit of struggle [and] hope[d] that one day we too would be able to take up guns and struggle against the capitalists in the mine.[28]

In addition to such explicitly theatrical performances, the Anyuan workers' club organized the writing and staging of thirty-one "costume lectures," described by Perry as "a hybrid form of didactic entertainment that was part drama and part lecture."[29] "With moralistic titles such as 'The Road to Awakening,' 'The Evils of Prostitution and Gambling,' 'The Patriotic Bandit,' and 'Our Victory,'" Perry writes, "the costume lectures were presented in evening performances in the workers' club auditorium to enthusiastic audiences numbering a thousand or more."[30] Local opera had long been popular among Chinese villagers, and the theater and costume-lecture formats became widely deployed as CCP organizing efforts spread from such industrial cities as Anyuan to the countryside. As one worker recalled, every Sunday "the head of the workers' club … led us to nearby villages to perform." "Whenever we arrived someplace, the band members would beat drums and play trumpets and flutes to attract a crowd. Then we would perform a program after which there would be a lecture [that] was warmly welcomed by the peasants."[31]

American journalist Edgar Snow argued: "There was no more powerful weapon of propaganda in the Communist movement than the Reds' dramatic troupes." He observed that "when the Reds occupied new areas, it was the Red Theater that calmed the fears of the people, gave them rudimentary ideas of the Red program, and dispensed great quantities of revolutionary thoughts, to win the people's confidence."[32] A self-proclaimed cheerleader for the Chinese revolution, Snow's account gives the misleading impression of easy performative success. Making use of internal party documents, the historian Yung-fa Chen argues that, on the contrary, the Chinese peasantry was a tough audience to crack. Centuries of Confucian teaching gave peasants "a tolerance for poverty and injustice that amounted to unquestioning devotion to harmony and passivity."[33] The peasants were conservative; they would have to be convinced to become revolutionaries.

As Feiyu Sun demonstrates in his 2013 *Social Suffering and Political Confession*, it was this reluctant, withholding quality of peasant-audiences that triggered the CCP's "speaking bitterness" campaign.[34] The strategy began with the *Fang Pin Wen Ku* method, which translates as "to visit poor families, to inquire of their sufferings."[35] CCP work teams entered peasant villages with what Sun calls the "experience technique" in hand. They visited poor families, asking probing questions about their personal lives. This was not purely a matter of unconstrained call and response; symbolic violence was involved, and the threat of physical violence never lay far behind:

> In order to avoid the perceived and real existential danger of being classified as reactionaries, the villagers had to present the work team with a personal narrative of their suffering as poor or hired peasants. If this narrative depiction of their personal suffering and oppression was convincing enough to overcome the mandatory skepticism of the work team and cadres, they would be rewarded with the "good peasant" classification.[36]

Ostensibly, such visits were about ideology, pedagogical exercises aimed at restructuring cognition. "It was the professed aim of this dialogue," Sun writes, "to teach the peasants how to reflect upon and

17

interpret their circumstances and identity in a ready-make narrative language which the political ideology of the CCP provided."[37]

The deeper ambition of *Fang Pin Wen Ku*, however, was dramaturgical; it aimed to induce the experience of "speaking bitterness," or *Suku*. According to official documents, *Suku* referred to sharing "an oral personal history about being persecuted by class enemies ... for the purpose of inspiring class hatred in the listeners [and] reaffirming one's own class standing."[38] Sun himself provides a more elaborate, decidedly dramaturgical definition:

> *Suku* is the practice of confessing individual suffering in a political context and in a collective public forum. In Chinese, the term *Suku* means to tell of one's suffering, or to pour out one's bitterness, in public. *Su* means to tell, to speak, to pour out, or to confess, while the term *Ku* means bitterness, pain, and suffering.[39]

One party organizer described *Suku* as "the blasting fuse of the mass *Fanshen* movement."[40] In the CCP's immense land reform campaign, *Fanshen* (literally, "turning over") referred to a complex organizational effort that moved peasants from tolerant fatalism to angry activism.

In William Hinton's monumental, rose-colored reconstruction of the land reform campaign in Long Bow village in 1948, he documents peasants' fearful reluctance to take aggressive action against landlords, and party cadres' determined efforts to retrain them. Despite Hinton's insistence that his account is realistic and documentarian, he implicitly employs a performative frame in his description of CCP efforts to expose landowners who had collaborated with Japanese occupiers:

> T'ien-ming called all the active young cadres and militiamen of Long Bow together and announced to them the policy of the county government, which was to confront all enemy collaborators and their backers at public meetings, expose their crimes, and turn them over to the country authorities for punishment ... The young men agreed to conduct a public meeting of the whole population the very next day. And so it was that Kuo Te-yu, running dog of the landlords, informer, torturer, grafter, and enemy stooge, found himself standing before a crowd of several hundred stolid peasants whom he had betrayed ... As the silent crowd contracted toward the spot where the accused man stood, T'ien-ming stepped forward. "Comrades, countrymen ... This is our chance. Remember how we were oppressed. The traitors seized our property and kicked us ... Let us speak out the bitter memories of the past. Let us see that the blood debt is repaid" ... The peasants were listening to every word but gave no sign as to how they felt ... No one moved and

18

no one spoke. "Come now, who has evidence against this man?" Again there was silence. Kuei-ts'ai, the new vice-chairman of the village, found it intolerable. He jumped up, struck Kuo Te-yu on the jaw with the flat of his hand. "Tell the meeting how much you stole," he demanded. The blow jarred the ragged crowd. It was as if an electric spark had tensed every muscle. Not in living memory had any peasant ever struck an official. A gasp, involuntary and barely audible, came from the people and above it a clear sharp "Ah" from an old man's throat. [But] the people in the square [still] waited, fascinated, as if watching a play. They did not realize that in order for the plot to unfold they themselves had to mount the stage and speak out what was on their minds.[41]

At the core of *Fanshen* was *Suku*, one of the Chinese revolution's most original and compelling social-cum-cultural inventions. In the course of village visits, party cadres located people whom they considered "exemplary narrators," proceeding to train them in emotionally arousing and confession-inducing storytelling techniques. With this well-rehearsed cast of political actors in hand, mass meetings were organized to let "suffering draw out suffering."[42] "An exemplary speaker during a *Suku* meeting would first touch the listeners emotionally," Sun explains, "to make them empathize with the *Suku* speaker's feelings – to feel sad listening to a story of misery and hardship and to feel hatred and outrage toward the speaker's persecutors and exploiters."[43] A handbook distributed by the CCP's People's Liberation Army in 1947, with the title *Suku and Revenge: Suku Education's Experience and Method*, offers detailed advice to CCP organizers about writing the script, setting the stage, preparing the audience, and gaining dramatic effect:

> All the people listening should feel and share in the suffering till everybody cries bitterly ... From suffering to pain, and from pain to hatred. The more suffering, the more pain, the more pain, the more hatred, and the more hatred the more powerful ... Use tasks such as preparing the *Suku* setting, organizing memorial ceremonies, preparing forms for recording revenge ... Create an atmosphere of suffering that is persuasive ... The following message of political consciousness should be instilled: The poor, all under the heavens, are all suffering; and the poor in this world are all one big family; we are brothers and sisters, and we should unite together to save ourselves, to abolish the roots of class exploitation and repression.[44]

Such cadre-organized dramas often seemed successful, producing political catharsis on a massive scale. An internal report, "Poor Peasants' Suku Assembly," also prepared in 1947, described what transpired during the Land Reform movement when "every district

19

started practicing Suku."[45] Despite its self-promotion and pseudo-numeracy, the cadre issued a report that strikingly illustrates their performative ambition and gives some indication of the scope of *Suku*'s dramatic success:

> In the Suku assembly in the town of Chengguan, after only one person's Suku, all those peasants had already started bellowing and to cry. Some people went back home, where the whole family again cried bitterly together ... According to incomplete statistics, there were 5184 peasants who did Suku in the whole of the year. 4551 of them cried bitterly during Suku ... There were 323 peasants speaking their bitterness about starvation; 546 speaking their bitterness about begging for food; 115 speaking their bitterness about scattered family; 116 speaking their bitterness about relatives being killed by bandits ... In the Suku Movement, cadres and people become one family; cadres felt an aching to see the people's crying; people persuaded the cadres to stop crying. People said: "This is the Communist Party! The Communist Party is also our poor!"[46]

While this discussion of *Suku* focuses on its performative deployment before the 1949 revolution, the same dramaturgical structure functioned as a powerful organizing tool with which Maoism sought to shape the self-perception and emotions of the masses after the revolution as well. The Cultural Revolution of the 1960s, for example, was fueled by the "*recalling* bitterness" campaign, which treated the pre-revolutionary episodes of speaking bitterness, not as performances, but as objective descriptions. Guo Wu documents how "individual memories of the formerly oppressed were gradually teased out by the Chinese socialist state to construct a class-based collective memory of the pre-1949 'old China' [that] aimed at reenacting class struggle and reinforcing class awareness by invoking collective memory."[47]

Past expressions of bitterness not only became the articulation of individual and collective memories, but also involved rituals and performance, and thus was successfully incorporated into the larger institution of propaganda and Chinese popular culture.[48] As a result, all depictions of the old society were dissociated from "objective realities" and became "representational realities."[49]

> The party-state sought to indoctrinate students through face-to-face oral reports by older people that emphasized their suffering before Liberation [in order] to educate students so that they would not forget the past ... Turning a personal, bitter story of an older person into a public political asset was the essence of the recalling-bitterness sessions around the country ... Selecting the right person to speak and creating the appropriate theatrical atmosphere was crucial to the success of

20

recalling bitterness and evoking emotional responses from the audience. ... Trained peasant orators would gulp wordlessly in pain when their narrations reached a climax ... The ability to touch the audience was the main criterion in selecting speakers. After being chosen, the speakers were trained further to ensure they were eloquent, emotional, and able to cry easily ... Many memoirs of the Cultural Revolution's sent-down youths, written in the 1980s and 1990s, recall how formerly urban students were re-educated by old peasants about past bitterness.[50]

The Chinese were able to make revolution, not because their Communist Party provided truthful information that responded to objective class interests, but rather because it forged a revolutionary art of protest that fused producers, scripts, actors, scenes, and audiences. The revolutionary drama may have seemed to exude realism and verisimilitude, but it worked to combine aesthetic and moral power in a manner that made it sublime.[51]

Civil Rights Protest in Mid-Twentieth-Century America: A New Social Actor

While revolutionary organizations need to be artful, they often possess levers of coercive power via party or state control, such that symbolic violence "adds value" to the dramatic power of ideological scripts. Bottom-up protests by relatively powerless movements have no such performative advantage, so the felicity of such protests becomes that much more difficult to sustain.

Consider, for example, the African American civil rights movement in the 1950–60s. A century earlier, the Civil War (1861–65) had abolished slavery, but with the end of Reconstruction, just a dozen years after northern victory, further black emancipation was blocked. Southern blacks became encaged by a caste system, even as blacks in the northern United States, a growing population, remained stigmatized and disempowered. In the 1950s and 1960s, an extraordinary social movement challenged this system of domination, achieving a great, if still only partial triumph.

In recent decades, social scientists have tended to interpret the civil rights movement as a struggle over "naked power,"[52] a strategic battle between southern blacks and their southern white oppressors for control over material resources.[53] In my own work, I've proposed an alternative explanation. Certainly, the civil rights movement was an effort to remove the barriers blocking black access to state power. But because of a complex mixture of racial fears and democratic politics, the movement's struggle to gain such power could be neither violent nor even implicitly coercive. The movement could have recourse only to persuasion. Aiming at influence, not power, it generated symbolic dramas, projecting them not to white southern state power, but to the audience of northern whites.[54]

This was not the direction in which the civil rights movement ostensibly aimed its message. Civil rights mobilizations seemed to be directed at southern institutions, but their real audience was a "third party," the white citizens who were watching this confrontation in the North. As opposed to the immediate audience of southern whites, civil rights campaigns seemed weak and, indeed, they were most often defeated. A few white southerners had their eyes opened, but the great majority was unmoved and turned away.

Modern audiences are dispersed, layered, and fragmented. Performers cannot hope to connect with all of them at the same time. Martin Luther King *publicly* claimed that nonviolent tactics were designed to persuade southern whites, appealing to their Christian and democratic hearts. As those inside the movement's leadership knew full well, however, King's tactics were actually designed to produce quite a different effect. True enough, King's thinking about nonviolence had come from his study of another master of the art of civil protest, Mahatma Gandhi. Gandhi believed that iterative performances of *satyagraha* – "insistence on truth" – would eventually soften imperial hearts and change British minds. But what worked for late imperial Britain was not felicitous in the America of Jim Crow. The racism of most southern whites, elite and mass, was far too ingrained for them to be responsive to Satyagraha of an African American kind. Despite his Christian idealism, King knew this in his bones. He had grown up in this South, but he had studied for his doctorate in New England. It was the Satyagraha of northern whites that King had in mind.[55]

From Frederick Douglass to Harriet Tubman to W. E. B. Du Bois, the leaders of African American protests were social actors who had a flare for the dramatic and could command the public stage. Though often sharply differing in ideology and ambition, all these leaders shared one, all-important capacity. They possessed an intuitive feeling for the American *collective conscience*, both white and black. They grasped what, in Saussure's terminology, might be called the American *langue*, the cultural language that set the background for the civil right movement's *paroles*, the speech acts by which African American movements engaged and protested against their oppressive social worlds, the strategic scripts they projected not only to fellow blacks but also to whites in the civil surround.

The deep cultural languages shared by black and white Americans were formed by secular strains of anti-authoritarian republican and liberal thought, alongside the religious themes of prophetic Christianity. Blacks identified with Jews in Pharaonic Egypt, seeing their own fate and possibility in the Exodus story. Whites traced their national mission to the rebellion against King George III, and in post-revolutionary times saw themselves locked in a battle for democracy against European aristocracy, empire, and despotism. During the first three centuries of the American experiment, however, racism prevented whites from identifying their own emancipation narrative with the black struggle for freedom. Only gradually, with the emergence of such persuasive African American performers as Douglass, Tubman, and Du Bois, and such publicizing organizations as the National Association for the Advancement of Colored People (NAACP), did the potential for such mutual identification develop.

A highly educated, deeply religious, personally gutsy, and preternaturally gifted dramaturge, the Reverend Martin Luther King set up southern whites as the ostensible audience for civil rights protests. In the actual practice of his protest dramas, however, King turned southern whites into mere foils. He transformed them from real enemies into imagined ones, larger than life figures in a morality play that he designed, scripted, and choreographed, in which he himself played the leading activist role. Time and time again, such movement dramas subverted southern white powers by seducing them to play the anti-democratic role of anti-Christ in their civil religious scripts.

When Rosa Parks refused to move to the back of the bus in Montgomery, Alabama, in December 1955, her courageous action had the appearance of a spontaneous individual protest. In fact, the move had long been planned by the local chapter of the NAACP, where Parks herself served as secretary. What could not be known beforehand, however, was that the choice to lead the upheaval that ensued would be a new arrival in the local ministry, a young preacher named Martin Luther King.

Sustaining the nonviolent Montgomery bus boycott over twelve long months required that a wide range of performances be fused felicitously together. The success of the protest depended on a tightly knit production team, a rigorous back stage rehearsal of civil actors, continuous direction of the unfolding *mises-en-scène*, scripting supple enough to maintain dramatic plotting and moral clarity through unpredictable ups and downs, and enough material power to provide thousands of financially straitened black people with private transportation, bail to get out of jail, and legal representation.[56] The social drama also required a heroic leading actor, one who could present himself as fearless in the face of police-state levels of repression and who was capable rhetorically of inspiring fervent emotional identification and moral inspiration.[57]

Not only did King project the black protest script locally, to the black masses who were cast and chorus for the Montgomery movement, but also nationally, to northern citizens, via white reporters powerfully affected by the transcendent notes struck by King in his civil religious script: "This bus situation was the precipitating factor, but there is something much deeper. There is deep determination ... to rise up against these oppressive forces."[58] Citing King's ringing declaration that "one of the glories of America" was "the right to protest for right," *Newsweek*, an influential weekly magazine at the time, framed the Montgomery protest in civil rather than racial or economic terms. After the success of the boycott, *Time* magazine put King on its cover, describing him as "what many a Negro – and, were it not for his color, many a white – would like to be."[59]

Montgomery was the first act in a series of protest events that steadily ramped up dramatic tension, a decades-long social drama that plotted the victory of civil good over anti-civil evil. There were the fraught, vividly reported lunch counter sit-ins of 1960, where wave after wave of nonviolent student protestors were arrested and jailed. There were the murderously risky Freedom Rides in 1961, which were met with horrendous beatings and were televised on the nightly news as courageous protests against criminal brutality.

When white police with their fire hoses and ferocious dogs attacked black school children in Birmingham, Alabama in the summer of 1964, it became a drama that captured and outraged the northern civil imagination as never before; and when, one year later, Alabama state police shot nonviolent marchers determined to cross a bridge in Selma, the drama aroused the deepest moral anxiety, exploding throughout the northern collective consciousness.[60] Movement leaders had chosen Birmingham and Selma precisely because they knew that the white leaders in these towns were particularly prone to racist outbursts and anti-democratic displays; and the protest events were scripted, rehearsed, choreographed, and artfully controlled throughout unfolding *mises-en-scène*. Yet, as Coleridge explained, the artifice of drama can never allow itself to be seen: dramatic effect depends upon the willing suspension of disbelief. Although Southern whites dismissed civil rights protests as trumped-up hype, white northern audiences viewed them as authentic and deeply sincere, as powerful dramatizations of the moral truth of racial oppression.

24

As northern whites witnessed these unfolding acts of the civil rights drama in what, thanks to television news, seemed like real time, their sentimental sympathy for the "lost cause" of southern whites gradually evaporated. "We have never ... scattered our efforts," King confided to a journalist in 1964, "but have focused upon specific symbolic objectives."[61] Symbolic power, King understood, has real effects. Empathizing with the black protagonists, not their southern white opponents, northern citizen-audiences demanded federal power be deployed to protect powerless blacks and punish their white oppressors. In 1964 and 1965, Congress, acting in the aftermath of JFK's assassination, abolished segregation laws and passed legislation enabling black civil and political rights. Northern state power invaded the states of the old Confederacy. Many called it the second Reconstruction.

"Black Lives Matter" in Twenty-first-Century America

The 1950s–60s civil rights movement was American focused, but it also inspired a global collective imaginary, projecting tableaux beyond local scenes to hundreds of millions who connected with the performances from outside. It initiated a narrative arc, a sequential iteration of utopian social performance that, over subsequent decades, became a deeply engrained culture structure, not only in the United States but also in global civil society.

The utopian ideal of civil solidarity sits uneasily in a world of social inequality, stigma, and repression.[62] Dissatisfaction with existing social arrangements is chronic, and the civil sphere is restless. Episodes of liminality, and social dramas demanding civil repair, are the periodic result: the Solidarity movement in Poland, the People Power Revolution in the Philippines, Velvet Revolutions in Central and Eastern Europe, Tiananmen Square, Barack Obama, the Arab Spring, the Occupy movement, the Umbrella protest in Hong Kong. Some of these movements succeeded in taking state power; they all generated extraordinary symbolic force. They were felicitous political dramas played out in the public arena, in their own locales and before the larger audience of "all humankind."[63]

In the final section of this chapter, however, I am concerned not with such global ramifications, nor the past few decades, but with a new civil rights movement that has only recently emerged on the American scene, Black Lives Matter. The iterative performances of the mid-century civil rights movement left behind a deeply ingrained culture structure, an intensely redolent set of background representations upon which later black protests felt compelled to draw. But, as I hope I have made clear, there is an enormous distance between background representations – the culture structures that provide the *langue* for symbolic action – and the concrete performances situated in time and space, which are informed by them. The latter are like pragmatic speech acts rather than emanations of cultural structures, and they require each of the other elements of performance to be brought into play.

Between the black protest tradition as crystallized in the mid-twentieth century and the conditions of poor black inhabitants of the inner cities in the early twenty-first century, there loomed the enormous challenge of forging new action-oriented scripts. These scripts would also have to be made to walk and talk, informing dramatic scenes that could appeal to, energize, and in some part unify citizen-audiences fragmented by race and class and demoralized by political fatalism. There would also have to be strong leaders, dramaturges who could produce protest performances and directors who could manage their *mises-en-scène*. Successfully fusing audience, script, and actors would require, as well, access to the means of symbolic production; sympathetic interpretation of ongoing performances by critics, such as journalists and intellectuals; and sufficient leverage vis-à-vis material power to prevent states from blocking performances via repression.

These disparate elements have, indeed, been brought into place by the black movement against police violence that has gathered force since 2012. Extraordinary creativity was needed to create each performative element. Skill, fortitude, and *fortuna* were required to weave them together into the iterative sequence that has allowed African Americans, once again, to seize the nation's political stage.

The underclass becomes an acting subject

By the time the Black Lives Matter movement was formed, it had been decades since African Americans had been able to do so. If the victory of the mid-century civil rights movement had been decisive, it was also partial. The gates of the ghetto had been pried loose for African American workers, clerks, professionals, and businessmen.[64] Yet, although their freedom of movement was vastly expanded, such groups remained subject to far-reaching racial stigma.[65] When they left the ghetto, the uneducated, unskilled, and unemployed were left behind, in the inner city. A racial underclass formed, an often desperate admixture of a dominated class and the residue of a still despised

26

race. Racial and class prejudice built a cultural fence around this inner-city group; politicians, real estate agents, courts, police, and prisons exercised controls of an administrative, coercive, and material kind. [66] Young black males especially were incarcerated at alarmingly high rates, often for acts that would not lead to imprisonment if the perpetrators had been white.

Working- and middle-class African Americans had peopled the twentieth-century movement for civil rights, supplying crucial cultural capital. They brought education and professional skills to the task of protest, and the black church, with its powerful bonding and bridging institutions, provided not only generalized trust but protected spaces within which public performances could be rehearsed. [67] These kinds of resources were not nearly as available to the new racial underclass, however; so its capacity for exercising political agency was severely curtailed.

In principle, if not in practice, the potential for social protest on behalf of the underclass remained, along with the possibility of leveraging widespread social criticism into civil repair of the institutions that have sustained its depredation. Despite fissures, contradictions, weak-kneed liberalism, and conservative backlash, the civil sphere in the United States remains potentially empowering, its ideals and institutions on call if the right social arrangements can be made. To create such arrangements requires a performatively powerful social movement, one that can so effectively dramatize underclass suffering that new networks of meaning can form between marginalized racial groups excluded from the civil sphere and the core groups who occupy secure and influential places within it.

In the years since 2012, such a performatively powerful black civil rights movement began taking shape. Police violence against black people had been routine for decades, but they had rarely been publicly marked. This changed when online organizers created evocative, highly condensed slogans and visual symbols, circulating them virtually on their social networks. When their cell phones and computers lit up, tens of thousands of black bodies took to the streets, producing choreographed demonstrations that contrasted black innocence with police brutality. Once routine, police shootings now became dramatized as egregious, undeniable abuses of civil authority. Paul Kuttner has it right:

Neither police violence in Black communities nor resistance to that violence are new. But something new *has* emerged: a new focus for anger and despair, a new source of critical hope, a new catalyst for

27

social imagination and creativity. There are surely many reasons that a movement has developed at this particular moment. [One] factor has certainly been the skill with which organizers have deployed symbols, hashtags, chants, metaphors, and images in order to communicate – quickly and powerfully – the underlying values and goals of the movement. Every social movement develops a cache of symbols. These symbols give coherence to dispersed grassroots efforts. They tap into our emotions and encourage us to learn more. We use them to mark our collective identity and to capture the attention of media outlets, with their famously short attention spans.[68]

"The Black Lives Matter movement," according to the *Huffington Post*, "has reframed the way Americans think about police treatment of people of color." The lives of poor black people began to matter:

> The Movement has managed to activate a sense of red alert around a chronic problem that, until, now, has remained mostly invisible outside the communities that suffer from it. ... Evidence does not suggest that shootings of black men by police officers have been significantly on the rise. Nevertheless, police killings have become front-page news and a political flash point, entirely because of the sense of emergency that movement has sustained.[69]

In the *New York Times*, Jay Caspian Kang describes the dramatic effect of the protests in a similar manner: "The swiftness with which the movement now acts, and the volume of people it can bring out to every protest, have turned every police killing into a national referendum on the value of black lives in America."[70]

The impact of such symbolic referenda has been to extend sympathy and identification to the underclass. Until recently, according to the Pew Research Center, "public opinion was ... closely divided" on the question of whether significant changes were still needed to achieve racial equality.[71] By July 2015, after three years of social mobilization, Americans who believed deep changes were needed outnumbered those satisfied with the status quo by two to one: "This shift in public opinion is seen across the board. Growing shares in all regions of the country, and across all demographic and partisan groups say both that racism is a big problem and that more needs to be done to achieve racial equality."[72]

Performing indignation and extending identification

How were such largely black protest performances able to affect the still majority white American citizen-audiences? As they unfolded on television and computer screens, the unprecedented wave of demonstrations against police brutality looked spontaneous, as if they came from the grassroots, springing up from the underclass victims themselves. Yet, this was not the case. Certainly, the demonstrations were heartfelt. Their authenticity, however, was choreographed, their verisimilitude the result of a singular fusion between actors and audience enhanced by performative effect.

When 17-year-old high school student Trayvon Martin was murdered by George Zimmerman, a neighborhood watch coordinator for a gated community in Sanford, Florida, on February 26, 2012, the national black community and its white supporters filled the airwaves with outrage over racism and civil irresponsibility. When the local police chief refused to arrest Zimmerman, claiming Florida's so-called Stand Your Ground statute allowed his exercise of armed self-defense, thousands protested, and their demonstrations surprised and riveted what turned out to be a broadly sympathetic nation. The reaction was as electrifying as it was unexpected, pushing the envelope of interracial moral responsibility and emotional identification further than it had ever been extended before. When President Obama publicly crystallized this identification, dramatically avowing, "When I think about this boy, I think about my own kids ... If I had a son, he would look like Trayvon,"[73] he was speaking not only for himself and other African American parents, but for a much broader swath of citizens whom he represented as President of the United States. The "Million Hoodies for Justice" protest group, formed a month after the shooting, organized a march in New York where protestors chanted "We want arrests!" and "We are all Trayvon," many clad in hooded sweatshirts "symbolic of the clothing Martin wore when he was killed."[74] Two weeks later, Zimmerman was charged with murder by a special prosecutor appointed by conservative Republican Governor Rick Scott.

Fifteen months later, when Zimmerman was acquitted, civil outrage once again ignited, boiling over with the news that Eric Garner, an African American father of six, had died when a white NYPD officer put him in a 20-second chokehold in the course of his arrest. In the days and weeks of protests that mushroomed across US cities, highly theatrical "die-ins" were staged; protestors lay down in the middle of busy streets, and demonstrators publicly chanted Garner's final words, "I Can't Breathe." When, just one month after Garner's killing, on August 9, 2014, a white police officer in Ferguson, Missouri, shot another young black man, Michael Brown, protests exploded again. Brown's last words were, "I don't have a gun, stop shooting!" These secular prayers of pleading and protest, "became a national rallying cry," according to the *New York Times*.[75] As protestors chanted these words in cities and campuses across the country, they also projected indexical gestures that would be immediately recognized as ritual re-enactment. For example, they raised their arms above their heads, in solidarity with Michael Brown, the black teenager who, according to witnesses, was surrendering when he was shot.

In December 2014, when a grand jury refused to issue indictments for Eric Garner's murder, urban protests heated to fever pitch. Performed with anger and resolve by African Americans in the face of potentially dangerous police repression, their dramatic words and choreographed movements, streamed live by social media and reported by mainstream journalism, ricocheted around the nation. Chanting and raising their arms in archetypical gestures of solidarity and fear, demonstrators marched in public squares, blocked local and interstate highways, and interrupted shopping centers, religious holidays, and political events. Their slogans and gestures became totems – "Mike Brown is an emblem," a protestor in Philadelphia declared[76] – and were circulated by iconic black figures, celebrities from music, film, sport, theater, and politics. Across from the Broadway NYPD police station, African American actors staged a precision rap-and-dancing protest. Outside a Cleveland Cavaliers and Brooklyn Nets basketball game, thousands milled in protest, while, on the inside, superstar LeBron James donned an "I Can't Breathe" T-shirt, proclaiming to national media, "as a society, we have to do better ... for one another no matter what race you are." In the same *USA Today* article, Nets guard Jarret Jack explained: "We aren't just focused on ourselves as just athletes ... We collectively understand that this is an issue that needs to be addressed. The more attention we can bring and awareness to it is great. It's not a color issue, it's a people issue. It's a citizen issue." The demonstrators outside the Cleveland arena welcomed these gestures, seeing them as potentially connecting with a much wider audience beyond. "That's a result of them being educated brothers and having a slight moral compass," a protestor identifying himself only as L.B. said. "They know they're on their grand stage. Anybody that has any type of public voice needs to stand up and do something."[77]

Projecting gestures and voices from such grand stages had an impact. The ritual-like symbolic actions generated a collective effervescence that pulsated outward in great waves and was observed by political commentators who gauged shifting opinion. Donna Brazile, the influential African American media commentator and interim chair of the Democratic National Committee, declared:

"Hands up, Don't Shoot" has become a larger symbol of the desire to prove one's innocence ... In many ways, it will always resonate as a symbol of an unarmed dead teenager lying for hours on the street. Just like "I can't breathe" will never go away. They are forever etched in the complicated story of racial bias in our criminal justice system.[78]

Black Lives Matter seizes the stage

It was in the midst of the Ferguson protests that Black Lives Matter – the hashtag, the organization, and the broad eponymous movement – emerged on the public scene.[79] #BlackLivesMatter had been created the day George Zimmerman went free, but in the year following it was rarely evoked. After the murder of Michael Brown, #BLM led the Freedom Rides that fed the conflagration in Ferguson, and the number of visitors to its website jumped a hundredfold.[80] A breathless contemporary account by the activist Spanish-language website TeleSUR is revealing: "A national coalition determined to challenge state violence will convene in Ferguson over the next three days," TeleSUR reported; and described the purpose of the gathering in performative terms: "to re-envision a Black political platform in the United States." The group that would build this platform was Black Lives Matter. TeleSUR linked the organization to the sacred tradition of black civil rights, providing one of the organization's founders with a platform from which to declaim views about repression, resilience, and destiny.

> On Friday, close to 600 people will gather in Ferguson, Missouri from across the continental United States, part of the Black Life Matters (BLM) Ride. "The Black Life Matters (BLM) Ride is the Freedom Ride of our generation," explains co-organizer Patrisse Cullors ... The BLM Ride comes out of the spirit and history of the 1960s Freedom Rides to Mississippi that aimed to end racial segregation" ... "The BLM Ride is a call to action for Black people across the country to come together and re-articulate our destiny," stresses Cullors ... "We believe that in order to move this country out of a cycle of destruction and trauma, we have to rise up, both locally and nationally. Ferguson represents both the repression that exists in Black communities, and also our immense resilience," advocates BLM in their National Advocacy and Organizing Toolkit.[81]

A UCLA graduate in religion and philosophy, Patrisse Cullors was a full-time organizer for the Ella Baker Center for Human Rights in Oakland, a nonprofit dedicated to social justice issues in the inner city.[82] She created the hashtag #BlackLivesMatter from a Facebook post by her friend Alicia Garza on the day of George Zimmerman's acquittal. "The sad part is," Garza wrote, "there's a section of America who is cheering and celebrating right now. And that makes me sick to my stomach. We GOTTA get it together y'all." Garza later added: "btw stop saying we are not surprised. That's a damn shame in itself. I continue to be surprised at how little Black lives matter. And I will continue that. Stop giving up on black lives ... black people. I love you. I love us. Our lives matter."[83]

Garza studied anthropology and sociology at the University of California, San Diego, and worked as a special projects director in the Oakland office of the National Domestic Workers Alliance, representing 20,000 caregivers and housekeepers. The third member of #BLM's founding trio is Opal Tometi, a writer and immigration rights organizer in Brooklyn, who built a social media platform on Facebook and Twitter so that, in the words of *New Yorker* journalist Jelani Cobb, "activists" could use the hashtag to "connect with one another." As Cobb put it, the three women then "began thinking about how to turn the phrase into a movement."[84]

Organizers, producers, directors, and activists

Garza, Cullors, and Tometi became invisible dramaturges, writing scripts for the highly visible public performances of their organization. They were not on the scene, but behind it. Looking back, Cullors claimed the role of producer and director, distinguishing such responsibilities from participating in real-time performances and handling the *mise-en-scène*:

> I identify as an organizer versus an activist because I believe an organizer is the smallest unit that you build your team around. The organizer is the person who gets the press together and who builds new leaders, the person who helps to build and launch campaigns, and is the person who decides what the targets will be and how we're going to change this world.[85]

It was somebody from outside the founding group of invisible organizers, a Brooklyn-based activist and friend of Cullors named Daniel Moore, who actually coordinated the Freedom Rides to Missouri from New York, Chicago, Portland, Los Angeles, Philadelphia, and Boston. Moore was soon joined by DeRay Mckesson, then a 29-year-old former school administrator from Minneapolis who, transfixed by the images and texts unrolling on his Twitter feed, drove 600 miles to Ferguson to immerse himself in the actual protest scene.[86] In

Ferguson, at a street-medic training session, Mckesson met Johnetta Elzie, a 25-year-old St. Louis native who had studied journalism in college. The two became hands-on, all-in, street-level organizing partners, avidly sharing information and showing up for virtually every event in the weeks and months ahead.

> Elzie [was] one of the most reliable real-time observers of the confrontations between the protesters and the police. She took photos of the protest organizers, of the sandwiches she and her friends made to feed other protesters, of the Buddhist monks who showed up at the burned QuickTrip. Mckesson, too, was live-tweeting [and] integrating video and referring to protesters and police officers alike by name. McKesson's tweets were usually sober and detailed, whereas Elzie's were cheerfully sarcastic.[87]

Elzie and Mckesson soon became "the most recognizable figures in the movement in Ferguson."[88] As iterations of black protest unfolded in response to later police shootings, the two became publicly visible persona standing out from the emerging, but still largely anonymous, "black subject" whose gathering power was increasingly seen and heard over television and computer screens.

> Pretty soon, Mckesson and Elzie were appearing regularly on TV and radio. The two cultivated appealing personas, becoming easily recognizable to their many followers. Mckesson had begun wearing red shoes and a red shirt to protests. Later, he replaced this outfit with a bright blue Patagonia vest, which he now wears everywhere he goes. (Someone created a DeRay's vest Twitter account.) Elzie often wore dark lipstick, a pair of oversize sunglasses and a leather jacket: the beautician's daughter channeling a Black Panther.[89]

This passage is from a spread about Mckesson and Elzie in a 2015 issue of the *New York Times Magazine*, a lengthy account filled with appealing color photos and marked by an enthusiastic, even adulatory tone.[90] Mckesson later announced his candidacy to become Baltimore's mayor. Soon after, clad in signature red sneakers and blue vest, he made guest appearances on *The Late Show* with Steven Colbert and *The Daily Show* with Trevor Noah.

The double movement

When journalists and social scientists began to examine the new BLM protest movement, they highlighted its online presence, as if software savvy plus anger and grit were sufficient in themselves to initiate the shock waves pulsating throughout the broader civil surround.

Beguiled by technology, such understandings truncate the performative process, eliding the chasm separating scripts and actors, on one side, from audiences, on the other – making invisible, in other words, the very "defusion" of performative elements that underscores the cultural and pragmatic difficulties of achieving dramatic success.

That this gap was real, and immensely challenging, explains why the BLM protest movement was a series of interrelated but separated calls and responses, not one performance but several, each one temporally, spatially, and demographically independent even if topically interlinked. The triggering posts of anonymous leaders, such as Garza and Cullors, were elaborated by on-scene actors, such as Mckesson and Elzie, and retweeted to a network of hundreds of organizers who were viewed as "in place" and "ready to bring thousands of people into the streets with a tweet."[91] These first responders in the layered audience[92] were primed and committed, waiting to be "re-fused." Mckesson put it this way: "When I tweet, I'm mostly preaching to the choir."[93] He was confident the audience for his missives would become actors performing protest on the street. What this on-scene organizer was not quite so certain about, however, were the effects that such choreographed bodily displays would have on audiences at one layer removed, those watching and listening to the street performances via mainstream media. Mckesson hoped, of course, that this more distant audience would identify with the dramas he was organizing, but he confessed that, in this second phase, he was actually preaching against the choir.

> The heart of the movement is ... shutting down streets, shutting down Walmarts, shutting down any place where people feel comfortable. We want to make people feel as uncomfortable as we feel when we hear about Mike, about Eric Garner, about Tamir Rice. We want them to experience what we go through on a daily basis.[94]

The BLM street protests did not aim to seize power; most did not even have concrete demands. Their ambition, rather, was communicative, to create dramatic performances that would trigger sympathy for the suffering of underclass others, generating an emotional cathexis that would extend cultural identification, putting "ordinary people" (whites mostly) in the position of the oppressed, making them "experience what we go through on a daily basis."

To produce such vicarious symbolic experience, the portrayal of protest in the news media was key. This is the second act of the Black Lives Matter performance. It begins with journalists interpreting the protests and filing stories that their news organizations project outward via print, television, and the Internet. The first circuit of the double movement – social media directives to a committed network that brought black bodies into the streets – produced the performance of the racial underclass as a new black subject. The second performative circuit aimed to re-fuse this protest with a much more distant audience. The new black subject had to be recognized by influential white core groups, and in a sympathetic way.

In their massive study of 40.8 million movement-related tweets between June 1, 2014 and May 31, 2015, Freelon et al. reconstruct the network structure of BLM's digital communications.[95] Two findings suggest precisely the kind of double movement I am proposing here. The first is that the digital network was decidedly loose, composed of weak rather than strong ties, among which there was relatively little exchange back and forth. Instead of a "dense network with many reciprocal ties – conducive to building trust between connections" – the kind which, according to Freelon and his colleagues, would be ideal for "circulat[ing] ideas for how to mobilize" – the researchers found an "extremely diffuse" network, one much "clearly conducive to broadly distributing and circulating information."[96] The second finding concerns not the geography of the network, but the substantive identity of its nodes. By far the most frequently connected hubs were media organizations, not individuals or protest groups, and most of these media were mainstream. "In the case of the Black Lives Matter Web network," Freelon and colleagues conclude, "what primarily gets produced and distributed is news, which is meant to be widely distributed."[97]

This empirical information illuminates the neural structures of the double movement. Directives from protest organizers not only triggered street performances but massive retweetings among activists, which were subsequently posted directly, or redirected, to interested journalists. Alerted, reporters then put themselves immediately on the scene, virtually in real time or bodily in real space. Initiating the second performative circuit, reporters posted contemporaneous stories on media blogs. These were picked up by participants inside the demonstrations and, more or less simultaneously, by the tens, sometimes hundreds, of thousands of potentially attentive watchers on the outside, many of whom re(re)tweeted to new nodes on the network in turn.

This two-part performative structure remained in place even as the protest movement's organization and tactics changed. Later in 2015, the controversies concerning police killings seemed to abate.[98] "If the goal of Black Lives matter was ... to convince more Americans that police brutality existed," the *New York Times* reported, then "it was successful." With that success, the *Times* observed, "the momentum began to shift and transform into something else," and "there were fewer protests than before."[99] BLM's national organization broke into more than thirty relatively independent, locally based activist groups. While scattered street demonstrations continued, attention shifted to more targeted disruptions, especially of nationally visible political campaigns.[100] BLM demonstrators took control of a "Netroots Nation forum featuring [Bernie] Sanders and Martin O'Malley in Phoenix and began chanting slogans."[101] At a Sanders rally in Seattle, two female BLM activists took over the microphone, demanding the candidate extend his calls for radical reform from class to race. In Atlanta, BLM interrupted a speech by Hillary Clinton on criminal justice and race. At a rally in Philadelphia, her husband, former President Bill Clinton, tried facing down chants from angry activists who linked his 1994 crime bill to the massive incarceration of black men. "Black Activists Are Literally Stealing the Stage from 2016 Contenders – And It's Working," one liberal blog headlined.[102]

It certainly appeared to be the case that, in response to the disruptive confrontations, Democratic "contenders … recalibrated their messages and tone." O'Malley apologized for saying "all lives matter." Sanders added "racial justice" and penal reform to his list of political priorities.[103] Hillary Clinton began a "Mothers of the Movement" campaign, encouraging the mourning mothers of Trayvon Martin, Eric Garner, Michael Brown, Tamir Rice, and Sandra Bland "to organize and travel the country with her campaign" and paying their expenses so they could attend the Democratic presidential debates. Describing the impact of this dramatic tactic, the *New York Times* noted how it bolstered the authenticity of Hillary Clinton's character and the vitality and verisimilitude of her campaign's performance: "Having these women by her side has provided Mrs. Clinton with powerful and deeply sympathetic character witnesses as she makes her case to African American voters. And they have given her campaign, an often cautious and poll-tested operation, a raw, human, and sometimes gut-wrenching feeling."[104] Mr. Clinton, too, felt compelled to be publicly responsive, the *New York Times* headlining: "Bill Clinton Says He Regrets Showdown With Black Lives Matters Protesters."[105]

BLM's newly disruptive tactics were also directed at Republican candidates, but, rather than eliciting supportive responses, these protests appeared to be aimed at highlighting what activists regarded as the uncaring whiteness of the conservative movement. The tactic seemed particularly effective apropos the candidacy of Donald Trump. The violent responses of his white supporters to BLM's provocations intensified not only Democratic, but also Republican anxieties about the anti-civil, "over the line" character of the New York real estate developer's campaign.

While the *New York Times* described the sequence of iterative demonstrations analyzed in this section as "the most formidable American protest movement of the 21st century to date,"[106] BLM's performative power remained relatively constricted in comparison to what had been generated by its mid-twentieth-century predecessor. Critical elements of social performance were not quite there. There were problems, for example, with BLM's script. The persuasive reach of disruptive indignation is limited. A more powerful myth would have laid out a redemptive pathway from suffering to salvation, from underclass to social justice, perhaps underscoring "American exceptionalism" or the idea of America as God's chosen people. The secular tone of BLM, however, precluded any connection with American civil religion.[107]

The lack of larger-than-life characters proved another major obstacle. Protagonists must be embodied in order to become heroic; collective subjects, online discourses, and digital images are not enough. DeRay Mckesson may have been the only distinguishable persona to have emerged from a protest movement that remained remarkably anonymous, but his 2016 Baltimore mayoral campaign still floundered for want of "name recognition."[108] In late December 2015, CNN claimed Mckesson "drives the conversation."[109] Four months later, the *New York Times Magazine* reported Mckesson "was on Fortune's World's Greatest Leaders list last year" and "has been to the White House so many times that he says he doesn't get nervous anymore."[110] Such claims of charismatic authority, however, were vastly overstated. Mckesson registered on the American radar screen, but he didn't penetrate its sacred center. He did not become a collective representation of black suffering and hope, either for the racial underclass or the protest drama's multicultural and multiclass audience on the outside. Mckesson did not embody, in the words he spoke, the tone of his voice, or the lines of his face, contemporary African American aspirations for justice. An effective organizer who became a recognizable face, Mckesson was more a celebrity, famous for being famous, than a genuine hero.[111]

* * *

Social movements do not succeed because they are materially power-ful; they become materially powerful because they succeed. To explain this seeming paradox, I have argued that social movements should be understood as social performances. To seize power in the state, one must first seize the collective imagination, projecting dramas on the stage of social life that depict the triumph of justice, so powerfully fusing with distant audiences that dangerous insurrection becomes legitimate.

The Chinese communist movement claimed it arose from the clash of objective interests, but the party had to make these class contradictions come to dramatic life. Mao was transformed into a larger-than-life persona, a heroic savior, and the peasant masses had to be inspired to deep anger and bitter tears. Despite the protests of generations of critical intellectuals and legal reformers, African Americans suffered mostly in silence for decades after slavery. It was the performative genius of Martin Luther King and his supporting staff that finally gave them voice. The drama they forged projected a redemptive narrative that riveted the northern white audience, gained significant political power, and made major repairs in the rent racial garment of American life. Fifty years later, even as social scientists laid out the structural forces encircling the new black underclass, Black Lives Matter forged an active black subject. Deploying the newly digital means of symbolic production, its organizers projected com-pelling narratives, slogans, and gestures, triggering massive African American protest and, fusing with sympathetic journalists, bringing the racially affirmative demand that black lives matter as much as white lives into the heart of a reluctantly responsive nation.

— 2 —

REVOLUTIONARY PERFORMANCE IN EGYPT: THE 2011 UPRISING

Discussions about revolutions, from the social scientific to the journalistic, almost invariably occur in the realist mode. Whether nominalist or collectivist, materialist, political or institutional, it seems a point of honor to maintain that it is real issues, real groups, and real interests, and how these have affected relative power vis-à-vis the state, that determine who makes revolutions, who opposes them, and who wins at the end of the day.

At the very beginning of the "January 25 Revolution" in Egypt, in 2011, a reporter for the *New York Times* traced its temporal and spatial origins to the naturalistic causal power of a single event: "The beating of a young businessman named Khaled Said last year [in Alexandria] led to weeks of demonstrations against police brutality."[1] Said, a 28-year-old businessman, allegedly had filmed proof of police corruption; he was dragged from an Internet café on June 6, 2010, tortured, and beaten to death. Addressing the broader social origins of the revolution, the *New York Times* also ran the headline, "Jobs and Age Reign as Factors in Mideast Uprisings," with an op-ed columnist explaining that "these are solid measures, but I would add spending on essentials like food" and "income inequality and burgeoning Internet usage" as other factors.[2] A *Le Monde* journalist noted that, while the revolutionary slogans were primarily political, "recent price increases and rising unemployment have become powerful engines of Egyptian protest."[3] A *Guardian* reporter also situated the protests in material concerns, "a wave of protest, sparked by self-immolation, unemployment and high food prices, sweeps the Arab world from Mauritania to Saudi Arabia."[4] The BBC webpage "Twenty Reasons Why It's Kicking Off Everywhere" cited "economic failure" and the "demographic bulge," adding that "at the heart of it all is a new sociological type: the graduate with no future;" that "women [are] very numerous as the backbone;" that "people just know more than they used to" and "have a better understanding of power;" that "truth moves faster than lies;" that "technology has expanded;" and that "the network [is] more powerful than the hierarchy."[5]

Western news media were quick to assure readers that the Egyptian uprising was not "ideological" or "moralistic," that its demands were down to earth and "concrete."[6] There was a collapse of living conditions, suffering groups rebelled, demography mattered, and the sharing of information was crucial. Eventually, state repression faltered. As for what happened next, it was a matter for the stronger side to decide. Posing the question, "who is really controlling events," a *New York Times* essayist supplied the conventional wisdom: "Lenin understood that the ultimate question in each revolution is always the unfathomable alchemy of power: who controls whom." Lenin himself put it more succinctly: "Who whom?"[7] Academic explanations of revolutions differ in detail and sophistication, but not in kind. An influential French demographer linked the "Arab Spring" to falling birth rates and rising rates of literacy, citing these as sure indicators of modern democratic "*mentalités*."[8]

This chapter takes a different approach. I will not argue that such so-called social factors are without significance, but that, in themselves, social facts do not speak. It is representations of social facts that do the talking. When wages and unemployment, birth rates and literacy, youth, the new class and the old state, corruption, repression, and urban decay enter into the tumultuous back and forth of revolutionary social strife, they do so as signs, folding these empirical facts ("signifieds" in semiotic terms) into chains of already powerful symbols ("signifiers"). But, while their materiality is an illusion, their factuality is not: it is a useful fiction. The apparent naturalness of signified social facts gives symbolic constructions their extraordinary pragmatic and performative effect. Social facts enter into history as meanings, not only to outsiders but to revolutionaries themselves.[9]

Dreaming Civil Society

At the core of social meanings are cultural codes that categorize things in moral terms, as good and bad, as pure-sacred and as polluted-profane. When these deeply felt moral-cum-expressive evaluations are wrapped in the clothing of human protagonists and antagonists, they structure the dynamic social narratives marking revolutionary time. These stories establish the execrable origins of social suffering, the past from which contemporary revolutionary struggle has developed, and the endpoint of justice and social transformation, the future to which struggles in the present are plotted to proceed.[10]

"We Are All Khaled Said" Facebook Page[11]
"We Are All Khaled Said" – English translation
Administrator (Wael Ghonim) (January 27, 5:49 a.m.)
"Feeling that I'm Dreaming."
Eyad Irshaid (January 27, 5:50 a.m.)
"Something new?"
Mohammed Abo El-ella (January 27, 5:50 a.m.)
"Noooooooooooo, [It is] reality, not dream!"
Mido Sheba (January, 5:50 a.m.)
"Dream, the dream becomes true."
Taghreed Ahmed (January 27, 5:50 a.m.)
"By God, we all are feeling that we are in a dream."
Bannour Grodt (January 27, 5:50 a.m.)
"[And] How will you feel when Mubarak runs to Saudi [Arabia]?"
Esraa Hyman (January 27, 5:50 a.m.)
"It feels like I am in a war but victory is ours, by the will of God ... and God-willing things'll be good."

What was at stake for those who made the January 25 Revolution was not simply economic or narrowly political. What they were contesting, as one observer acutely reported, was something decidedly "intangible."[12] It was a matter of hopes and ideals, of the values of autonomy and solidarity that define a more civil society.[13] An Egyptian activist recounted the story of the Tunisian fruit-seller whose martyrdom, in the twilight of 2010, had fired the democratic protest in the Arab Spring of early 2011. It had been a matter, he carefully explained, not of money but of individual "dignity." Arrogant Tunisian officials had denied the street merchant a license, speaking "to him like he was a beggar."[14]

Neither was protest only an economic issue for the martyred Egyptian, Khaled Said. It had been a civil matter, of chronic and flagrant official corruption, that moved him to rebel. The immensely influential Arabic Facebook page established by Wael Ghonim to honor Said, in June 2010 – 'We Are All Khaled Said' (WAAKS) – is filled with video clips and newspaper articles about police violence, official corruption, and the regime's distorted media of communication. "This is your country," Ghonim insisted to his followers, "a government official is your employee who gets his salary from your tax money, and you have rights."[15] In a January 27 posting, Ghonim wrote about "Freedom *and* the Loaf," the latter referring to bread, the former to moral aspiration, and he added, as if to clarify:

الحرية و الرغيف.. مطلب كل مصر شريف.

All of Egypt is demanding honor/virtue.[16]

Five days later, one week into the January struggle, WAAKS (English) announced the "Egyptians [*sic*] Dignity Revolution," and six days after that proclaimed: "This is not a political revolution. This is not a religious revolution. This is an all Egyptians [*sic*] revolution. This is the dignity and freedom revolution."[17] Interviewed by Al Jazeera (English-language version), a demonstrator named Mohammed explained: "We are prepared to live on the bare minimum, as long as we feel like we have our dignity, that we are walking down the streets with our dignity."[18] According to an editorial in *Le Monde,* the Egyptian people were saying "no to misery and corruption and yes to dignity and freedom."[19] Mahmoud Gouda, a Cairo sales director, remembered how his brother had been tortured by Egyptian police: "In the name of my brother's dignity, I now demand the departure of Mubarak."[20] Shadia Abdelrahim, a 26-year-old Cairo doctor, repeated a similar idea: "It isn't a question of politics, but of dignity."[21] According to the *Guardian,* "the Egyptian regime has deprived the people of everything, including freedom and dignity, and has failed to supply them with their daily needs." *La Repubblica* agreed: "They ask for bread, work, justice and dignity." In the days after the government's most extreme effort at repressing the revolution, a *New York Times* reporter observed that "dignity" was "a word often used."[22]

Individual freedom and dignity depend for their existence upon a certain kind of community, more civil than primordial. A New Jersey man asked in a letter to the *New York Times*: "Is it possible that those who believe that every Muslim could be a terrorist might now at least be wondering if the Middle East is populated by people craving what all of us want, a world built upon basic freedoms with respect for divergent views?"[23] One of the organizations leading the Egyptian uprising, the April 6 Youth Movement, declared on its Arabic website that it was not sectional or individual interests, but a shared commitment to reconstructing a beloved community that drove the revolution: "Nothing brings us together except our love for this country and the desire to reform it."[24] Day after day, the revolutionaries represented themselves as a cross-section of Egyptian society, as weaving together a community that was universalistic in the most expansive and idealized sense. "The reality that emerged from interviews with protestors," the *New York Times* reported after the first day of agitation, was that "opposition to Mr. Mubarak's rule spreads across ideological lines [and] came from all social classes," that the protestors "did not belong to any particular group," and that many "were attending their first demonstration."[25] Lowly Egyptian foot soldiers declared, "this is the revolution of all the people."[26] Wealthy Egyptians, while acknowledging that "elites like us will say, 'Oh, we're going to lose out,'" insisted "we may have to lose out in order to give something back to ourselves."[27]

In the extraordinarily stratified context of contemporary Egypt, such observations elicited continual surprise. That participants in the revolution were motivated by a broadly encompassing, civil, and universalistic solidarity, rather than by narrower, primordial, and more particularistic concerns, was a central motif of the *New York Times* coverage over the movement's eighteen days:

> Friday's protest was the largest and most diverse yet, including young and old, women with Louis Vuitton bags and men in galabeyas, factory workers and film stars.[28]

> Hopes of Egyptians, Poor and Wealthy, Converge in Fight for Cairo Bridge.[29]

> The protestors came from every social class and included even wealthy Egyptians who are often dismissed as apolitical, or too comfortable to mobilize. For some of them in the crowd on Friday, the brutality of the security forces was a revelation. "Dogs!" they yelled at the riot police, as they saw bloodied protesters dragged away. "These people are Egyptians!"[30]

> There seemed to be a simple national consensus, felt by car mechanics in Upper Egypt and the café society in Cairo: the government has failed them.[31]

> Over the last several days, hundreds of thousands of Egyptians – from indigent fruit peddlers and doormen to students and engineers, even wealthy landlords – poured into the streets together.[32]

> Most of the week's protests appeared to represent a nearly universal cross section of the public.[33]

> The battle was waged by Mohammed Gamil, a dentist in a blue tie who ran toward the barricades of Tahrir Square. It was joined by Fayeqa Hussein, a veiled mother of seven who filled a Styrofoam container with rocks. Magdi Abdel-Rahman, a 60-year-old grandfather, kissed the ground before throwing himself against crowds [and] the charge was led by Yasser Hamdi, who said his 2-year-old daughter would live a life better than the one he endured. "Aren't you men?" he shouted. "Let's go!"[34]

The uprising [was] the last option for not only the young and dispossessed but also virtually every element of Egypt's population – turbaned clerics, businessmen from wealthy suburbs, film directors and well-to-do engineers.[35]

Such observations were hardly confined to correspondents and columnists from the American newspaper. That the solidarity driving the revolution was civil and expansive was noted far and wide. An Al Jazeera (English) correspondent observed that "the people we have seen taking to the streets today are not the 50 or 60 activists that we have been seeing protesting in Egypt for the past five or six years," but "normal Egyptians, older women, younger men, even children."[36] A comment on its English website insisted:

The pro-democracy protest in Tahrir Square was the most diverse gathering that I have ever witnessed in Egypt ... There were plenty of mid-teens to early 30s men and women in the pro-democracy camp. But with them were children, the elderly, the ultra-pious and the slickest cosmopolitans, workers, farmers, professionals, intellectuals, artists, long-time activists, complete neophytes to political protest, and representatives of all political persuasions.[37]

The *Guardian* reported on "an unlikely alliance of youth activists, political Islamists, industrial workers and football fans":[38]

Young people of every background and social class marched and sang together. Older, respected figures went round with food and blankets. Cigarette-smoking women in jeans sat next to their niqab-wearing sisters on the pavement. Old comrades from the student movement of the 1970s met for the first time in decades. Young people went round collecting litter. People who stayed at home phoned nearby restaurants with orders to deliver food to the protesters. Not one religious or sectarian slogan was heard. The solidarity was palpable. And if this sounds romantic, well, it was and is.[39]

La Repubblica reminded its readers that Egypt's civic tradition was older than Italy's: "We understand more that Egyptians are beginning to think of their Muslim faith as secondary in respect to their political convictions, just as they have in history ... Egypt had a parliament four years before Italy."[40]

On the third day of upheaval, Wael Ghonim underscored the civil nature of solidarity on WAAKS:

الكنيسة المصرية تجعو المسيحيين لحضور المظاهرات السلمية مع إخوتهم المسلمين ... الحمد لله .

و كلنا ايد واحدة لأن كلنا عايزين حقوقنا.

44

The Egyptian church invites Christians to attend peaceful demonstrations with their Muslim brothers ... Praise God and we all are supported as one for we all desire our rights.[41]

On the following day, this message went out on WAAKS (English): "For our brothers and sisters in Egypt. The winds of change are blowing – all Egyptians – Christians, Muslims, Everyone ... are together as one" (January 28, 2011). Two days before, as the movement prepared for its first mass confrontation, Ghonim had declared a similar theme on WAAKS (Arabic):

سنخرج بمسيرات في كل مساجد وكنائس مصر الكبرى متجهين ناحية الميادين العامة ومعتصمين حتى ننال حقوقنا المسلوبة. مصر ستخرج مسلميها ومسيحييها من أجل محاربة الفساد والبطالة والظلم وغياب الحرية. سيتم تحديد المساجد والكنائس ليلة الخميس.

We will exit into marches in all the great mosques and churches of Egypt heading toward public squares and staying until we receive our denied rights. Egypt will exit, its Muslims and its Christians, to fight corruption, unemployment, injustice, and the absence of freedom. Chosen mosques and churches will be announced Thursday night.[42]

From the very first day of the uprising, revolutionary leaders presented themselves and their organizations as providing an impermeable shield around the emerging civil sphere of the nation, one that would protect not only the individual but the broader community upon which individuality depends. Warning that "abuse of any individual is against the entire nation," the April 6 Youth Movement warned the regime that, in the event of such abuse, "unforeseen results will come that cannot be controlled."[43]

Here are some quotes from Al Jazeera (Arabic):

وأضاف البيان ـالذي تلقت الجزيرة نت نسخة منه ـ أن الحركة ستتخذ التدابير اللازمة لحماية الجميع قدر المستطاع، وقالت "قمنا بتجهيز دروع واقية وكذلك أطباء وصيادلة" لإسعاف أي مواطن قد يتعرض لإيذاء جسدي. وتم تجهيز غرفة عمليات خاصة باليوم.

The statement [by April 6 Youth Movement] – a copy of which was received by Al Jazeera Net – added that the movement will adopt necessary measures to protect everyone as much as possible, and it said "We have employed protective shields as well as doctors and pharmacists" to rescue any citizen that may be exposed to physical harm.

ووصفت الحركة تصريحات وزارة الداخلية المصرية ـالتي قالت فيها إنها ستتصدى بكل حزم للمظاهرة ـ بأنها "متغطرسة وليست جديدة، فالحكومة تأبى إعطاء التصاريح اللازمة، ثم تتعامل بطريقة قمعية مع الجماهير بحجة عدم الحصول على تصريح بالمظاهرة."

The movement described the statements of the Interior Ministry – that said that the ministry would address/thwart any determination to protest – as "arrogant and nothing new, the government refuses to give the necessary permits, then deals repressively with the masses under the pretext of failing to obtain permits for a protest."[44]

Cultural Background: Binary Moral Classifications

For participants and observers alike, revolutionary conflicts are experienced as a life and death struggle between not just social groups but social representations, one representing the sacred, the other the profane. A *Guardian* writer called the Egyptian regime "a quagmire of tyranny."[45] "This is a titanic struggle," one *New York Times* columnist reported during the uprising's final days, "between the tired but still powerful, top down 1952 Egyptian Army-led revolution and a new vibrant, but chaotic, 2011 people-led revolution from the bottom up."[46] Another *Times* columnist declared: "Rarely have we seen such epic clashes between the forces of light and darkness."[47]

For the Egyptian state and its ideological apparatus – Mubarak's secret police, his corrupt administration, puppet parliament, and house intellectuals – the events of the eighteen-day revolution, and the actors who drove them, were represented as deeply polluting; they were constructed by a negative discourse that legitimated, in fact demanded, their repression.[48] After the assassination of his predecessor Anwar Sadat in 1981, Mubarak had projected a progressive narrative. Against the forces of fundamentalism, violence, and reaction, he would modernize Egypt and bring it into the future. "We will embark on our great path," he promised in his 1981 inaugural speech, "not stopping or hesitating, building and not destroying, protecting and not threatening, preserving and not squandering."[49] During the 1990s, fighting a low-level war against Islamist groups, Mubarak's regime represented itself not only as the guarantor of social order, but also as the defender of modernity and even democratic reform, as working against the anti-democratic character of the Islamicist side.[50] A leading intellectual whom Mubarak appointed general secretary of the Supreme Council of Culture, for example, authored books with such titles as *Defending Enlightenment* and *Against Fanaticism*.[51] In 2006, even as Mubarak announced he would retain his presidency for life, he framed his decision in a progressive manner, promising the Parliament, "I will pursue with you the march of transition into the future, shouldering the responsibility and burdens as long as I draw breath."[52]

Such rhetoric would seem to defy the natural laws of social realism, but five years later Mubarak applied the same binary grid of moral signifiers to the unfolding signifieds of the January 25 Revolution. Those opposing the regime were "instigators," "foreigners" and "spies," not true "Egyptians," not the sincere "patriots" who constituted the "vast majority." While outside agitators engaged in "sabotage" and created "chaos," the state would maintain "stability" and "security." The street activists were a small "minority" of "outlaws," an "illegitimate and illegal" group who employed "force." The state, by contrast, was lawful, had "the popular support of the vast majority," and displayed an "ability to listen." Critics engaged in "propaganda," but Mubarak's regime was "careful" and "deliberate," willing to initiate "dialogue." The revolutionaries, by contrast, were taking "uncalculated and hasty steps that would produce more irrationality." They were "intellectual adolescents" with "little standing," while the state was "big" and "strong." The protests were quickly becoming "exhausted," even as Mubarak and his regime remained "resilient." Those who challenged the government were "dangerous," but the regime was "safe."[53]

While there is evidence that Egyptian elites and masses initially had evinced some sympathy for such regime coding, as Mubarak's reign

Table 2.1 The Mubarak regime's classifications

Profane protest	Sacred regime
Instigators	Egyptians
Foreigners, spies	Patriots
Chaos	Security, stability
Force	Willingness to listen
Hasty	Careful
Uncalculated	Deliberate
Irrational	Dialogue
Minority	Popular majority
Exhausted	Resilient
Little standing	Big, strong
Dangerous	Safe
Primitive	Modern
Sectarian	Rational
Illegitimate	
Illegal	
Outlaws	
Sabotage	
Propaganda	
Intellectual adolescents	

lengthened and his emergency decrees remained in place, his shaky connection to the collective consciousness faded along with his promises of modernization. Until the January 25 outbreak, however, there had been scarcely any public opportunity to articulate an alternative symbolic system, one that matched the regime's secularism and went toe-to-toe with it in a morally agonistic way. Demonstrations such as the Cairo Spring of 2005 and the 2008 food riots in El-Mahalla el-Kubra had been summarily quashed.[54] By contrast, from the beginning of the January 25 Revolution, protestors were able to seize the public stage, and they broadcast an alternative symbolic classification. Their moral categories were not, in themselves, sharply divergent from the ones that Mubarak himself employed. What changed was the relative weighting of one quality over another, and how these discursive signifiers were socially applied. Democracy and freedom became much more prominent, the state pushed over to the polluted side. Revolutionary discourse also found fresh tropes for speaking the sacred and profane, and they were now able to perform them practically, in time and space, in extraordinarily effective ways.

Inside the sacred and profane classification of the revolutionaries, Mubarak was exercising "repression" and "brute force," while the demonstrators called for "freedom" and "communication." The revolutionaries denounced the "barbaric" Egyptian state headed by a "modern-day Pharaoh," interpreting his moves as "carefully calibrated." They characterized their own movement, by contrast, as "leaderless," choosing time and again to emphasize the "spontaneous" character of their activities. While regime officials were "dogs" and "thugs," the protesters were described as "the people." Mubarak had launched a "crackdown" to "throttle" the people's voice with "violence," but protestors remained "courageous" and "undaunted," and their ambition was said to be "communication." The "arrogant" autocrat addressed his subjects as "sons and daughters"; the revolutionaries spoke of one another as "citizens." The demonstrators were "youthful"; the regime was "petrified." Mubarak's was a "dictatorial" regime; the revolution demanded "democracy."[55]

If the Egyptian revolutionaries could represent themselves so effectively inside this binary discourse of civil society – speaking fluently about their democratic motives, relations, and imagined institutions – this was due in no small part to a broader intellectual revolution in Arab political life, a dramatic shift in the fundaments of political language that provided the background representations for contemporaries' public speech. In the decades preceding the events of January 25, the vanguard of Arab political culture had changed. The

Table 2.2 The revolutionaries' classifications

Profane regime	Sacred protestors
Repression	Freedom
Choking brute force	Communication
Modern-day pharaoh	Leaderless
Calibrated	Spontaneous
Petrified	Youth
Dogs, thugs	The people
Mubarak and cronies	Most Egyptians
Sons and daughters	Citizens
Dictator	Democracy
Arrogant	
Violence	

postcolonial promises of militant Arab nationalism lost their luster,[56] and currents inside political Islam were shifting. Debates about civil society and democracy permeated books, newspaper articles, magazines, websites, and the talking heads and interviews on Al Jazeera TV. Some secular intellectuals became "court liberals" who projected democracy as a distant ideal but kept quiet about contemporary Arab regimes. Others went into internal or external exile, publicly attacked Arab authoritarianism, and stridently demanded immediate radical, democratic change.[57] Such core Islamic ideas as *hurriya* (freedom) were expanded from the religious into the political sphere, and even Sharia law and Islamic justice began to be interpreted in civil ways.[58] Despite fears among such conservative interpreters as *USA Today* – that the Muslim Brotherhood would assume leadership and that it would be a "calamity"[59] – other Western journalists recognized that Islamism was leavened with a "variety of positions," many of which were explicitly democratic: "There are Orthodox and heretical Nasserites, communists, trade union Labor Party members, Labor Muslim, liberals ... and certainly there are Islamists, but split into factions, and certainly much more complicated than we imagine them to be."[60] *La Repubblica* stressed the secular nature of the demonstrations: "Yesterday, Friday, the day of prayer, the crowd chanted the usual cry of Allah'u Akhbar, Allah is great. But the slogan of the revolt, the one that filled the streets, is another: 'Illegitimate!' Mubarak is an illegitimate president (because his election was a fraud)."[61]

An Egyptian leader of the Muslim Brotherhood wrote a *New York Times* op-ed piece stressing this democratic turn in Arab and Muslim intellectual opinion in the present day: "We envision the establishment of a democratic, civil state that draws on universal measures of freedom and justice, which are central Islamic values ... We embrace democracy not as a foreign concept ... but as a set of principles and objectives that are inherently compatible with and reinforce Islamic tenets."[62]

Nowhere was this Arab intellectual revolution more visible, and its effects more palpable, than in the coverage of the revolution that Al Jazeera (Arabic) broadcast to the Egyptian people and beyond. Its journalists and editors strongly identified with the activists' civil and democratic aspirations, and their reporting, while professional, often seemed to be speaking in the movement's name. On the first day of the uprising, January 25, the Arabic network provided a framework for the events that identified the protestors as sacred carriers of honest and principled democratic activism, stigmatizing its regime opponents as arrogant, fraudulent, repressive, aggressive, and violent.

Here are some quotes from Al Jazeera (Arabic):

حذرت حركة شباب 6 أبريل وزارة الداخلية المصرية من التعامل بعنف مع النشطاء والمتظاهرين الذين سينزلون إلى الشوارع اليوم في احتجاج يصادف يوم عيد الشرطة، في الوقت الذي أنذرت فيه الحكومة المصرية المتظاهرين بأنهم سيواجهون الاعتقال إن هم مضوا قدماً في تنظيم الاحتجاجات.

The April 6 Youth Movement was warned by the Egyptian Interior ministry that it will deal violently with activists and protesters that will take to the streets today in a protest falling upon National Police Day [January 25], at a time that the Egyptian government warned protesters that they would face arrest if they went ahead in organizing the protests.

حذرت حركة شباب 6 أبريل وزارة الداخلية المصرية من التعامل بعنف مع النشطاء والمتظاهرين الذين سينزلون إلى

وحذر بيان أصدرته الحركة وزارة الداخلية من ممارسة "الاحتيال القديم بدس عملائها من البلطجية داخل صفوف المتظاهرين لإحداث مشاجرات واعتداءات على الممتلكات العامة، ثم اتخاذ ذلك ذريعة لسحق المتظاهرين ونعتهم بالمخربين والخارجين على القانون".

And a statement issued by the April 6 Movement warned the Interior Ministry of its practice of "the old fraud of poking its clients, thugs, inside the ranks of the protestors in order to create fights and attacks on public property, taking that as a pretext for crushing the protestors, labeling them as vandals and outlaws."

وخاطب البيان قوات الأمن بأن "يلتزموا بحدود القانون"، و"ألا يمارسوا ما تعودوا على ممارسته من قبل، لأن ذلك الزمن قد مضى وانقضى، والاعتداء على أي فرد هو اعتداء على الأمة بأكملها، وقد يأتي بنتائج غير متوقعة ولا تمكن السيطرة عليها

And the statement addressed the security forces to "commit themselves to the limits of the law"

...ووصفت الحركة تصريحات وزارة الداخلية المصرية ـ التي قالت فيها إنها ستتصدى بكل حزم للمظاهرة ـ بأنها "متغطرسة وليست جديدة، فالحكومة تأبى إعطاء التصاريح اللازمة، ثم تتعامل بطريقة قمعية مع الجماهير بحجة عدم الحصول على تصريح بالمظاهرة".

The movement described the statements of the Interior Ministry – that said that the ministry would address/thwart any determination to protest – as "arrogant and nothing new, the government refuses to give the necessary permits, then deals repressively with the masses under the pretext of failing to obtain permits for a protest."[63]

For many Western observers, these intellectual developments in the Arab world were obscured by the anti-American and anti-Zionist sentiments that often accompanied their fervent expression, as well as by the violence of radical Islamic fundamentalists that crystallized during the same period of time. Writing about the January 25 Revolution, for example, *USA Today* characterized the Muslim Brotherhood as "a banned political movement that wants a government run strictly as an Islamic state."[64] The impact of these shifts in Arab intellectual life was obscured, as well, by the subtle power that long-lasting dictatorships can exercise over the mentalities of those they dominate, sometimes causing them to doubt their own capacities for rule. Mohammed ElBaradei, the Nobel laureate who had returned to Egypt to organize public opposition against the Mubarak regime, observed that "people were taught not to think or act," acknowledging "frankly, I didn't think people were ready." Expressing surprise when members of the Egyptian elite participated in the demonstrations, one protestor commented, "This is the class that never spoke out before."[65]

The January 25 Revolution began when a people who had seemed an "apolitical and largely apathetic public" found their voice.[66] It was not only resistance to the state's physical repression that propelled and sustained the rebellion, but outrage against a regime discourse that polluted the Egyptian people as abject and its activists as evil. Because social signification is arbitrary and socially constructed, it is always in play. Binary moral classification may seem static, but it is not. Its social anchoring is restless and undecided, its interpretation dynamic and potentially explosive. Binary structures pollute those who may think of themselves as sacred, and purify those whom others passionately judge to be profane. As "January 25" gained momentum, the movement became more subject to depredations from the regime's polluting symbols, and indignation at such humiliating misapprehension increased in kind. "A people who once complained of their quiescence," the *New York Times* observed, "would no longer stay quiet." It was because they finally could speak out that "they seized control of their lives."[67] In the process, Al Jazeera (Arabic) reported, "the Egyptians in the street surprised observers and analysts [and]

Table 2.3 Tension between moral antinomies

Mubarak classification		Revolutionary classification	
Profane protest	Sacred regime	Profane regime	Sacred protestors
Instigators	Egyptians	Repression	Freedom
Foreigners, spies	Patriots	Choking brute force	Communication
Chaos	Security, stability	Modern-day pharaoh	Leaderless
Force	Willingness to listen	Carefully calibrated	Spontaneous
Hasty	Careful	Petrified	Youth
Uncalculated	Deliberate	Dogs, thugs	The people
Irrational	Dialogue	Mubarak and cronies	Vast majority of Egypt
Minority	Popular majority	Sons and daughters	Citizens
Exhausted	Resilient	Dictator	Democracy
Little standing	Big, strong	Arrogant	
Dangerous	Safe	Violence	
Primitive	Modern		
Sectarian	Rational		
Illegitimate			
Illegal			
Outlaws			
Sabotage			
Propaganda			
Intellectual adolescents			

the Egyptian president and government," and "they surprised even themselves."[68]

Narratives of National Decline and Salvation

Much as counterpoint propels baroque music, so the agonism of juxtaposed moral codes energizes social upheaval. The protestors of January 25 aimed to purify themselves and pollute the regime engaged in their moral depredation. In order to do so, they folded the morally charged binaries into a temporal language of before and after, a narrative organized by conflict between social actors who represented their respective moral sides. The revolutionary narrative inscribed the events of the insurgency inside a plot of national decline and resurrection. There was broad and fervent idealization of the Egypt of old. Once, Egypt had been a great nation and civilization. Despite some imprecision about the beginning of the golden age, the date of Egypt's decline is clear: it was during Mubarak's reign. "All Egyptian people believe that their country is a great country with very deep roots in history," a Cairo University professor explained, "but the Mubarak regime broke our dignity in the Arab world and in the whole world."[69] When the Associated Press interviewed Ismail Syed, the hotel worker allowed: "this is the first time I am protesting, but we have been a cowardly nation. We have to finally say no."[70] Mohammed ElBaradei lamented: "Egypt, the land of the Library of Alexandria, of a culture that contributed groundbreaking advances in mathematics, medicine, and science, has fallen far behind."[71] A protestor in the street put it more simply: "I want to say this to the regime: Thirty years is more than enough. Our country is going down and down because of your policies."[72] Many others expressed similar sentiments: "For thirty years, Egypt lost its place. We've been ruled by mercenaries and rulers who stole from our treasuries. It's over now, the people have woken up, and they're going to rise again. Egypt is going to be the example again."[73] As a coffee-shop owner joined protesters in Shubra, northern Cairo, he shouted: "Egypt is waking up."[74] In the early morning of January 27, after the first days of successful mobilization and confrontation, Wael Ghonim rallied insurgent forces for more sacrifices in the days ahead. "We won't be intimidated," he tapped on WAAKS (Arabic):

كلنا سنموت لتحيا مصر

"We shall die for Egypt to live."[75]

A week later, Al Jazeera (Arabic) broadcast a segment called "Wishes of a number of Protesters in Tahrir Square" – أراء عدد من المعتصمين في ميدان التحرير. – a series of face-to-face interviews with fiercely determined protestors in Tahrir Square. An older woman in black in the entrance to a tent told the interviewer:

لو أعدنا سنة هنا لاحدي ما نأخذ هائنا عشنا كثير محرومين و ذلنا بلدنا كثير.

Even if we stayed here for a whole year, we would stay until we get what is rightfully ours. We have lived for so long deprived and our country has been humiliated very much.

A woman carrying an Egyptian flag declared:

إن شاء الله هنأخذ هريتنا و نحرر مصر من ظلم حسني مبارك.

God willing we shall seize our freedom and free Egypt from the injustice/oppression of Hosni Mubarak.[76]

Journalists interpreted the revolutionary narration in the same way. According to the *New York Times*, Egypt was a "nation that once saw itself as the center of civilization and the Arab world," and it recorded "the country's erosion over decades of authoritarian rule," how it had "gone from being a cosmopolitan showcase to a poor, struggling city that evokes barely a vestige of its former grandeur." Egypt had once been "the cradle of civilization and a one-time leader of the Arab world," but now it "had slipped towards backwardness and irrelevance."[77]

The lowest point in this inverted parabola was the present. Contemporary Egypt was narrated as the worst of times. A secular protest leader decried the "hell we are in right now." A media adviser for the Muslim Brotherhood declared "everyone is suffering from social problems, unemployment, inflation, corruption and oppression." A popular playwright poeticized: "Every Egyptian is carrying inside of them 100 short stories of pain and novels of grievance." The antagonist in this narrative of declension was clear: Mubarak was to blame. "This nightmare is the ruling party and the current regime," a former Brotherhood member who had quit from frustration explained: "This is everyone's nightmare."[78] According to a former Egyptian political prisoner, the sociologist Saad Ibrahim:

Those in Tahrir Square have had their fill of the pharaoh's deception … This aging pharaoh is trying to create the false impression that without his steady hand, Egypt will descend into chaos. The carefully orchestrated and well-armed mobs of "pro-Mubarak demonstrators" are just the latest acts in his three decades of deception.[79]

The *Wall Street Journal* described how "two teenagers on a marble pedestal in the adjacent park held up a cardboard placard, as eloquent as it was blunt: 'Hosni Mubarak isn't president anymore. He is the Devil.'" *La Repubblica* wrote, "The president is now a head without a future, a symbol, a shadow, embarrassing," describing Mubarak's failure to resign as "the final joke of a plastic pharaoh."[80]

The January 25 Revolution was a new plotline driven by world-transforming protagonists carrying on their shoulders hopes for national renewal. On the morning of the first day of the uprising, the April 6 Youth Movement warned security forces "to not exercise what was exercised before, because that time has already gone by and passed."[81] The *Guardian* documented the same national narrative in the streets:

> In the narrow side streets protesters regrouped, while well-wishers on their balconies above threw down water for those with streaming eyes from the tear gas. "Wake up Egypt, your silence is killing us," came the yells from below. Others shouted: "Egyptians, come down to join us." Their appeals were answered with people streaming down from the apartment blocks: "We are change" and "Gamal (Mubarak) tell your father Egyptians hate him," were the cries.[82]

Overthrowing the Mubarak regime would move Egypt from darkness to light. "There are a lot of things wrong with this country," an unemployed protestor remarked, explaining "the president has been here for thirty years."[83] *Le Monde* reported Mohammed ElBaradei's comment, upon his most recent return to Egypt: "This is a critical moment in the history of Egypt … The will of change must be respected."[84] *La Repubblica* headlined "ElBaradei Man of Destiny 'Today a New Country is Born'."[85] Expelling Mubarak would push Egypt from one side to the other of the binary code. It would allow Egyptians to reinscribe their nation on the sacred side. Regime and protestors both loved the nation, but only one conceived this nationalism in a civil way.[86] The *New York Times* reported:[87]

> "This is our country," said Maram Jani, a 33-year old wearing a pink veil who returned after working as a psychologist for three years in the Persian Gulf. "We want to stay in our country. We want to share in its wealth, we want to be part of its land. They can only laugh at us so long, make fun of us for so long."[88]

The atmosphere in Tahrir Square reverted from embattled to jubilant. The protesters abandoned their makeshift barriers to chant, pray and sing the national anthem around the center of the square.[89]

"We took our freedom," Mustafa Abudrasheed Muhanna said. "Egypt is born again." So was the Egyptian flag, no longer seen as a symbol of a stagnant state, a bureaucrat's wall decoration or a backdrop for state television broadcasts of Mr. Mubarak's meetings. In the square on Friday, it was a woman's shawl, a child's plaything and a cherished accessory. Sold for $2, it was marked in black pen with political slogans or signed like a yearbook. Everywhere, the flags waved ... One sign held by a young man said: "Mubarak: Enter + Shift + Delete." Moawia Mohamed, 20, held another that said, "welcome to the New Egypt."[90]

Samar Ali, a 23-year-old graduate of the University of Fine Arts in Cairo, recounted that, "I decided to go to Tahrir Square," but "I was afraid of the Islamists or that I would be sexually harassed by the men in the street." What she found when she got to the square was a different Egypt, a country on the rise: "I was shocked to see that those Egyptians who made me so afraid are the ones who now protect me, with so much dignity. I discovered another Egypt, the one my father had told me about."[91]

Declaring that the demonstrators "broke the barrier of fear," novelist Alaa al-Aswany commented to Al Jazeera (English) that "the writers of the regime were saying Egypt is not Tunisia and Egyptians are less educated than Tunisians." He countered: "Here is the thing: these young people proved they can take their rights forcefully."[92] Firas al-Atraqchi, a former Al Jazeera (English) journalist, linked the revolution to national revival in the same way:

> In more than 18 years of living in Cairo, I have never felt the sense of excited hope that exists in Egypt tonight. From speaking to colleagues (many of whom are journalists covering the protests), friends and neighbors, they all feel that despite the number of teargas canisters fired at protesters and the number of those who have been beaten and detained, a long-dormant patriotism and pride has been finally awakened.[93]

The BBC reported that, during the culminating demonstrations in Tahrir Square on February 11, "three chants were dominant – and very telling."

> One – "Lift your head up high, you're Egyptian" – was a response to how humiliated, how hopeless we'd been made to feel over the last four decades. The second was: "We'll get married, We'll have kids," and reflected the hopes of the millions whose desperate need for jobs and homes had been driving them to risk their lives to illegally cross the sea to Europe or the desert to Libya. The third chant was: "Everyone who loves Egypt, come and rebuild Egypt."[94]

Revolution would resurrect Egypt's golden age. During one demonstration, activists distributed a fake version of *Al Ahram*, the state-owned newspaper. On its front page was a picture of a mummy from the pharaonic days. The text below read: "To the grandchildren of our grandchildren in Tahrir Square. You gave me back my spirit."[95]

The Script and the Carrier Group

These were the collective representations that formed the background for the revolutionary upheaval in Egypt – its moralizing binaries, energizing narratives, and intellectual antecedents.[96] The upheaval that became the January 25 Revolution began as an effort to perform these background representations, to move from symbolic construction to symbolic action. For the collective action to succeed, symbols had to be projected from their creators to layered audiences: to gather followers and foot soldiers from the more committed, to engage the elites, to seduce the middle, and to gain attention outside, from the Arab region and the global civil sphere.

The agents who were at the core of this performative project formed the revolution's "carrier group." It was they who projected the symbols and, after they made the connection with audiences, directed the revolutionary *mise-en-scène*. Hundreds of thousands of protestors peopled the "scene" of the revolutionary drama, but it was directed by movement intellectuals[97] who made every effort to script and choreograph street actions in advance.

Because the mere existence of such a directorate, even a relatively loosely organized one, seemed threatening to the revolution's representation as democratic, its leaders tried to keep their strategizing invisible and even their very existence under wraps. The first media mentions of a revolutionary directorate did not surface in the Western media until nearly a week after the movement began. Despite claims of being spontaneous and leaderless, it was reported that not only throughout the events, but well before them, "a small group of Internet-savvy young political organizers" had been meeting frequently with one another. On Sunday, January 30, for example, overlapping members of the leadership network reconnoitered at three different times and locations. Every evening, leaders would prepare a blueprint for the next day's events.[98] Distributed the next morning via email and text message, and updated throughout the day, the script provided slogans, suggested routes and movements, and assigned key actors roles to play and words to say.[99]

Organizers used photocopies to disseminate information. Anonymous leaflets circulating in Cairo ... provide practical and tactical advice for mass demonstrations, confronting riot police, and besieging and taking control of government offices. Signed "long live Egypt," the slickly produced 26-page document calls on demonstrators to begin with peaceful protests, carrying roses but no banners, and march on official buildings while persuading policemen and soldiers to join their ranks. The leaflet asks recipients to redistribute it by email and photocopy, but not to use social media such as Facebook and Twitter, which are being monitored by the security forces. Protesters in Cairo are advised to gather in large numbers in their own neighborhoods away from police and troops and then move toward key installations such as the state broadcasting HQ on the Nile-side Corniche and try to take control "in the name of the people." Other priority targets are the presidential palace and police stations in several parts of central Cairo. The leaflet includes aerial photographs with approach routes marked and diagrams on crowd formations. Suggested "positive" slogans include "long live Egypt" and "down with the corrupt regime." There are no signs of slogans reflecting the agenda of the powerful Muslim Brotherhood. It advises demonstrators to wear clothing such as hooded jackets, running shoes, goggles, and scarves to protect against teargas, and to carry dustbin lids – to ward off baton blows and rubber bullets – first aid kits, and roses to symbolize their peaceful intentions. Diagrams show how to defend against riot police and push in waves to break through their ranks. "The most important thing is to protect each other," the leaflet says.[100]

Even after older and more established opposition leaders joined the insurrection, it was these "young internet pioneers" who were "still calling the shots," and who remained "the vanguard behind the scenes."[101] At the end of the eighteen days of protest, the *New York Times* headlined: "Wired, Educated, and Shrewd, Young Egyptians Guide Revolt."[102]

Stories about the young leadership network emerged in bits and pieces over the course of the revolution's second and third weeks: revelations about their friendships, backgrounds, and ambitions, how they had met, their organizing history, and the roles they now played. Their identities, interests, and solidarity were typically described from a materialist perspective, as those of a new class[103] whose technological labor and higher education inscribed in them a critical orientation[104] that they could now put on display.[105] It seems clear, however, that the revolutionary leadership was much more and much less than that. Their day jobs were many and varied. Some worked in high-tech, but others were full-time political organizers; some ran NGOs, others were feminist and labor activists; some had businesses, others were religious leaders. In fact, the only demographic they did share was their relative youth. They were truly a carrier group – for the Arab intellectual revolution, for the moral binaries of civil society, and for the narrative of national resurrection that promised to save the Egyptian nation from further decline. It was shared ideas that brought this group together, cultural perceptions forged from the searing heat of common experiences and propelled by an uncommon willingness to sacrifice their privileges for some greater good.

The collective identity of these youthful activists was "years in the making,"[106] transforming the nascent carrier group from more traditional, working-class oriented activists into radical advocates for civil society.[107] Their loose association began with the "*Kefaya*" (Enough) movement in 2005, and the "Youth for Change" brigade they organized within it landed many in prison. By 2008, many had retreated to their computers, becoming politicized bloggers calling for a wave of anti-regime strikes. They set up their first Facebook page to promote the Mahalla protest in March 2008. In the face of the violent repression of workers and their families, some youthful activists formed the April 6 Youth Movement and went back to the drawing board. Under the influence not only of their practical experience, but surging intellectual interest in civil society, the revolutionaries began reading up on strategic nonviolence, particularly the ideas of Gene Sharpe, the American whose philosophy of radical civil protest derived from Mahatma Gandhi and Martin Luther King and whose strategic thinking had inspired the Serbian youth group Otpor's struggle against Slobodan Milošević. Some Egyptian activists actually travelled to Serbia for political re-education; others set up an organization called the Academy of Change in Qatar to promote Sharpe's ideas.[108] "The Academy of Change is sort of like our Marx and we are like Lenin," a youthful member of the leadership group offered during the events of January 25. Days before the January 25 Revolution, organizers from both Serbia and the Egyptian Academy of Change helped the directorate train protest organizers in Cairo.[109] They were intent on teaching activists to resolutely maintain a stance of nonviolence; otherwise, it would become impossible to perform a democratic civil sphere. As the first day's demonstrations began, a WAAKS (English) administrator made these commitments strikingly clear:

> Some members believe that a peaceful protest in Egypt will not do much. All our protests are peaceful and legal ones. If you have a different opinion please feel free to say it, but I have never and will never call for or support a protest anywhere unless it is 100% legal and peaceful. (January 18, 2011; 12:15 p.m.)

Struggle and *Mise-en-Scène*

Social performances have many elements, each necessary but none alone sufficient. Revolutions need carrier groups, and these groups make every effort to compose compelling scripts. The next step is to make the scripts walk and talk. Walking and talking means putting a script into practice, creating actual events, with real human beings, which unfold in time and space. Social dramas, unlike theatrical ones, are open-ended and contingent. They can be staged, but nobody is certain whether the actors will arrive, who they will be, how events will unfold, which side will win a confrontation, and what the drama's effects on the audience will be. In relatively democratic societies, where there exists some independence for the civil sphere, the effect of political performance is contingent, but its staging and dramatization – the walking and talking of scripted action – is not particularly difficult to pull off. In more repressive societies, where civil spheres are suppressed, performative success must be measured more minimally. In some real part, an opposition performance is successful merely by the fact of its having taken place. Autocracies aim to prevent oppositional political performances from occurring. In order to block the transition from scripting to walking and talking, the regime puts its threats of dire punishment into place – from the destruction of life routines to imprisonment, torture, and death. Simply to stage a public performance in such a repressive society is already an achievement. It marks its effect, as philosopher John Austin might have said, in the very act of its own doing: from being merely words with meanings, opposition becomes words that do things. Meanings are instantiated in time and place, and the symbols signifying a situation move from the subjunctive to present tense.[110]

One of the best ways to stop public performances, to keep organizers from being able to do things with words, is to prevent those staging opposition from communicating with others who might wish to attend. Without the means of symbolic production, communication beyond immediate face-to-face contact becomes impossible.

Even as the Mubarak regime monopolized and manipulated print and television media, its insistent investment in a progressive, modernizing narrative compelled it to be thoroughly "wired" at the same time. Some twenty million of Egypt's eighty million population owned computers or social networking devices, guaranteeing regular access to the World Wide Web. In 2006, the Mubarak government proudly hosted Wikipedia's annual global convention.

Wiring the nation presented an Achilles heel to which the carrier group of Egyptian dissidents took careful aim. In early 2010, Wael Ghonim, a 31-year-old Google executive who had been part of the circle around Mohammed ElBaradei, joined the group. Director of the global Internet company's marketing for North Africa and the Middle East, Ghonim was expert in techniques of symbolic projection, in moving a digital message from speaker to audience:[111] "I worked in marketing, and I knew that if you build a brand you get people to trust the brand."[112] Communicating with hundreds of thousands of WAAKS (Arabic) followers, Ghonim conducted online exercises in democratic participation, dress rehearsals for the uprising to come. After the victory of the Tunisian revolution on January 14, 2011, leaders sensed that the time for performing mass public opposition had finally arrived. If 50,000 persons signed up, the Facebook page messaged, the first public protest would be staged. More than 100,000 responded. January 25 was Police Day, a national holiday honoring a police revolt suppressed by the British colonialists. The carrier group transformed it into an uprising against the postcolonial state. Before launching a full-fledged demonstration, however, the organizers tried one more "out of town" run, to test how far into the layered audiences[113] their radical performance of opposition would reach:

> When the 25th came, the coalition of young activists, almost all of them affluent, wanted to tap into the widespread frustration with the country's autocracy, and also the grinding poverty of Egyptian life. They started by trying to rally poor people with complaints about pocketbook issues: "They are eating pigeon and chicken, but we eat beans every day."[114]

Marching through the narrow streets and alleys of working-class Cairo, the organizers discovered an extraordinary response. Egyptians leaned out of windows shouting encouragement, banging pots and pans in support. Thousands left their apartments and poured into the streets to join the demonstration.[115] Two of Mubarak's National Party buildings were set on fire. Placing a call to his fellow organizers who had gathered to await the results of this trial run, Ghonim reported it a massive success. The carrier group now had clear evidence that their movement could connect a wider audience.

The revolution could begin. Routes to Tahrir Square were chosen, street leaders assigned, and a massive, public, aggressive, yet insistently nonviolent confrontation with the autocratic state began later that day. "Freedom, Freedom, Freedom," the swelling crowds chanted, as they coursed through the streets on their way to Tahrir (Liberation) Square.[116] As the demonstration built on January 25, a series of postings on WAAKS (English) juxtaposed the protest drama's sacred civil purpose with the profane, anti-democratic response of the regime.

> Protesters at the High Court break down the Police siege and run toward Tahrir Square. (1:23 p.m.)
> Protesters moving to opera house from Tahrir Square. Their number is well over 1,000. (1:38 p.m.)
> Police moved in on protesters and attacking protesters badly. Using batons and water cannons. (3:50 p.m.)
> Confirmed: Tahrir Square is now COMPLETELY ours. Egyptian Police now is only worried about protecting their headquarters: Ministry of interior. (4:55 p.m.)
>
> BREAKING NEWS: Police in Egypt open fire on protesters … Our correspondent was hit in his head … with rubber bullets. (6:12 p.m., 6:19 p.m.)
>
> Confirmed reports: Restaurants in Tahrir Square are giving away food for free to protesters. What more are you waiting for to go to join your fellow countrymen in Tahrir? You'll get a free meal at least! (8:39 p.m.)
>
> For all Egyptians: Twitter is closed as you know, Facebook will close very soon. Please All use proxies and tell ALL your friends in Egypt to use proxy to connect. (11:29 p.m.)

By the end of that January 25 evening, the carrier group knew that they had been able to make their script walk and talk. The closest rows of layered audiences had identified with their performance. An Egyptian observer reported how, on the first day of the demonstrations, the once disparate organizing groups had "fused, and with them multitudes of Egyptians young and old":

> For Cairo they chose three locations: Shubra, Matariyya, and Arab League Street. These were strategic choices: naturally crowded neighborhoods, with lots of side streets. Young activists started their march in nearby areas, collected a following and by the time they reached, for example, Arab League Street, they were 20,000 marching. The Central Security Forces were in chaos; when they formed cordons the people just broke through them. When they raised their riot shields and batons the young people walked right up to them with their hands up chanting "Silmiyyah! (Peaceful) Silmiyyah!"[117]

These early responders to the revolution now become part of a newly enlarged collective actor, forming a massive social movement that, over the next seventeen days, would battle Mubarak and his state for performative power.

From that afternoon forward, the carrier group directed, and the expanding Egyptian participant-audience enacted, a gradually ascending, day-after-day drama of good challenging evil, of an outraged but peaceful community of citizen-activists who had the courage not only to keep demonstrating and speaking for democracy, but to die for it. The size and enthusiasm waxed and waned, but the slope was upward. Seemingly inevitably, the emotional weighting of the sacred revolutionary drama gradually increased. On January 23, journalists had predicted the imminent rebellion would mark the beginning of a "political evolution."[118] Political experts cautioned, however, against an analogy with the anti-communist democratic uprisings of 1989. After listing the ways in which the Jasmine revolution in Tunisia was a one-off, a neoconservative intellectual remarked: "There are plenty of reasons to think we are not on the cusp of a democratic avalanche."[119] Three days later, the media were reporting that "tens of thousands" of demonstrators had "filled the streets" in "the largest display of popular dissatisfaction since the bread riots of 1977,"[120] and that, "as evening fell, thousands of people converged on Tahrir Square, in the center of Cairo, and began an occupation."[121] Six days later: "Egypt quakes beneath the fury of a huge public uprising."[122] Three days after that, journalists reported, "from the perspective of the protestors and many others ... the uprising had become what they called a 'popular revolution',"[123] and a blogger for the *Guardian* proclaimed, "we are witnessing a true revolution."[124] The next day was declared "one of the most spectacular popular movements in Egypt's history."[125] As one of the youthful organizers, Salma Said, told *USA Today*, the growing scale was such that the organizers had to turn to "young Cairo soccer fans to help them organize against police actions," because they "had experience with unruly mobs and police."[126]

The denotative content of the demonstrators' chants and placards was clear. They called on their fellow members of the national community to join them in their civil crusade and for the dangerously anti-democratic regime on the other side to resign.

Where are all the Egyptian people?![127]
People, people, take to the streets.[128]
Tomorrow all the Egyptians are going to be in the streets.[129]
Mubarak, your plane is waiting.[130]
Game over Mubarak! Democracy now![131]

But the emotional and symbolic connotations of the swelling streams of movement and confrontation also mattered, not only the literal message. What was unfolding before the layered audience, both near and far, was an extraordinary social drama. Participants and observers alike evoked the language of theater. In the midst of the first afternoon's march, WAAKS (English) tapped, "Amazing scenes" (January 25; 1:23 p.m.), a phrase echoed in the *Guardian*.[132] Journalists described the revolutionary demonstrations as tableaux – a "day of drama,"[133] "the Egyptian Drama,"[134] and "Thursday's drama."[135] And they, too, recorded the "remarkable scenes"[136] and "dramatic scenes."[137]

While the revolutionary performances spread to several Egyptian cities, they were concentrated in Cairo's Tahrir Square, the geographical center of Egypt's capital city that now became its symbolic center as well. The *Guardian* described the square as the "scene of the ongoing mass demonstrations,"[138] and the *Wall Street Journal* suggested the revolt "had found a stage worthy of its ambitions."[139] The revolutionary *mise-en-scène* consisted largely of marches into and out of the square, speeches and demonstrations inside it, and pitched battles to retain control of this physical-cum-symbolic stage. Dramas rolled across this stage hour after hour, day after day, evening after evening, and they became riveting public events.

A compelling plot needs twists and turns, with audiences on the edge of their seats, never knowing what's next. Suspense rivets attention. "The Drama in Egypt: What Is the Next Act?," the *New York Times* headlined in its letters section at the drama's halfway point, on February 4.[140] That same day, the *Times* news columns reported that "control of the streets" had "cycled through a dizzying succession of stages."[141] The day-to-day plot unfolded via journalistic time:

January 25: Zeinab Mohamed, an Egyptian blogger, commented, "I got a Facebook invitation for January 25, 'Anger' day, at the same time I was covering the Tunisian revolution ... I felt they were overestimating the situation: revolutions do not happen on Facebook or on a specific date. I thought it would be just another day of small protests downtown where protesters are harassed by the security forces as usual. But how wrong I was."[142]

January 26: It was not clear whether the size and intensity of the demonstrations ... would or could be sustained.[143]

January 28: The government seems to be using a version of a rope-a-dope strategy Muhammad Ali used to defeat George Foreman in 1974. Mr. Ali spent round after round against the ropes as Mr. Foreman pounded himself into exhaustion.[144]

January 29: The crisis in Egypt has reached a critical turning point.[145]

Even as armored military vehicles deployed around important Egyptian government institutions on Friday for the first time in decades, it remained difficult to predict what role the armed forces might play in either quelling the disturbances or easing President Hosni Mubarak from power.[146]

"We don't know if the army is with us or against us."[147]

Revolution, transition, coup? Whatever the outcome of the chaos which was rampant yesterday in the streets of Cairo, one thing is clear, Egypt will never be the same.[148]

January 30: "The president is ... on shaky ground [and] he doesn't know what will happen tomorrow."[149]

There is a current of anxiety over what the protests would lead to.[150]

No one seemed sure where the movement would lead.[151]

February 2: "It is not possible to say what will happen next. Everything is up in the air."[152]

February 4: The momentum of the opposition movement has ebbed and flowed.[153]

February 5: Egypt's revolution is far from decided.[154]

February 7: "It's exciting but also a little bit scary ... People are getting hurt and also, I don't know what will happen next."[155]

February 8: It is not easy to predict what will happen next in Egypt's uprising.[156]

Momentum has seemed to shift by the day in a climactic struggle.[157]

Protesters and the government are locked in a battle for momentum.[158]

February 12: We are a long way from knowing how Egypt will turn out.[159]

As events zigzagged forth and back, journalists narrated the pulsating uncertainty as a sequence of chapters, numbered by week and day.

February 1: "This is the first day of the Egyptian revolution," said Karim Rizk, at one of the Cairo rallies.[160]

The six-day-old protest here entered a new stage.[161]

February 2: On Tuesday, the eighth day of demonstrations, hundreds of thousands went to Liberation Square.[162]

A dramatic eighth day of mass protests.[163]

February 4: Nine days after a diverse band of protestors mobilized on the Internet and gathered by the thousands.[164]

On the ninth day of the uprising ...[165]

February 5: For eleven days ... the dominating demand [has been] that Mubarak should go away.[166]

In the eleven days since the Cairo uprising began ...[167]

The twelfth day of protest ...[168]

February 6: Twelve days into an uprising in Egypt ...[169]

February 8: As Egypt's revolt entered its third week ...[170]

February 9: On the fifteenth day of protests ...[171]

February 11: After seventeen days ...[172]

February 20: Eighteen Days in Tahrir Square ...[173]

In the most compelling dramatic plots, the contingent becomes the teleological. Strong narratives, *pace* Aristotle, must have not only a beginning and a middle, but also an end. The sense of an ending permeates the present, sustaining the protagonists in their struggle against evil others, propelling the densely organized action forward so that meaning can be transformed on the other side. Even as they were engulfed in the anxiety of dramatic interaction, revolutionary demonstrators believed they would ultimately triumph.

> "Our protest on the 25th is the beginning of the end," wrote organizers on the Arabic "We are all Khaled Said" Facebook group that day. "It is the end of silence, acquiescence and submission to what is happening in our country. It will be the start of a new page in Egypt's history, one of activism and demanding our rights."[174]

> After we walked from Tahrir Square across the Nile bridge, Professor Mamoun Fandy remarked to me that there is an old Egyptian poem that says: "The Nile can bend and turn, but what is impossible is that it would ever dry up." The same is true of the river of freedom that is loose here now. Maybe you can bend it for a while, or turn it, but it is not going to dry up.[175]

> A long dead North African poet's most famous poem has become the anthem of the movement. His work seems to define the protests and their ambitions ... "If one day, a people desires to live, their fate will answer their call, and their night will then begin to fade, and their chains break and fall." A veteran dissident remarked, "He is leading us from the grave."[176]

In these representations, individuals spoke as if the outcome were determined, the civil side fated to win.

Repressive Counter-Performances

No matter their suggestive narrative power, the struggles that constituted the *mise-en-scène* did not have to end with victory for the revolutionary side. There really were twists and turns, and the Mubarak regime, even when it could not achieve a knockout punch, often seemed ahead on points. For three decades, its rule had been successful in purely pragmatic terms, and its staying power had not been effectuated by brute power alone. Mubarak tortured and killed some of his most determined opponents, but mostly he employed bribery, administrative control, and police power to co-opt his enemies and to prevent public performances of opposition. And he himself was always careful to keep up appearances, presenting himself as a strong and caring father for his citizen-children, hewing to his narrative that the regime devoted itself not only symbolically, but materially, to bringing Egypt from the dark night of backwardness to the bright light of the modern day. As Machiavelli once put it, "some men cherish something that seems like the real thing as much as they do the real thing itself."[177]

We have seen earlier that, far from presenting himself as the knife-edge of naked power, Mubarak inserted his regime into the heart of moral classification. He now attacked the insurgency as a blocking character to his narrative of national progress and liberation. Throughout the eighteen days of twisting and turning, this conservative vision of purity and danger – this repressive sense of the narrative stake – informed every public speech-act in which the regime engaged. In "news" stories printed by state-controlled newspapers and in the "reports" of correspondents on state television and radio; in official statements by Mubarak's administrative staff; and in the president's own carefully crafted and widely broadcast speeches of January 20 and February 10: in all these, Mubarak strove mightily to match his language of repression with the facts on the ground. "The government's strategy," the *New York Times* reported, "seems motivated at turning broader public opinion in the country against the protestors."[178] The dictator wished to connect emerging social facts to the right kind of signifiers, transforming them into signs that would speak in his chosen way. But the conjuring tricks of this master ventriloquist were losing their magical effect. Egypt's layered audiences seemed ever more distant from his megaphone. There was another powerful speaker in the national echo chamber, and the means of symbolic production were no longer Mubarak's to control. As journalists discovered to their surprise in the early days of the demonstrations, "Mubarak and his officials seemed to stumble in formulating a response to the most serious challenge to his rule."[179]

When Mubarak found it rhetorically more difficult to match his words with things, he exercised the levers of power to change the situation on the ground. On the fifth day of the confrontation, the regime removed the police presence from the streets of Egypt's major cities and let thousands of hardened criminals out of four prisons – to predictable effect.

> In a collapse of authority, the police withdrew from major cities on Saturday, giving rein to gangs that stole and burned cars, looted ships, and ransacked a fashionable mall, where dismembered mannequins for conservative Islamic dress were strewn over broken glass and puddles of water. Thousands of inmates poured out of four prisons, including the country's most notorious, Abu Zaabal and Wadi Natroun.[180]

In light of this state of affairs – with real rampaging and disorder in neighborhoods and streets –Mubarak hoped that his regime's polluting moral assignations could finally take hold. "Egypt challenges anarchy!" a government-owned newspaper hopefully shouted the next day. Some members of the national audience were convinced. "At first, the words were right," a driver named Abu Sayyid al-Sayyid confided to a reporter, referring to the early promises and performances of the demonstrations. But faced with the new social situation – the dangerous and newly unstable facts on the ground – al-Sayyid explained he had now changed his mind: "The protests were peaceful – freedom, jobs, and all that. But then the looting came and the thugs and thieves with it. Someone has to step in before there's nothing left to step into." Nagi Ahmed, a schoolteacher in Cairo, hoped the demonstrations would end soon: "I want to go back to work … The money I have is almost gone."[181] Shenouda Badawi, a 20-year-old Coptic Christian engineering student expressed concern: "My mother and my sister are terrified. We need calm. The message has been heard. Mubarak must stay in power as long as the opposition needs to form a new structure. Otherwise there will be chaos."[182] On January 31, Mubarak appeared on state television, "in a meeting with military chiefs in what was portrayed as business as usual."[183] Throughout that Sunday, state television broadcast calls from Egyptians who claimed to be 100 percent loyal to the regime. "Behind you are eighty million people, saying yes to Mubarak!" one exclaimed.[184] Abdelaziz Ibrahim Fayed, a camel-owner and perfume-shop salesman at the pyramids stated: "One million don't need Mubarak, and 84 million don't want him to leave."[185] According to the *New York Times*, however, such full-throated support was among the "rarest of comments across Cairo."[186]

The regime's effort to legitimate the discourse of repression – by actually making neighborhoods and streets dangerous – had failed.

The movement's discourse of liberation proved resilient, its pro-jection via alternative means of symbolic production effective and broad. An independent newspaper portrayed the new dangers on the ground this way: "A Conspiracy by Security to Support the Scenario of Chaos."[187] Rather than connecting the anti-regime demonstrators to the rising disorder, in fact, Cairo residents were much more likely to blame the regime itself. "We're worried about the chaos, sure," remarked a film director, Selma al-Tarzi, as she joined friends in Tahrir Square. "But everyone is aware the chaos is generated by the government. The revolution is not generating the chaos."[188]

Thomas Hobbes's warning about performative failure still rings true: "That which taketh away the reputation of Sincerity," wrote the theorist of *Leviathan*,[189] "is the doing or saying of such things, as appear to be signes, that what they require other men to believe, is not believed by themselves." Once the Mubarak regime's signify-ing efforts were made to seem deeply hypocritical, its final layer of legitimacy peeled off like old house paint in the hot summer sun. The steel edge of the knife blade was all that was left. As it turned out, Mubarak could not make full use of the knife, which was ultimately in the hands of the Egyptian army; but he brandished his blade with a flourish and employed it in a menacing way.

From the first day of the January 25 Revolution, Mubarak had deployed force to prevent radical public performances, and he redou-bled his efforts at physical repression as the insurrection expanded. Police fired water cannons to disperse the massing of protestors; when demonstrators continued to surge forward, Mubarak's forces fired rubber bullets; and, when nothing seemed to work, they used real bullets to shoot and kill. Activists were abducted from the streets for days and weeks, put into lock down, tortured, and sometimes mur-dered. Hundreds of protestors were shot, many of them mortally, in the streets. On January 28, the fourth day of the protests, the leader-ship planned a "Day of Rage" for Friday, the holy day of the Islamic week. Intertwining the sacred and secular, hundreds of thousands of audience-participants marched towards Tahrir Square. Mubarak's forces responded with the most brutal crackdown of the eighteen-day revolt. The day began with a near total blackout of communica-tions. "The Internet suddenly showed no sign of life," *La Repubblica* reported, and "a couple of hours later even mobile phones, local and international lines collapsed."[190] Soon after, Egypt's counterterrorism forces were deployed and the interior ministry warned of "deci-sive measures."[191] The day proceeded with brigades of riot police, black-shirted security police, and undercover forces in civilian dress battering protestors at mosques, bridges, and intersections, as part of a massive effort to prevent them from reaching Tahrir Square.[192]

After miles of peaceful marching, demonstrators were confronted by 1,000 armed police, along with five armored vehicles and two fire trucks. There ensued a fierce struggle over access to a bridge leading into the center. In "The Battle of Kasr el-Nil Bridge," protestors ripped bricks from the streets to throw at policemen and defended themselves with handmade shields; and armed security forces charged them with water cannon, tear gas, rubber bullets, and eventually live ammunition. In all, 900 people were hurt, 400 hospitalized with critical injuries. Observers described the streets as "covered with pools of blood."[193] The pitched battle ended in the early hours of the next morning, with the Mubarak forces in full retreat and tens of thousands of protestors staying in the square. Mohammed ElBaradei called it the battle of "the people versus the thugs," adding, "this is the work of a barbaric regime that is doomed."[194] It turned out he was right.

The Moment and the Place

For the hundreds of thousands of demonstrators, and for many among their riveted audiences at home and abroad, the violent confrontation that extended from the afternoon of January 28 to early the next morning was a palpitating experience of fear and righteous rage, and their eventual victory was cathartic. The battle's denouement marked an epiphanic moment in the revolutionary narrative. It was a rupture that created a sense of liminality, a time out of time.[195] The routines of everyday temporality were shattered, the future brought into the present, and time opened up to the possibility of utopian change. Announcing a "new era," Mohammed ElBaradei declared: "today we are proud of Egyptians. We have restored our rights, restored our freedom, and what we have begun cannot be reversed."[196] "It's our 'independence day,' a true independence," exalted Popi, an accountant from Suez.[197] Ahmed, owner of a medical laboratory in Suez, proclaimed: "the barrier of fear has fallen."[198] A hole had been punched in historical time, and the opening would not be closed until the revolutionary curtain fell. From now until Mubarak's capitulation on February 11, participants and observers would speak of being inside a "moment."

January 28: This is truly a historical moment, one that undoubtedly will be seen in hindsight as the beginning of when Egyptians took their country back from corrupt, out-of-touch leaders who knew not the people they claimed to rule.[199]

January 29: A day of "fury and freedom" – a historic moment for an Egypt that has seen anger and fury aplenty.[200]

January 30: The revolt which changes the history of the Middle East.[201]

The sweaty young men were fired by the euphoria of what they called a revolutionary moment.[202]

No one seemed to be sure where the moment would lead. But everyone understood that it was, in fact, a moment.[203]

A moment the most enthusiastic call revolutionary.[204]

January 31: Anti-Mubarak protest brings moment of truth for U.S.[205]

February 2: In the euphoria of the moment.[206]

An historic moment, and it is teaching the Arab world everything.[207]

February 3: The Middle East watched breathlessly at a moment as compelling as any in the Arab world in a lifetime.[208]

Many ... said they had experienced this day as a moment of grace.[209]

February 4: "Our current revolutionary moment."[210]

February 5: "This is our moment, our time, Mubarak has to go. He will never know how we feel. We want to live, not to struggle."[211]

February 7: "No one seems willing to surrender a moment that feels imbued with the idealism of defiance."[212]

February 8: "One brief shining moment."[213]

February 11: "A moment of transformation."[214]

February 12: Egypt's Moment.[215]

As stunning a moment as the Arab world has witnessed.[216]

This moment out of time was concentrated and consecrated in an epiphanic place: Tahrir Square. In ordinary times, the square was "cacophonous and dirty, full of crazed motorists in dilapidated cars," the buildings were aged, and the place "carried a bit of menace."[217] After its consecration, Tahrir Square became a "parallel capital" that was "an idea as much as a place,"[218] "the center of the center of Cairo."[219] Inside the square, one Egyptian remarked, "my vision goes a lot farther than my eyes can see."[220] Already on the first day a demonstrator named Mohammed Saleh stated: "This is an historic day in Egypt's history, because we have started to say 'no'. I'll tell my children someday that I was standing here in Tahrir Square."[221] The *Guardian* wrote: "In Tahrir Square, in the center of Cairo, on Tuesday night [January 25], Egypt refound and celebrated its diversity. The activists formed a minor part of the gathering, what was there was The People."[222] After the protestors survived the Battle of Kasr el-Nil Bridge, these historic feelings became more deeply weighted:

> Tents housed artists, one of whom declared that Tahrir was the Revolution of Light. There was something fitting in the description, an idea of the ephemeral and fleeting. "God has cured my ailments here," said Ali Seif, 52, a photographer who has been here since the uprising began, and who said he had diabetes and heart problems. "That's what freedom feels like," said Ibrahim Hamid, standing next to him ... Mohamed Farouq stood at the entrance to the Kasr el-Nil Bridge, the passageway to Tahrir. "You feel like this is the society you want to live in," he said."[223]

> "It's like a giant party, there is a strong feeling of happiness. For a week, I've barely slept because I participate in night patrols to secure the area. And yet I'm not tired, because one can breathe normally because the fear is gone," said Aza, a 38 year old Suez resident and manager of a maritime shipping company.[224]

Tahrir Square had become a living and breathing microcosm of a civil sphere, the idealized world of dignity, equality, and expanded solidarity for which the democratic activists fought. The following is a post from WAAKS (English):

> Welcome to the Republic of Tahrir square, Cairo: In addition to Freedom of speech [sic] and Democracy for all, we have the following FREE services: hospital, daily newspaper, kitchen for hot meals, security, artists corner, singing and slogans club, poetry competitions, border control, signs exhibition and political brainstorming. (February 9, 2011)

A broadcaster on Al Jazeera (English) commented that "the square has become a mini-utopia in central Cairo. Political opinions aired, gender and sectarian divisions nowhere to be found. People feed and clothe each other here."[225] Another story on Al Jazeera (English) reported that, while "it is hard to say how the protesters' civic engagement is viewed outside the Tahrir Square," conversations "in several residential neighborhoods over the last week" praised "the communal atmosphere" in the square. "'There is no strife in the square between Christians and Muslims,' said an elderly man named Omar, sitting in a coffee shop in the capital's Agouza neighborhood. 'This is how it used to be in all of Egypt'."[226] *Le Monde* also described Tahrir Square in a utopian manner:

> Despite concerns, the bad omens and the dead, the irreducible Tahrir Square cultivates a friendly atmosphere where, for the moment, politi-

cal differences are silent in order to focus on the common goal: the leader's departure. Volunteers pick up trash, sweep the streets, distributing water and blankets. Improvised soccer matches happen at night to keep warm. Two teams were created: "Bread" and "Freedom." On Sunday, "Bread" won.[227]

For the *New York Times*, the square had become "the epicenter of the uprising and a platform, writ small, for the frustrations, ambitions and resurgent pride of a generation claiming the country's mantle."[228]

In a sun-basked square, [the] sense of empowerment has radiated across the downtown, where volunteers passed out free wafers, tea and cake. Youths swept streets, organized security and checked identification at checkpoints in a show of popular mobilization ... 'For the first time, people feel like they belong to this place,' said Selma al-Tarzi, a 33-year old film director.[229]

The streets of Cairo are famously unkempt; people scatter their trash in the streets. But in the square, a minimum ground for expectations was set and met ... Abdel Reheem ... was walking with a garbage bag, systematically leaning over to collect the empty plastic cups, cigarette butts, and dirty tissues left by the tide of protesters who came every day. "I am cleaning because this is my home," he said, adding that it was not until he went to Tahrir that he began to think of himself as a citizen. "I am Egyptian again, not marginalized, not without value or dignity," he said. "I feel like I have planted a tree. Now I need to look after it."[230]

"You see all these people, with no stealing, no girls being bothered, and no violence," said Omar Saleh. "He's trying to tell us that without me, without the regime, you will fall into anarchy, but we have all told him, 'No.'"[231]

In a country made miserable by the petty humiliations of authority, Egyptians were welcomed to the square with boisterous greetings. "Thank God for your safety," men organized as guards declared. "Welcome, heroes!" others cried. "Come on and join the square." Most poignantly, they simply chanted, "These are the Egyptian people."[232]

Everyone in the society is here.[233]

A graphic design on WAAKS (English) mixed the Western Superman icon with the newly luminous Egyptian image of democratic protesters overflowing Tahrir Square. Pulling open his white Oxford shirt and rep-stripe tie, Superman reveals not the traditional body-hugging blue shirt with big red "S," but a "liberated" Tahrir Square.

Four days after the first wave of repression had been rebuffed, on February 2 and 3, the Mubarak regime engaged in one last violent

28 Jan

Freedom, Change & Justice

Friday of Anger
uprizing against Corruption, injustice

"We Are All Khaled Said"

spasmodic effort to route the assembled demonstrators and retake the square: 1,500 more people were injured and new deaths reported.[234] The government's invasion was again repulsed. This time around, however, there was no catharsis. The epiphanic moment had already arrived, and it already had a place.

> This is the revolution in our country, the revolution in our minds. Mubarak can stay for days or weeks but he cannot change that. We cannot go back."[235]

> "We're not afraid," said Ashraf Abdel Razeq, 37, who works as a carpenter and watches the tanks at night. "We want to clean our society, and we're not going to let the tanks stop us."[236]

> "Right now, it's all here, protecting Tahrir Square," said Hisham Kassem, a veteran activist and publisher, who kept a wary eye on barricades built with corrugated tin, wrecked cars and trucks, barrels, buckets filled with sand and metal railing torn from the curb. "We keep it tonight, and tomorrow the whole country is going to come out."[237]

To interpret this final spasm of violence, Al Jazeera reached for the signifying language of the democratic protest movement. Casting the event as yet another episode of brutal state repression, the Arabic television station broadcast a passionate narrative about purity confronting evil, and it promised that the moment of revelation – the true identity of protagonists and antagonists – was imminent:

حقيقة البلطجية المتصدون للتظاهرات المصرية
على ظهور خيول و جمال جاؤو دخلو ميدان التحرير شاهرين الصياط و العصي و القضان و
ترشح التقديرات أن عددهم يفوت 3000. فمن يكون هؤلائ الذين فاجؤو الجميع بهجومهم... و
الذين قالوا إنهم إعتقلوا بعض المهاجمين و عثروا معهم على بطاقات تثبت أنهم من رجال الشرطة.
فقد ذكرت حركة السادس من أبريل أن المهاجمين هم رجال لشرطة بلباس مدني و بلطجية
مأجورون من رجال أعمال. و قال محمد البردعي إن لديه أدلة على أن المهاجمين من الشرطة أما
مصطفا الفقي من الحزب الحاكم فقال أنه من مأجوري بعض الأعمال من الحزب الحاكم...
مطالبات سلمية للشباب تقمع بالحديد و النار و الأسلحة الميلة للدموع و حصيلة القتلى و سنات من
الجرحى. والداخلية تنفي – و الجيش على الحياد و يبقى الجواب عن هوية القامعين أو المجرمين
حسب المنظمات الحقوقية في طي الأيام المقبلة و في أحكام القضاء.

Thugs Confront Egyptian Protestors
On the backs of horses and camels they came, entering into Tahrir Square, brandishing whips, crowbars, and other weapons, their numbers running to an estimated 3,000. So who are those that came attacking? ... Protesters say that they have captured some of the attackers and find on them cards certifying that they are policemen. The April 6 Movement claimed that the attackers are plain clothes policemen and thugs hired by businessmen. Mohamed ElBaradei said that he had evidence that the attackers were from among the police. Mustafa AlFaqi from the ruling party said that some are on the payroll of businessmen from the ruling party ... The demands of peaceful young people are suppressed with iron and fire, with tear gas, resulting in many killed and hundreds wounded. And the Interior ministry denies it all – the army remains neutral and the answer ... as to the identity of criminals and oppressors ... will be left up to judgment of the next few days.[238]

The Sense of an Ending

With the symbolic center firmly secured, the victory of the revolution became only a matter of time. Mubarak made one more effort to alter the facts on the ground, trying once again to match the regime's words with things. At the beginning of week three, on the eighteenth day of the revolutionary time, the government staged another performance of "normalization." The revolutionary occupation of Tahrir Square was now taken as a *fait accompli*, so rather than engage in a futile effort at polluting it, the government tried making it seem mundane. Before January 25, Cairo's overflowing cars had passed with difficulty through the square's traffic-jammed streets; after that date, passage was blocked by the confluence of revolutionaries, barbed wire, home-made barricades, army trucks, and tanks. The regime now proposed to restore traffic by routing it around the square rather than through it. Banks made schedules to reopen, newspapers were taken down from shop windows, and Egypt's stock market was going to start doing business for the first time in many days.[239] With these practical altera-tions under way, the regime once again tried reconnecting its social signifiers with social facts. Officials declared the revolt a thing of the past, and two days later Mubarak gave a rambling and paternalistic speech. Wheeling out tired and hoary platitudes, the regime polluted the revolutionaries by working the binaries one last time. Framing the massive civil disobedience as "extremely dangerous," the recently appointed vice-president Omar Suleiman claimed that continued revolt would lead to "uncalculated and hasty steps that produce more irrationality." To prevent such degradation, the insurrection must be shut down and the regime allowed to thrive. "There will be no ending of the regime," Suleiman declared, "because that means chaos," and "we absolutely do not tolerate it."[240]

But the voice and the actions of the dictatorship no longer had performative traction. The failure of Mubarak's earlier fact-altering efforts had compelled him to unsheathe the cold edge of the knife blade. If that violence had proven unable to shut down the revolu-tionary performance, how could the regime now declare normality and just move on?

One performance on February 7 did succeed in garnering sym-pathetic public attention. It was the fairytale of Wael Ghonim's release. Twelve days earlier, the Facebook organizer had been kid-napped, secreted in a government location, imprisoned, and kept in blindfolded isolation. His last tweet before his disappearance had ominously evoked martyrdom: "Pray for #Egypt. Very worried as it seems that government planning a war crime against people. We are all ready to die #Jan25."[241] His first tweet after liberation evoked the sacrality of the civil struggle: "Freedom is a bless that deserves fighting for it [sic]." The evening of his release, Ghonim appeared on Egypt's most popular interview show, 10 P.M., broadcast by satellite televi-sion. Resolving a long-standing mystery, he identified himself as the creator of "We Are All Khalid Said." The Facebook page that helped build and direct the participant-audience of the revolution now had 486,000 registered followers.[242] As the tearful and handsome young man recounted his suffering and resurrection, he gestured to the revo-lutionary narrative and the protagonists who had died for it.

"Please do not make me a hero," Mr. Ghonim said in a voice trembling with emotion, and later completely breaking down when told of the hundreds of people who have died in clashes since the Jan. 25 protests began. "I want to express my condolences for all the Egyptians who died. We were down there for peaceful demonstrations," he added. "The heroes were the ones on the street."[243]

The interview helped transform Ghonim into what one observer called the "movement's reluctant icon." The next day, he and the talk show host Mona el-Shazly, a star in her own right, made a pilgrimage to Tahrir Square. When demonstrators converged in greater numbers than ever before, Ghonim and el-Shazly "were the ones many came to cheer."[244]

Two days after that, on February 10, with worker strikes outside Cairo adding to the momentum and giant demonstrations continuing in the square, Mubarak scheduled a nationally televised address, and leaks from inside and outside Egypt created sky-high expectations that he would resign. Instead, the president tried one more time to match his authoritarian version of the progressive narrative with the new facts on the Egyptian ground. Assuring demonstrators "your demands are ... legitimate and just," he praised them "for being a symbolic generation that is calling for change to the better, that is dreaming for a better future, and is making the future." Refusing to budge, he placed his historical persona on the side of the future: "I'm determined to execute and carry out what I have promised without going back to the past."[245]

The hundreds of thousands in Tahrir Square fairly bellowed in frustration and rage, shaking their shoes at his televised image. Earlier that day, the Supreme Council of the Armed Forces had issued a document called "Communique Number 1," on behalf of which, on state television, an army spokesman affirmed "support for the legitimate demands of the people" and pledged to "remain in continuous session to consider what procedures and measures ... may be taken to protect the nation, and the achievements and aspirations of the great people of Egypt."[246] Afterward, the army chief of staff came to Tahrir Square and made similar assurances, and the crowd roared in celebration. The steel edge of the knife blade was sheathed. Not coercive, but civil power would determine the outcome of this historic confrontation.

Hosni Mubarak resigned early the next evening. Under the heading "Collective Effervescence," the *New York Times* wrote how "tens of thousands who had bowed down for evening prayers leapt to their feet, bouncing and dancing in joy," that "revising the sense of the revolution's rallying cry, they chanted, 'the people, at last have brought down the regime'."[247] The courageous protagonists had won, and the inverted arc of national history would rise again. An Egyptian told the *Wall Street Journal*:

> Gamal Abdul Nasser and Anwar Al Sadat and Hosni Mubarak had taken away from me the love of my country ... I despaired of our people, thought they had given up liberty for this mediocre tyranny. Then on January 28, leaving the Friday prayer, I saw an endless stream of humanity, heading to Liberation Square. I never thought I would live to see this moment, these people in that vast crowd, they gave me back my love of my country.[248]

The epiphanic character of the revolution was celebrated and its sacrality affirmed. Writing for the *Guardian*, the novelist Ahdaf Soueif observed: "The joy cries filled the air – across Egypt the joy cries filled the air ... Look at the streets of Egypt; this is what hope looks like."[249] A protestor exalted, "the sun will rise on a more beautiful Egypt."[250] "I'm in Tahrir Square!" a young man yelled into his cell phone, spreading the word, "in freedom, in freedom, in freedom."[251] The *Wall Street Journal* ran these captions beneath photographs portraying the regime's denouement.[252]

> People celebrating in Alexandria waved signs, hung out car windows, and danced on the sea wall.
>
> A man kneeled in a road and prayed in Alexandria.
>
> Many families joined in the celebration in Alexandria.
>
> People celebrating in Tahrir Square in Cairo used aerosol cans to create streaks of fire.
>
> A man gazed towards a screen in Tahrir Square.
>
> A man in Cairo held up a laptop displaying an image of celebrations in Egypt after hearing the news that Mr. Mubarak was resigning.
>
> Two men embraced in Tahrir Square after hearing that Mr. Mubarak was resigning.
>
> People lighted flares in Tahrir Square.
>
> Flares illuminated the crowd in Tahrir Square.

The sense of an out-of-time moment could not be contained. An Egyptian announcer on the Hezbollah-run television in Al-Manar wept on air. "Allahu Akbar, the pharaoh is dead," he announced, asking "Am I dreaming? I'm afraid to be dreaming."[253] Wael Ghonim had marked the first day of revolution by tapping to his WAAKS followers his "feeling that I'm in a dream." When the revolutionary performance succeeded, Ghonim insisted to his fellow Egyptians that dreaming was a civil obligation: "It shows how civilized the Egyptian people are. Now our nightmare is over. It's time to dream."[254]

Of Power Physical, Interpretive, and Global

Meanings make revolutions. But the collective and individual actors who crystallize and perform revolutionary meanings do not do so in circumstances of their own choosing. Only rarely do they possess the communicative means to project their interpretations effectively, much less the physical means to protect their performances from violence by the powers that be.

The means of symbolic production

Effective social performances rely on powerful background representations, skillful directors who can write and direct scripts, motivated and convincing actors, and a twisting and turning *mise-en-scène* to build the suspense that makes an audience rapt. None of this matters, however, if a performance does not have access to the means of symbolic production. In the first place, performers must have a stage. But even with a stage – like the streets and squares of Cairo – social performance needs access to the media of mass communication. Without distributive power, the revolution cannot have interpretive power: it cannot project to audiences who remain at one remove from the immediate face-to-face.

On the evening of January 28, during the ferocious struggles between demonstrators and armed civilians and police, state television broadcast a "quiet tableau of the night sky in downtown Cairo, with the message that a curfew had been imposed."[255] That morning the government had tried pulling the plug on Egypt's Internet connection, aiming to remove the nation from the global grid. Yet, despite these efforts, Al Jazeera (Arabic) managed to run live video of the raging battle right up to the victory of demonstrators early in the morning of 29 January.

In the midst of the battle, on its Arabic channel's program *Egypt's Revolution*, Al Jazeera journalist Fawzi al-Bushra delivered his report alongside dramatic televised scenes: tear gas being fired; plain-clothes police officers beating a young man; massed demonstrators fighting against an armored vehicle firing tear gas which then ran over them; individual protestors being shot; and old men and women, with emotionally stricken faces and voices, demanding the ousting of Mubarak.

Al-Bushra's takeaway from the ugly confrontations illuminated the filaments of civil society. "After many dead, wounded, and arrested numbering in the thousands," he observed, "the people discovered ... that the police aren't always in the service of the people and can sometimes resort to oppression when the people don't line up with the will of the rulers." Because "the government became estranged from its people, secluded, and incapable," it had "kept quiet about the events," but now they were being "broadcast to television screens around the world."[256]

At one point, Al Jazeera's Arabic and English channels both displayed a split screen that juxtaposed the peaceful scene broadcast by state television with pictures of a police van set on fire by protestors defying the curfew, amid sounds of gunfire and explosions.[257] These sounds and images of state repression and courageous resistance were beamed up from Tahrir Square to satellites circulating the earth, distributed to sympathetic Arab audiences outside Cairo, flashed across the entire globe, and broadcast back to some protesters inside.

The omnipresence of such alternative images and texts would have been unthinkable two decades earlier, when the capacity for dictatorships to censor broadcasts was virtually airtight.[258] In 1989, the Chinese army carried out deadly killings of Tiananmen protestors under conditions of a blackout so total that documentary evidence of the repression is not available to this day. Contemporary digital technology has destroyed such governmental capacity to monopolize the means of broadcast communication.[259] It has facilitated the rise of alternative media, whether commercial entertainment television, private or independent news journalism, or web-based media such as blogs and social media. During the January 25 Revolution, each of these digital-based technologies, at one time or another and in varying degrees of intensity, played a critical role in allowing radical political performances to project themselves beyond their immediate staging, reaching potentially sympathetic audiences on the outside. The operational capacity for these alternative media transcended Egyptian territory. They all employed satellites, so one source of their distributive machinery circled the globe beyond national control. Yet, each of these media also depended on ground receivers, on downloadable and uploadable capacities, either cell phone or computer-based. Attacking these on-the-ground elements of digital technologies, the Egyptian state traded its immediate economic interest – much of its wealth also depended on digital communication – for a shot at destroying its opponent's ability to wage an effective symbolic fight.

The response to these efforts at controlling the means of symbolic production demonstrates how the anti-authoritarian capacity of digital media depends not only on technological ingenuity, but on democratic commitment. For the moral outrage of technicians, managers, and owners, as much as their technical abilities, was required to combat the repressive effects of government might.

> A senior strategist at National Public Radio, whose day job was in digital media, turned his personal Twitter account into a news wire. Seeking out voices and videos inside Egypt, he made 400 new posts a day to some 20,800 followers, many of whom were professional journalists with access to new media from around the world.[260]
>
> After the Egyptian state shutdown uploading to Twitter, activists inside Twitter and Google developed a news service, Speak2tweet, that allowed Egyptians without access to digital media to leave cell phone voice messages that could be filed as updates to Twitter.[261]
>
> After the Internet went back up, managers at YouTube working with Storyful, a social media curatorial service, discovered a way to retrieve and store the thousands of videos pouring out of Tahrir Square and to make them quickly accessible on CitizenTube, its news and politics channel.[262]

Each of the above items represents an ingenious technological achievement, but each also depended on its enablers having a will, not only a way. The owners of digital media could have cooperated with the Egyptian government and shut down their media without a fight. Egyptian performances of democracy influenced them to behave in exactly the opposite way.

> "Like many people, we've been glued to the news unfolding in Egypt and thinking of what we could do to help people on the ground," said a joint statement posted Monday by Ujjwal Singh, the co-founder of SayNow, and Abdel Karim Mardini, Google's product manager for the Middle East and North Africa. "Over the weekend we came up with the idea of a speak-to-tweet device – the ability for anyone to tweet using just a voice connection," the statement said. "We hope that this will go some way to helping people in Egypt stay connected at this very difficult time. Our thoughts are with everyone there."[263]

The Global Civil Sphere

It is notable that such supportive comments came from controllers of media technology located outside of Egypt. That the revolutionary performance inside Egypt unfolded before not only local but

81

international audiences was a critical reason, not just for its ultimate success, but for its very ability to proceed. In the middle of the worst days of government repression, an Egyptian novelist confided to a Western journalist that, "even if the regime continues to bombard us with bullets and tear gas, and continues to block Internet access and cut off our mobile phones, we will find ways to get our voices across the world and to demand freedom and justice."[264] He was confident the brutal physical power of the Egyptian regime could be restrained if protestors connected to the broader civil sphere outside. He was correct that, in the age of digital media, he and his colleagues could find ways to continue to project their civil productions beyond the national territory. He was also right that there would be a massive world audience to respond to demands for freedom and justice.[265] Yet, the global audience is fragmented, the perception of geopolitical interest matters as much as civil ideals, and the invocation of both global public opinion and sanctions is skewed in hegemonic, north-versus-south, west-versus-east sorts of ways.[266]

Capitalist democracies compromise their internal commitments to civil society in order to protect what they conceive as geopolitical interests, and in the Egyptian case there seemed to be many such interests indeed, from supporting Israel to fighting Islamic terrorism to maintaining stable oil production and prices. Some of these national interests are material, having to do with matters of life and limb and economic concerns of the gravest kind; others are moral, having to do with protecting a Jewish state in the post-Holocaust world. Whether material or ideal, during the days of the January 25 Revolution such interests formed an external environment in relation to which the American nation-state felt compelled to act in an instrumentally rational way. Regardless of commitments in principle to a civil society, national leaders felt American interests would be damaged by a revolutionary upheaval. At first, they opposed the democratic movement and supported Mubarak's continuing reign. After the first day of demonstrations in Egypt, US Secretary of State Hillary Clinton, even while protesting "we support the fundamental right of expression and assembly for all people," and while urging "all parties" to "exercise restraint and refrain from violence," offered an extraordinarily realpolitik "assessment" of the situation: "The Egyptian Government is stable and is looking for ways to respond to the legitimate needs and interests of the Egyptian people."[267] Nor did other democratic states offer Egyptian insurgents immediate support.

On the global level, despite Japan's democratic capitalism and China's rise, the global exercise of economic and military power remains largely limited to a handful of Western states, states that have chosen to bind their internal exercise of political power in a democratic way.[268] In Britain, France, and the United States, the civil sphere exercises ultimate control over the state. Civil power manifests itself in public opinion, which is powerfully affected by independent journalism. In the earliest days of Egypt's January 25 Revolution, Western media coverage was torn between two metaphors. In the poetics that sought to make sense of this titanic struggle, one finds the stark metaphorical contrast between 1979 and 1989.[269] "If Egyptian protesters overcome the government," the *New York Times* asked, "would this be 1979 or 1989?"[270] Which historical memory should be analogically applied? Were the events in 2011 Egypt like the anticommunist revolutions in Europe of 1989? Or did they resemble 1979 Iran, when the overthrow of the Shah, which at first seemed democratic, quickly gave way to a violent and repressive theocratic dictatorship? In 2011, a *New York Times* editorial warned "the Iranian Revolution is seared in our memories,"[271] one of its columnists recalling how "in 1979, a grass-roots uprising in Iran led to an undemocratic regime that oppresses women and minorities and destabilizes the region."[272] Perhaps, however, Egyptians were experiencing a revolution like the one in 1989. As the *New York Times* reminds its readers, "in 1989, uprisings in Eastern Europe led to the rise of stable democracies."[273] If the 1979 metaphor applied, then the contentious events in Egypt would be signified as wild, out of control, and sinister. If, however, Egyptians were actually inside a "1989" revolution, then events in 2011, while still contentious and often chaotic, could be coded as civil, and eminently worthy of identification and respect.

As the revolutionary performance inside Egypt became more powerful and sharply etched, the metaphorical confusion waned. The insurgency was less ambiguously framed. It became the "Arab Spring," and the 1989 metaphor applied. One *Le Monde* report put it this way:

> We're not in 1979. The Islamic revolution was a great disappointment. Young Arabs connected to the Internet have seen the videos of these young Iranians killed by the henchmen of Ahmadinejad. They identify more with them, or young Tunisians, than with the "beards." In the streets, the few "Allah Akbar" are drowned out by cries of "freedom."[274]

Another *Le Monde* report was even more generous, linking the events in Egypt with the nation's own sacred date of 1789, the year of the French Revolution.[275] *La Repubblica* also became less ambivalent:

Egyptian civil society has been growing and restructuring. Certainly, there is the Muslim Brotherhood, an archipelago of a thousand ambiguities, which Mubarak has sold successfully as a band of terrorists. But there are also non-Christians, nationalists, socialists, people who can no longer simply tolerate the "hereditary republic". The less we listen to and support their demands, the more the risk of an Islamist drift becomes concrete."[276]

This metaphorical shift was not limited to the left. Conservative media also began to manifest enthusiasm for the civil, revolutionary side.[277] An editorial in *USA Today* announced that "Egypt is not post-Shah Iran"[278] and another concluded that "a foreign policy that stands in opposition to American ideals – in Egypt as elsewhere – is one that is doomed to failure."[279]

Indeed, the enthusiasm of Western media for the Egyptian revolution has been on display throughout the pages of this chapter, evidenced in the hundreds of citations to influential media in France, Italy, the United Kingdom, and the United States, and to the broadcasts beamed into these domestic civil spheres from Al Jazeera (English). While the reports from these professional journalists were detached, they were less "objective" than interpretive judgments. Journalists evaluated the revolution's unfolding events in relation to the overarching discourse of civil society, a standard that reflected not only the professional ethics of journalists but also the commitments of democratic constituencies back home. In turn, such reporting affected opinion in the civil spheres of Western nations.[280] Al Jazeera's Arabic reporting powerfully influenced Egypt's emerging civil sphere in a similar way. Presenting themselves as both professionally independent and deeply democratic, Al Jazeera journalists deployed the moral binaries of civil discourse to sentimentalize the revolution's protagonists and stigmatize its enemies.[281] Between such Arabic and Western journalism there was, in fact, a marked intertextuality, with each side referring frequently to the other's reporting to make its own points. In a broadcast early on January 25, for example, Al Jazeera (Arabic) reported that "an American reporter in Cairo for *Time* magazine described the protests that are expected to take place today [as] similar to the popular outpouring that caused the fall of Zine El Abidine Ben Ali in Tunis," and as an "historical event with respect to popular political activity in the age of Hosni Mubarak." The broadcast ended with this news:

وقد حثت منظمة العفو الدولية السلطات المصرية على "السماح بالاحتجاجات السلمية"، وقال متعاطفون من مختلف أنحاء العالم إنهم يعتزمون تنظيم احتجاجات للتضامن مع الاحتجاجات في مصر.

And Amnesty International urged the Egyptian authorities to "allow peaceful protests," and sympathizers from around the world said that they intend to organize protests in solidarity with protests in Egypt.[282]

Western journalists, for their part, often referred to Arabic reports in Al Jazeera to provide evidence of the depth and breadth of the democratic uprising among the Egyptian people.

No wonder that Egyptian state authorities threatened, intimidated, and often physically attacked journalists throughout the revolutionary fight. Such incidents generally had a boomerang effect, however, transforming journalists from implicit into explicit protagonists in the dramatic struggle between liberty and repression, a transformation that supplied "global civil society" with new heroes in its critical reaction to the Egyptian state. In the UK, the *Guardian* provided a detailed first-hand account of correspondent Jack Shenker's physical assault and arrest by security forces alongside Egyptian protestors.[283] Al Jazeera and CNN broadcast similar stories about attacks on their leading correspondents.[284]

The Army

Social performances are always mediated by power, and not only of the interpretive kind. That the Egyptian army refrained from exercising its physical power is what allowed the agonistic performances of government and protestors to play out, for the revolutionary confrontation to be in greater part symbolic, and for the radicals to make such an arresting case that civil power compelled Mubarak to leave the scene.

In democracies, the civil sphere places extraordinary physical, administrative, legal, and cultural constraints upon the exercise of mass violence inside the territory of the nation-state. A nation's armed forces have the physical power many times over to control domestic disputes, but even in civil emergencies, when the internal activation of military force is authorized, officers of the civil sphere issue orders that greatly inhibit physical fire power. Because authoritarian societies do not possess such civil constraints, the armed forces often exercise, and more frequently threaten to exercise, massive physical power on the domestic scene. Certainly, this was the case in postcolonial Egypt, where presidents Nasser, Sadat, and Mubarak all rose from the ranks of the army and made use of its physical capacities for all sorts of domestic tasks.

Why the army failed to intervene during the January 25 Revolution has often been explained by material interest. That the army wished to preserve its wealth and status is certainly not to be denied. If these were its primary motives, however, military leaders would have sided with autocracy, for Mubarak fed, clothed, and pampered them, and wished them always at his side. But perhaps they refrained from repression from fear they would be injured by the backlash from democratic public opinion. This might indeed have happened, but why would the army have cared, if they lived in a privileged and isolated manner, had the physical power to protect themselves, and only its material self-interest were at stake?

In fact, there is evidence that many army officers, as well as the mass of draftees, were attracted to the emotions and ideals projected by revolutionary performances. The staff were trained by, and spent long periods of time in, Western democratic countries, particularly the United States, where contentious democratic conflicts are rife and civil inhibitions still rule. For the first time in decades, Mubarak did order army troops actively to intervene in Egypt's political life, yet the army, while agreeing to be present, chose to remain aloof. Not the army, but Mubarak's secret police and specially recruited civilians were the forces that violently intervened. In the epiphanic moment that followed the January 28 battle between revolutionaries trying to enter Tahrir Square and police forces blocking it, the army declared its respect for the civil cause of the protestors and refused to physically intervene:

> The six-day uprising here entered a new stage about 9 p.m. when a uniformed spokesman declared on state television that "the armed forces will not resort to the use of force against our great people" ... The military understood "the legitimacy of your demands" and "affirms that freedom of expression through peaceful means is guaranteed to everybody."[285]

By the evening of January 29, the side that the army was taking had become manifest and clear.

> On the 6th October bridge, as darkness fell, a couple of dozen police were attempting to hold their positions confronted by a crowd of several thousands. It was under this bridge that the *Guardian* saw the first army vehicles, two armoured infantry carriers, motoring down the Nile Corniche, news of their arrival cheered by demonstrators. By 7:45 p.m. a column of army tanks was visible, rumbling across the Abd El Moniem Riyad overpass, flying Egyptian flags. Some of them had protesters dancing on them as they drove along.[286]

For their part, throughout the demonstrations, protestors expressed solidarity with the army:

> Egyptian protesters in Cairo chanted slogans calling for the army to support them, complaining of police violence during clashes on Friday in which security forces fired teargas and rubber bullets. "Where is the army? Come and see what the police are doing to us. We want the army."[287]

> Adel, an engineer conscripted into the army, had shed his military uniform and joined the protesters, watching as the tanks rolled across the street. He warned that deaths were inevitable. "Some soldiers won't fire on the Egyptian people, but others are too scared to disobey orders. You have no idea what rebelling in the army can mean for you." He continued: "I am supposed to be on the 7am train to my barracks, but we are witnessing the final hours of Mubarak and his regime."[288]

> ElBaradei, who is now backed by the powerful Muslim Brotherhood and other opposition groups, said he wanted to negotiate about a new government with the army, which he described as "part of the Egyptian people."[289]

> Tanks surround Tahrir Square but the army has declared it will never attack the people. Young Egyptians surround the tanks, chatting with the soldiers. Last night there was a football game – "the people versus the army" – with a tank as the prize. The people won. They did not get the tank. But then one of the most popular chants in Tahrir today is: "The people, the army as one hand."[290]

> Mostafa Hussein, a rights activist, said: "I have to admit I feel anxious about the future. I worry the military will try to control the country with an iron fist. The only thing I can be certain of is that they won't open fire and try to kill us en masse."[291]

> Tawfik El-Mardenly ... 62, managing director of a telecom company, served as a private before the 1973 war against Israel. "We never say anything bad about the army," he said. "They gave us the only victory in our life," he said, referring to the 1973 war that led to strategic gains for Egypt. "People don't see them as corrupt, unlike the police." He added, "We respect the army, and we would like to keep this respect as long as we can. This is not the army's role."[292]

It was when the army publicly reaffirmed its commitment to the civil cause, on the penultimate day of the confrontation, that Egypt's dictator had no practical option but to resign.

The argument for material interest can also be externally made. The reason for the army's exercise of self-constraint may be seen as responding to threats from hegemonic powers, if not from global civil society. It is a fact that nation-states and their armies monopolize the means of violence on the global scene. In a global order more Hobbesian that Lockean, hegemonic control operates at both regional and international levels. With many times the national military budget of other nations, significant technological advantages, a vast military network of alliances, and robust if often precarious international prestige, the US government often uses threats of military intervention, and sometimes the real thing, to gain international control. While it did not threaten directly to intervene in Egypt, the American military still had significant effect. Early on, Vice-President Joe Biden publically warned the Egyptian army that, if it did intervene against the protestors, the United States would "review its commitments" to supplying its annual $1.3 billion military aid. From that point on, American military officers at every level made frequent informal contacts with their Egyptian counterparts, warning them against intervention.[293]

This exercise of American power over the Egyptian army was significant. It begs the question, however, of why the United States should wish to prevent the army's physical intervention in the first place. Answering this question takes the search for an explanation back from the material to the ideal side. The democratic reporting of journalists affected domestic public opinion, which then exerted civil power against government support for Mubarak. Reporters' sympathetic interpretations, outraged letters to editors,[294] influential op-ed columnists, and the deeply held civil distaste for anti-democratic oppression had a cumulative effect. "Faced with images of riot police using tear gas and water cannons," the *New York Times* reported, "President Obama moved from support to distancing."[295] Before long, the world's most powerful democratic nations were engaged in speech acts strongly sanctioning Mubarak and supporting the revolutionary movement. President Barack Obama and Secretary of State Hillary Clinton continually warned Egyptian officials to "allow peaceful public demonstrations" and reminded them that people needed "mechanisms to express legitimate grievances." When the plug was pulled on the Internet, US officials immediately issued blunt criticisms. As the revolutionary process traveled farther down the road, Secretary Clinton began repeating, "We have been very clear that we want to see an orderly transition to democracy,"[296] and key European leaders also publicly urged "restraint."[297] By the second week of the insurrection, as Mubarak became increasingly polluted by the protest, the *New York Times* reported that "Obama seemed determined to put as much daylight as possible" between himself and the Egyptian president.[298] Government sources leaked the story that, months before the January crisis, the American president had ordered an intensive secret policy review of the US Egyptian policy, which resulted in a classified eighteen-page "Presidential Study Directive," and that, during the crisis, Obama had devoted thirty-eight meetings to the topic.[299] In a televised speech to the American people hours after Mubarak's resignation, Obama projected deep sympathy for the civil struggle of the Egyptian revolution. "Egyptians have made it clear that nothing less than genuine democracy will carry the day," he declared. Evoking the iconic language of Martin Luther King, Jr., Obama connected the Egyptian struggle to the most revered movement of civil repair in America's own recent history. In Egypt, he declared, "it was the moral force of nonviolence – not terrorism and mindless killing – that bent the arc of history toward justice once more."[300]

Because public opinion in Western democratic societies mattered, Egyptian protestors directed messages to the communicative institutions of the global civil sphere. Explaining why English was the principal language other than Arabic in which the Tahrir Square protestors inscribed their signs, an academic said it was "to assert the country is modern and its citizens know the global language" and to combat "Western stereotypes about being backward and traditional."[301] In part because of the United States' hegemonic power, but also because of Obama's race and family background and the way he had reached out to Islamic civilization with his earlier "Cairo speech," the American president often received disproportionate attention from the Egyptian protesters:

> Many of the protesters were critical of the United States and complained about American government support for Mr. Mubarak [but] many of the protesters expressed their criticisms by telling American journalists that they had something to tell the president, directly. "I want to send a message to President Obama," said Mohamed el-Mesry, a middle-aged professional. "I call on President Obama, at least in his statements, to be in solidarity with the Egyptian people and freedom, truly like he says."[302]

WAAKS (English) projected a continuous stream of text, image, and sound from inside the heart of the revolution to English-reading and listening audiences in the wider world around. After the first day of confrontations, on January 25, the Facebook page sent out this message:

> Good night everyone. A kind request to our international supporters: Make your voice heard, tell your representatives and members of

parliament that you do not wish for your government to support dictatorships like Mubarak's. (January 26, 2011; 1:56 a.m.)

Early on January 28, the day of massive confrontation, WAAKS (English) posted:

It really feels like World population is becoming one nation. The amount of support we are getting from brave international individuals and groups is enormous. Wikileaks has just published fresh cables about Egyptian police brutality. Nothing new to us, but let the world see. I'll be posting a lot of news very soon. get ready. (January 28, 2011; 12:49 p.m.)

Some hours later, this post:

Many many thanks for the international solidarity. Individuals from all over the world have proved to themselves & to all of us that we are just ONE human race despite any differences. Please watch this excellent video by our supporters: A Guerilla Projection and "Remove Mubarak" on the UN building in New York. (January 28, 2011; 7:43 p.m.)

Finally, toward the end of the January 28 battle:

Please everyone. Don't let Egyptians suffer alone. Your support and pressure does make a lot of difference. Protest peacefully in your country, lobby your leaders & government, if the world turns on Mubarak, he will have to leave under pressure. (January 29, 2011; 1:53 a.m.)

On 11 February, WAAKS (English) posted this revolutionary denouement:

THANK GOD. THANKS TO ALL THOSE WHO DIED FOR US TO LIVE IN FREEDOM. THANKS TO ALL EGYPTIANS WHO SLEPT ROUGH IN TAHRIR, ALEXANDRIA AND EVERYWHERE. THANK YOU ALL ON THIS PAGE FOR YOUR SUPPORT AND YOUR AMAZING GREATNESS AND HELP. THANKS TO EVERYONE WHO CALLED HIS LEADER AND HIS REPRESENTATIVE. THANK YOU TUNISIA. (February 11, 2011; 6.54 p.m.; capitals in original)

— 3 —

POLITICAL PERFORMANCE IN THE US: OBAMA'S 2012 RE-ELECTION

From the Greeks and American Founding Fathers to modern political scientists, democracy has been misunderstood as an exercise in rationality. Voters are portrayed as employing unencumbered intellects, as looking at issues and weighing their interests, as having the ability to understand truth and see through the distortions of the other side. But this simply isn't the way political society works.

Over the last century, there has been an increasingly theatrical self-consciousness displayed in the pursuit of political power, both on behalf of and against the state. In my own work (Alexander 2010, 2011; Alexander and Jaworsky 2014),[1] I have deployed the concept "citizen-audience" to transform the deliberative theory of democracy in a culturally pragmatic way, examining the emergence of such distinctive performative elements as speech writers, performance coaches, advance men, focus groups, polls, and videographers, not only in the struggle for power but in the exercise of institutionalized power itself. Each of these new elements has become a focus of political specialization, responding to the increasing difficulty of creating political performances that seem convincing and authentic, a challenge exacerbated by social media, which creates active audiences and immediate critical feedback.

Voters do not decide whom to vote for by weighing their objective costs and benefits. They are not calculating machines, but emotional and moral human beings. Searching for the meanings of things, they want to make sense of political life, working out grand narratives about where we've been, where we are now, where we're going in the future.

Political candidates project themselves into these social dramas as "characters," casting themselves as heroic protagonists and their

91

opponents as wearing black hats. Citizen-audiences evaluate these shape-shifting performances, making identifications, not calculations. They support characters that seem life affirming and hopeful, and oppose those who appear evil and dangerous.

Those auditioning for presidential power aim to become collective representations, symbols that embody the best qualities of citizens and the nation. If a candidate succeeds in symbolizing the shared collectivity – America, Korea, Mexico, Ukraine – for enough voters, he or she will be allowed to control the nation's highest office.

Obama Character in Poetry and Prose

In 2008, during his first presidential campaign, Barack Obama created a truly inspiring character that compelled mass identification. In the first two years of his presidency, however, the emotional fusion binding this character to Americans on the left and center became attenuated. In some part, such loosening was inevitable. The symbolic intensity of Obama-character as it performed on the campaign trail could not possibly be sustained when Obama-President began manipulating the machinery of government.

There were also self-inflicted wounds. Obama's political autobiography was all about healing the polarizing wounds of the 1960s, but he deeply underestimated the difficulty of creating such a vital center inside Congress. During the 2009 year-long health care debate, post-partisan compromise was merely a figment of the president's imagination. He came away empty-handed, without a shred of Republican support. While Obama-character played the fiddle of reconciliation, the radical right Tea Party made America burn. Obama-character seemed cool and out of touch, neglecting narrative – as he later acknowledged – for the weeds of public health planning and economic policy. The political result of this performative failure? The Republicans smashed the Democrats in the Congressional midterm elections of 2010.

In the wake of their cathartic triumph, Republican leaders had the emotional energy of millions of angry, disappointed Americans in their hands. They had only to find a vessel for these seething emotions, a candidate who would become such a compelling collective representation that he could take back power in the 2012 elections. Republicans failed to rise to this creative challenge, emerging from the 2012 primary season with a cipher, not a symbol. Mitt Romney possessed a mile-long CV and a well-oiled political machine, but nary a shadow of charisma. He saw himself as a tool, not a vessel, an instrument of economic management rather than a vehicle for emotional and moral representation.

Instead of symbolizing, Romney disappeared into the role of the problem-solving businessman, offering pragmatism as reason enough to elect him. But voters wrap practical promises inside gauzy symbolic blankets. What matters is what citizens can feel, the character of the candidate and his story. They can't rationally evaluate the validity of promises. Is candidate Romney one of us? Is he up-from-the-bootstraps, a self-made American hero like Lyndon Johnson, Richard Nixon, or Bill Clinton? Is he a warrior hero like Eisenhower or Bush? Is he an aristocratic hero sacrificing personal comfort to work for the American people, like Teddy Roosevelt, FDR, or JFK?

It didn't matter who Mitt Romney actually was, only what his character seemed to be. With some shrewd rebranding by Obama and the Democratic production team, Romney-character emerged as "Bain Capitalist," the quarter-billionaire who wouldn't come clean about his taxes, parked hidden money offshore, and loaded a dog atop his car. Romney may have had brainpower, but he seemed to be missing soul. The Romney-character signified self over community, a glad hander who'd tell the American people what he wanted them to hear, not what he himself deeply believed.

The Obama-character presented a sharp contrast. The 2008 campaign had been poetry in motion, a hero promising salvation, but President Obama governed in prose, with no relief in sight. Whatever the practical failings of Obama-the-President, however, Obama-as-campaigner was still viewed as idealistic and honest, devoted to helping others rather than feathering his own nest.

Would Americans eventually come to see Obama-the-candidate as a good-hearted flop? The Republican performance team would have had it so. The dramaturgical challenge for the Democratic opposition was to transform the 2008 narrative so that Obama could be a transformative hero once again. The key was symbolizing economics. In 2008, Obama had promised to resolve the Great Recession and to restore America's economic might. Four years later, this had still not come to pass. Republicans portrayed Obama as a failed hero, a good-hearted flop. The Democrats repositioned Obama as inheriting, not creating, the nation's current economic mess. When former President Bill Clinton addressed the Democratic nominating convention in August, 2012, he declared that the economic crisis had already begun before the Obama presidency, shouting: "750,000 jobs were lost in January 2008 alone!" No human being could have done any better job, Clinton assured the American citizen-audience, than Obama had managed in the four years since. When, on the day following, President Obama formally accepted his party's nomination for a second term, he proclaimed that the nation was actually in the middle of an economic recovery, suggesting a new timeline according to which economic redemption would not be fully achieved for years to come, and only if he were elected for a second time.

The bounce in the polls that followed the Democratic nominating convention indicated that Obama-character had regained some traction with the center and suggested some refusion with the activist left. Even if Obama could no longer be an avidly romantic hero, he could, at the very least, be represented as working heroically for the people. The shape of the presidential contest had finally crystallized. According to the polls, President Obama had stretched his lead over challenger Romney, narrowly at the national level but decisively in the critical swing states.

Campaigns are all about hope and bluff. Though no one could hear a discouraging word from the Romney campaign, the writing was on the wall.

In the two-month-long dramaturgical space that stretched from the nominating conventions to election day in early November 2012, however, conspicuous opportunities remained for performative failures and successes. Looming largest among them were the presidential and vice-presidential debates, televised live and unscripted. No other events in the American political calendar so crystallize the triumph of ritual and dramaturgy over rational argument.

The *Huffington Post* invited me to comment on these critical performative encounters.[2] In the early morning of October 3, 2012, I posted "Obama's Downcast Eyes,"[3] describing the initial presidential debate as one that created dramatic reversal:

> The French poet Baudelaire spoke of "the grandiloquent truth of gestures on life's great occasions." Last night's debate marked one of the formulaic great occasions of American political life. But President Obama's gestures were not eloquent, and because of this theatrical failure he couldn't get a handle on political truth.
>
> Presidential debates are plays within a play. Campaigns are dramas, not fact-finding missions, and debates are theatrical episodes, not academic tests. Everybody knows the televised debates are artificial, scripted, rehearsed, and choreographed. Rhetorical, not deliberative, more professional wrestling than political argument.
>
> Yet the fifty million Americans who tune into these feigned encounters willingly suspend their disbelief. They are looking for a different, less

rational kind of truth. By drama's end they will find it – a feeling truth that depends on identification, character, drama, and catharsis – truth in an aesthetic sense, a matter of performance, not about who is right.

In last night's drama, the president reprised a role that, two years ago, nearly destroyed his presidency. He played The Last Rational Man, the policy wonk, the distanced professor. He worried over proper explanations. He spoke about numbers not adding up, about math and arithmetic.

Romney's numbers did not add up. The born again conservative blithely shrugged off Republican tax policy – which would balloon the deficit and slash entitlements – like an old suit that had become too tight: That's not my plan. I won't raise the deficit by 5 trillion dollars. I won't cut taxes for the rich. I won't reduce Medicare. I won't stop 26-year-olds from being ensured or cut off people with pre-existing conditions.

Bold lies! The Last Rational Man seemed taken aback. He tried explaining and reasoning, so the American people could see the Republican's numbers just didn't add up. "For eighteen months he's been talking about his tax cutting plan, now, five weeks before the election, he says never mind." Soon, it was back to the numbers. "It's a matter of arithmetic." Obama kept asking Americans to do the math.

The president should have told stories, to illustrate with narratives not explain with facts. Romney did exactly that. When the exasperated president insisted on the size of Republican tax cuts and deficits, the Governor replied: "I've got five boys, I'm used to people saying what isn't true!" Figuratively, he became the father, and Obama the wishful, wistful, and wayward prodigal son.

There was more to Obama's dramaturgical failure than bad lines and an out-of-date script. Political performances are also about eyes and energy, about looking and being looked at, about seeming eager and interested and caring.

Romney-character was animated, clearly relishing this fight. He was pink and cheerful and almost chirpy. Brimming with confidence, he could barely contain himself. His eyes were wide and open; he displayed a passionate mane.

Obama-character kept his eyes downcast. He seemed sad and passive, smiling wryly as if to admit he was weathering painful blows. When he looked up, his answers were often agonizingly slow. He searched for words and they didn't come easily.

When President Obama did find his voice, he spoke quietly of "balance" and "responsibility." Governor Romney, eyes wide open and energized by a fire within, spoke fervently of apocalypse and salvation. He concluded with soaring rhetoric about the "two different paths for our future as a nation." Obama ended by gesturing to the same old, same old, the dreary past, not a bright shining future.

The president kicked off the public debate with a private message to his "Sweetie" on the evening of their 20th anniversary. "There are a lot of points I want to make tonight, but the most important one is that 20 years ago I became the luckiest man on Earth." Ninety minutes later, it seemed painfully clear that the Barack Obama would have preferred to be out on a date. Mitt Romney was the happy warrior last night.

In response to these sharply contrasting political performances, polls recorded Obama's popularity tanking and Romney's on the rise. Obama's startled supporters accused the Democratic performance team of malfeasance. They had been confident; now they felt kicked in the stomach.

Just one week later, the parties' vice-presidential candidates had their own debate. In one corner was the Republican Paul Ryan, a youthful, extremely conservative Congressman from Wisconsin; in the other corner was Joe Biden, the venerable sitting vice-president, formerly a Democratic senator from Delaware. In the wake of President Obama's stumbling performance in the first debate, a great deal was now dramaturgically at stake. Early in the morning of October 11, I posted "Laughing Man and Choir Boy"[4] on the *Huffington Post*:

> Last night, Paul Ryan played the choir boy. Blue eyed and innocent, pretending to be a flowing font of sympathy for his fellow citizens' pain, seeming guileless, all he wanted to do was help Americans get a job and speak God's truth.
>
> Joe Biden laughed his head off.
>
> Paul tried telling his story of sincerity and concern. Joe sat in the back of the class, grinning, smirking, and grunting his amusement, often shouting out incredulous disbelief: You're kidding us, right?! Hey, we're in on the fun. We know it's a joke. It is a joke, right Paul? You don't think we're going to take this guff seriously, do you? It's all a bunch of malarkey!
>
> Every school kid in American knows how this trick is played. Some fakey student siting in the front row raises his hand, stands up, and drones on and on, trying to get on the teacher's good side. You and your friends glance at each other and start snickering in the back row. You don't have to say anything, but you steal the show. The attention of the class is diverted, and turns to you.
>
> Biden played the joker, but he wasn't being funny. Like Shakespeare's fool, there was method to his apparent madness. As Ryan said his lines, our attention was pulled away by the audacity, the sheer riskiness, of the Vice-President of the United States acting out in public. With his comic antics, Biden took himself outside the text, but not off the stage. He ended up front and center. His subversive tactics gave us permission to be snide about Ryan's performance too.

Of course, dramatic plots can have only one hero. In the performance of American politics, that's the president. But every hero has a side-kick, a spear carrier who passes the ammunition, takes a pratfall for the team and always comes up good natured and smiling (but one step behind) in the end. The job description is to make the big guy look good. The Lone Ranger and Tonto, Johnny Carson and Ed McMahon, Superman and Jimmy Olsen, Don Quixote and Sancho Panza.

Last night, Biden and Ryan auditioned for this secondary role.

For Ryan, this meant keeping the recently scrip-doctored Republican story going. The Democratic standard bearers are not heroes but whimpy failures. They're listless, don't care about America, have lost their purpose and energy. We Republicans are fighting ready. The Democrats portray us as wolves, but we actually are moderate democrats in disguise. It's we who are on the people's side; the Democrats are on the side of the state.

Biden's task was to engage in a blocking maneuver. He aimed to stop the surging Republican performance of competence and caring by showing it to be just that – a performance. Not by reasoning but by gesturing. In a dramatic language more powerful than speech, he suggested Republicans are telling a just-so story that's too funny for words, and that it's okay to laugh!

Blocking Ryan's story, Biden gave Obama a chance to rewind his own. The president lost last week's debate by playing the prissy Explainer-in-Chief who would rather reason than fight. He listened politely, allowing Romney to pivot to the new Republican story.

Last night, Obama's side kick gave the would-be hero a swift kick in the behind. Joe pulled Barack up off the ground, told him to stop being a doormat, to take off his shirt and flex his muscles and take back the role of partisan fighter who can throw a punch.

He did this by getting in choir boy's face. Paul Ryan played the studious nerd, the sincere, blue-eyed innocent trying to please the teacher by knowing all the facts. Big Old Joe called him out, continuously interrupted, gave no quarter, controlled the debate.

Joe sat in the back of the room and laughed. He was a holy fool and a brilliant bully. If he didn't deliver a knock-out, he certainly blocked the pilgrim's progress. Has he set the stage for the return of the hero next week?

This now became the burning focal point of the long-running presidential campaign. Could the hero come back? Barack Obama possessed an extraordinary gift for political performance, but time and time again he had also demonstrated a capacity to shoot himself in the foot, to crawl back into the shell of the Last Rational Man, leaving the performance of politics behind. This desire to de-dramatize – emotionally understandable but politically self-destructive – had shattered the presidential performance in the first Obama–Romney debate. If Obama could not recover his balance in the second, party leaders and pundits on all sides agreed, the presidential contest might be irrevocably tilted to the conservative side.

This didn't happen. Obama found his dancing shoes. In front of 70 million viewers, he exuded confidence and poise. On the *Huffington Post* site, in the early morning of October 17, 2012, I posted "Courtroom Drama of Truth and Lies."[5]

> In a democratic society, the struggle for power is not about force but ideals and aspirations, about the dream of justice and who has the courage to tell the truth.
>
> The right-wing individualism of Republican free market policies has crippled that party's ability to talk about justice while speaking the truth. Until Labor Day, Mitt Romney attacked redistribution, defended the wealthy, and described half the society as whining bottom dwellers. After Labor Day, Romney pulled the sheet off his Etch-A-Sketch and started over. New Romney is all about justice. Good jobs for all. Maintain taxes on the wealthy, middle class tax breaks, and popular parts of Obama Care. New Romney even supports abortion, didn't you know?
>
> Last week, good old Joe called this New Republicanism a bunch of malarkey. He's right, but the problem is how to get voters in the middle to agree? The empirical arguments are complex, the numbers numbing. Shouting "it's all lies" doesn't convince anybody who isn't already.
>
> The challenge for Democrats is to dramatize Republican deception, not to assert it factually. "He said, she said" isn't a winning strategy. Theater is about showing, not telling.
>
> Last week, Biden showed Republican deception by grinning and snorting and laughing.
>
> Last night, during the first two-thirds of debate, President Obama used numbers and, on four different occasions, tried simply telling his audience about New Romney's untruth: "What Governor Romney said just isn't true." "Not true, Governor Romney." "Not true." "It's just not true."
>
> Then Obama got a chance to show, not tell.
>
> Drastically miscalculating, Romney bitch-slapped the president: "When we have four Americans killed [in the American Embassy in Benghazi, Libya] ... the president, the day after that happened, flies off to Las Vegas for a political fundraiser, then the next day to Colorado for another ... political event."
>
> Obama was a shameless pol, not a patriot.
>
> Tough stuff. Rather than apologizing, or even explaining, the president had the wit to call the lying Republican's bluff.

Obama: "The day after the attack, Governor, I stood in the Rose Garden and I told the American people and the world that this was an act of terror." Far from being weak-kneed, the president had been angry, and had told the unvarnished truth. Not only then but now. Playing the hard man, the president stared Romney's insinuating insult down.

Obama: "The suggestion that anybody on my team ... would play politics or mislead when we've lost four of our own, Governor, is offensive. That's not what we do. That's not what I do as president, that's not what I do as commander-in-chief."

Romney maintained this was just what the president did do. Obama had backed down in the Rose Garden, and he was going to have to back down last night. The president was lying, not the New Republican side.

Romney: "I think [it's] interesting that the president just said ... that on the day after the attack he went into the Rose Garden and said this was an act of terror."

The president's reply was pure as ice, and just as cold.

Obama: "That's what I said."

The exchange had become a confrontation, the stakes starkly raised. It was no longer about who was right about facts, but who was a liar. A direct accusation had been made against the president of the United States, who then called his accuser out. The narrative struggle between good and evil tightened, and the drama ratcheted up.

Now this was not a debate but a courtroom drama. The theater plays nightly on TV as the tense struggle between crime and justice, with prosecutors and defense lawyers fighting to discover who is the shadow faced liar and who the truth teller dressed in white.

Prosecutor Romney pressed his case: "You said in the Rose Garden [that] it was not a spontaneous demonstration, is that what you're saying?

Obama's reply seemed scripted for a courtroom fight: "Please proceed, Governor."

Falling for the trap, Romney resorted to dramaturgical legalese: "I want to make sure we get that for the record because it took 14 days before he called the attack on Benghazi an act of terror."

The defending attorney now pulled the noose tight.

Obama: "Get the transcript."

Here comes the judge. CNN [debate] moderator Candy Crowley ruled for the defense. She didn't need to go to the Rose Garden transcript to confirm the truthfulness of the defendant's side.

At first, however, Judge Crowley hesitated. So much was on the line.

Crowley: "It - it - it – he did, in fact, sir. So let me – let me call it an act of terror."

Obama seized this third party testimony of Romney's bad faith, but he wanted it more dramatically made.

Obama: "Can you say that a little louder, Cindy?"
She could: "He did call it an act of terror."
Objection sustained.
Dramatic plots turn on epiphanic moments of revelation. Republicans know how to lie with statistics, but they may find it difficult to resist last night's dramatic moment of moral truth. Their leader had called the president out, but the judge caught him in a stark and snarky bold-faced lie. Romney staked his integrity on humiliating Obama, but it was he who was humbled.
Last night, the Republic standard bearer didn't just stumble. In full view of 70 million Americans, he spectacularly fell from grace.

Two weeks later, President Obama decisively won re-election. As in 2008, he received more than 50 per cent of the popular vote, the first Democratic candidate to do so in nearly 70 years. Not only media commentators, but social scientists too made a great brouhaha about the shifting demographics of the American electorate, claiming that its increasingly nonwhite, non-Anglo composition had guaranteed Obama victory. Yet, while such factors are hardly without consequence, they can no more guarantee an effective political performance than financial backing guarantees the success of a Broadway play on opening night. Everything is open, in politics as in theater. There is no warranty. The play's the thing.

During adolescence and young adulthood, Barack Obama had stripped off layers of social convention in order to establish a singular identity. Becoming his own man, he launched an inner-directed political career. How frustrating to discover, as he reached for the political zenith, that he had become a character in some melodrama that he would prefer not to play.

But for all his role-distancing and existential dread, Barack Obama knew that political success depended on becoming a central character in the publican play. Democracy does not engage the populace in a debating society but a stage. Political campaigns are epics splashed across a panorama that plays out in mythical, not historical, time. Citizen-audiences come into contact not with actual candidates, but with their symbolic representation. These semblances are projected by media outlets, supplied with content by political campaigns. The ambition of campaigns is to control the image. And the challenge of political performance is to become the protagonist in your own play. Politicians enact scripts that coil expectations, stoke anxious fears, and raise high hopes. As these social texts roll out, they offer themselves as candidates for lead in the play.

While creating a powerful narrative requires a highly developed feeling for the times, the role for which candidates audition is pretty much standardized. To be elected president, you must be a hero, or at least be seen as one. Heroes are extraordinary individuals with a touch of immortality about them. Taking great risks, they save people in dark times. Heroes transform and save. They lead people from darkness to light.

In 2008, the Democratic production team wrote a fresh and audacious script that seemed perfectly fitted to the spirit of the times, and Obama-character played the role of hero with flare, passion, and redeeming authenticity. Under the reign of evil Bush II, America had endured a dark era of duplicity, war, and corruption, and an arrogant refusal to address democratic domestic needs. Enter Barack Obama stage left. Casting himself in the image of Martin Luther King, Jr., Obama the youthful hero could also proclaim "I have a dream," as he promised fundamental change. He would create justice and reverse the rising tide of inequality. He would stop the oceans from rising and make the cities green.

Obama's "Performance of Politics 2008" was a brilliant success, but neither the narrative nor its protagonist survived the prose of Obama-the-President's "Performance of Power." In art, challenging twists and turns of plot are carefully calibrated to reveal the hero's qualities. In life, heroes can be played the fool. Events spin out of control, presenting outsized challenges that can be difficult or impossible to overcome.

Faced with a spoiled identity, the only option for the president's 2012 re-election campaign was to rewrite the play. Instead of the conquering hero, Obama played the little Dutch boy with his finger in the dike. Rather than promising to transform America, the 2012 Obama-character pledged, if elected, that things wouldn't get worse. Rather than promising to reason with recalcitrant Republicans, Obama *Deux* embarked on a battle to destroy their faithless, feckless leader. This 2012 plot depended less on pumping up the protagonist than dumbing down the antagonist and blackening him with a polluting brush. Through summer and convention time, this asymmetrical warfare worked. Romney was painted as unscrupulous, elitist, extremist. He was not only against women, minorities, and the 47 percent, but democracy itself.

But as summer turned into autumn, and conventions gave way to debates, the brutal exigencies of social – as compared with theatrical – performance came back into play. In social performance, you can write a script for your antagonist, but you can't make him play. Your team can plot a winning role for the protagonist, but there is no assurance he'll ably act it out.

101

For months, Romney-character had been giving gifts to the Obama production team, falling neatly into their traps. Meanwhile, the Obama-character was being feisty and aggressive, connecting with audiences, seeming authentic, not a hero but a striver who well stood his ground. All this changed with the first debate. The Democratic plot turned inside out, protagonist and antagonist seeming to switch sides. The Obama-character was suddenly deflated with cast down eyes, while the Romney-character swelled and expanded with power. Before 70 million Americans, in what seemed an unscripted moment, Mitt Romney gave the performance of his life. The Republican successfully auditioned for the role of president.

In the weeks that followed, the Performance of Politics 2012 became a more even and deadly fight. Amidst Democrat moaning about lies and "Romnesia," the Republicans' lead character remained robust, white teeth shining, hair glistening, voice charged, and gestures ramped up.

The ancient Greeks distinguished between *Kairos* and *Chronos*. *Chronos* is calendar time, orderly and linear. *Kairos* is the right time, the opportune moment, improvised for the occasion. In early October, Romney had seized the day. Taking control of *Kairos*, he pushed Obama into mere calendar time. The Obama-character struggled to get back into mythos. Though damaged, his wound did not prove mortal. In the second debate, the hero returned to the stage. Like King Arthur, Obama became not only the once, but the future king.

The Dramatization of Consciousness

Four decades ago, in a proclamation that seemed counterintuitive for a Marxist theorist, Raymond Williams insisted that contemporary societies must still dramatize social consciousness. Williams acknowledged that the transition from ritual to theater – what I have called performative defusion – was a process that had nurtured critical intervention: "Drama broke from fixed signs, established its permanent distance from myth and ritual and from the hierarchical figures and processions of state."[6] Yet, even if drama "separated," Williams suggested, it "did not separate out altogether"; for "beyond what many people can see as the theatricality of our image-conscious public world, there is a more serious, more effective, more deeply rooted drama: the dramatization of consciousness itself."

Drama is fundamental to the search for meaning and solidarity in a post-ritual world. How else can character, virtue, and morality be sustained when the metaphysics of cosmological religion has broken down and social rituals are sporadic and incomplete? Drama displaces yet also encompasses shreds of the premodern religious order. Before theater, the pragmatics of social performance was relatively simple. With the emergence of theater, in the post-cosmological world of complexity and defusion, social performances became extraordinarily difficult. Social theory must understand and conceptualize these difficulties, examining how dramatic techniques not only separate and shape the elements of performance, but seek to put them back together again.

— 4 —

DRAMATIC INTELLECTUALS

This chapter is concerned not with intellectuals as creators of important ideas, but with creators of important ideas who become compelling actors in a social scene – men and women whose ideas can make social things happen, either when they're alive and kicking (such intellectuals do kick) or after their corporal bodies have passed from the scene. This is not intellectual history, but a sociological approach to the historical achievements of certain kinds of intellectuals.

Reflecting Ideas: Sociology of Culture

Explaining such intellectuals does mean explaining something about the form and formation of their ideas, but much more as well – why their ideas had large effect. Most social scientists and theorists addressing these questions have offered reductionist models that make social-structural position determining. From Marx to Bourdieu, the focus has been on the *non*-ideational circumstances that the creators of ideas find themselves in: capitalism replacing feudalism; industrialism creating a working class; massification flattening society; the emergence of new ruling classes, middle classes, or power elites; nations losing wars, suffering economic depression, or runaway inflation. Such emergent situations are portrayed as stealth conditions, lying in wait until they could properly be seen. Eventually, a smart, talented, and ambitious intellectual comes along who – finally! – can correctly read the social scene. *Et voila*! It is because intellectual theories mirror the nature of society,[1] so the structuralist story goes, that they can affect it so.

A limpid statement of such reflection theory can be found in

The Communist Manifesto. "The theoretical conclusions of the Communists," Marx and Engels assert,[2] "are in no way based on principles that have been invited, or discovered, by this or that would-be reformer," but "merely express in general terms actual relations springing from an existing class struggle, from a historical movement going on under our very eyes." The *Manifesto* provides a structural approach not only to the ideas of intellectuals but to their motivation. Radical intellectuals are described as representing a "small section of the ruling class" who had once been "bourgeois ideologists" but whose class position has now been so reduced that they have become proletarianized.[3] The "process of dissolution going on within the ruling class," Marx and Engels suggest, is of such a "violent and glaring character" that the economic basis of bourgeois life has disappeared. Just as external reality explains the content of intellectual ideas, so does external circumstance explain why intellectuals have created it.

According to this model of *déclassé*, ideas are pathways for intellectuals who have lost their social position to gain compensation. Employing skills from their once privileged life, they enable a lower group to rise, and themselves along with it. Thus is a model of social determinism transformed into the semblance of a theory of agency. In the hands of such thinkers as Pierre Bourdieu and Michele Lamont, intellectuals become unconscious strategizers.[4] When conceived in this manner, however, agency is illusory. Ideas become simply a nonmaterial means for profit-maximization. There is no reference to the impact of ideas themselves, to the contingency of their creation, or the symbolic power of their effect.[5] Reflection theory blocks a dramaturgical approach to intellectuals and a voluntaristic[6] understanding of ideational creation.

Two variations of the structural model have sought to modify its deterministic and reductionist cast. One approaches intellectuals as a new middle class. Once-respected members of the *Bildungsbürgertum*, intellectuals have now become the best-educated members of an information-processing class. Working with information, Alvin Gouldner claimed, creates the "culture of critical discourse."[7] But if a discourse is a reflection of the labor process, can it actually be a critical reflection upon it? In *Intellectuals on the Road to Class Power*, George Konrad and Ivan Szelenyi are more blunt.[8] Their displaced middle-class thinkers are not ideationally, but self-motivated: their ideas have no causal independence from intellectuals' political and economic interest.

Yet another variation of the structural model approaches

intellectuals as spiritually alienated and socially envious; they are expected to supply cultural patina, but possess neither political nor economic power. Edward Shils reasoned that such dislocation inspires a gnostic yearning among intellectuals: they demand a utopian but thoroughly impractical transcendence. Intellectuals are out of touch with actually existing possibilities for changing society in mundane but practical ways.[9]

Structural approaches to intellectuals identify elements central to any sociological explanation. Highly educated persons are deeply affected by changing social circumstances. But only a tiny few among such persons respond by creating compelling systems of new ideas, and fewer still have the skill and good fortune to ensure that their ideas have dramatic effect. Structural approaches cannot explain how ideas become causes. They exemplify what I have called a sociology *of* culture in contrast with a cultural *sociology*.[10] Noncultural, social factors are prerequisites of effective intellectual action, but they predict neither the content of intellectual ideas nor the process of intellectual action, much less their social effects. Structural models do not help us understand the drama of intellectual life and the performative possibilities of progressive and reactionary ideas.

Performing Ideas: Cultural Sociology

To achieve such understandings, we must turn from sociology of culture to cultural sociology, from a theory of external circumstances to a meaning-centered theory, one that models how social meaning is instantiated via social performance.[11] Intellectual actors orient themselves to meaning. They want to enact mythos and engage in symbolic action, but they must also be acutely sensitive to pragmatics and strategy. Social performance theory conceptualizes such cultural pragmatics. It develops a macro-sociology of how social meanings can become dramatic in the complex contexts of contingent social life.

Intellectuals play powerful social roles insofar as (1) their ideas provide poetically potent scripts; (2) the scripts not only read well but have the potential to "walk and talk," thus contributing to the staging of social dramas; and (3) the enacted scripts so affect the meanings and motivations of audiences that social actors are motivated to participate in social movements and build new institutions. To the degree that these conditions are met, to that degree do intellectuals become dramatic personae in the deeply affecting performances their ideas have created. Their persons become iconic, condensed, simplified, and charismatic collective representations of the transformational models they themselves propose – contemporarily, in real time, or retrospectively, in memory.

When human societies were small and relatively unified, they had no need for intellectuals; the metaphysical, social, and natural worlds that composed such societies seemed tied together in an immanent way. The social performances that give body and direction to organic social worlds do not require reflection and innovation. They are rituals, scheduled social performances, habitual and consensual, that call out stereotyped emotions and meanings and produce predictable social effects. When organic societies decompose, under the pressures of social rationalization, institutional differentiation, and cultural fragmentation, the elements fused together in ritualistic performance begin to unwind. As the elements of performance defuse, mythos becomes more separated from mundane society and audiences become separated from actors. For social understandings to become widely shared, they must now be projected and elaborately staged. In conditions of defusion, it becomes more difficult to project authentic and persuasive performances, to bring the elements of performance back together, to make symbolic action stick. Shamans give way to priests and theologians and eventually to intellectuals, the first historical creators of ideas who have the burden of making things up.[12]

Powerful intellectuals create symbolic frameworks that re-fuse fragmented meanings, actions, and institutions. They provide a new horizon of meaning for social actors who, having lost the "sense" of social and cultural circumstance, experience emotional anxiety and existential stress. To command dramatic ideational power, intellectuals must code and narrate newly emerging social realities in a manner that offers salvation.[13]

To make meaning in synchronic terms, intellectuals define binaries of good and evil. They identify contemporary social arrangements as dangerous and polluting, and conjure up utopian alternatives, antidotes that promise to purify and save. To be forceful, however, intellectual ideas must also be diachronic. They must place sacred and profane social forces into historical time, and narrate them as protagonists and antagonists. The past becomes a golden age; the present is framed as a fateful falling away into oppression, nihilism, or anomie. Socially effective intellectuals persuade us that a far different future is possible. The present is not an end point but a hinge of history. While necessarily connected to the past from which it emerges as a present,

107

contemporary time may swing either way. It may thrust forward to future salvation or remain caught inside the present, soon to become a corrupted past.

When intellectuals create narratives that juxtapose heroic protagonists with dangerous antagonists, the tension is portrayed not only as social struggle, but as storied plot. Sacred and profane binaries thus become dramatic, energized by all-or-nothing battles that decide our shared human fate. They have inspiring ups and harrowing downs. There is a battle for position, and history can go either way.[14] When virtue wins, the sacred is protected and evil slain. When social crisis leads to collective catharsis, blocking elements are pushed aside and ordinary time becomes *Weltgeschichte*. Social protagonists become heroes; so do the intellectuals who created the theory scripting the struggle and its transformative denouement.

Intellectual Heroes of the American Left

In *Seeds of the Sixties*, their singular account of American social critics in the 1950s, Ron Eyerman and Andrew Jameson describe these intellectuals in exactly such heroic terms.[15] "This is a book about dissident intellectuals and the breathing spaces that they carved out of the postwar landscape." As heroes, these 1950s intellectuals are praised for creating compelling binaries, for having had the courage to draw a sharp line between the human sacred and the dehumanizing profane. C. Wright Mills and Hannah Arendt are portrayed as condemning the "age of conformity," "defending the right of dissent," and "reinventing partisanship." Lewis Mumford and Rachel Carson "gave voice to the deviant and downtrodden" at a time "when most intellectuals were falling in line." Herbert Marcuse and Margaret Mead "kept open the critical processes of debate" in a world of "industrialized science and bureaucratic ... knowledge." The courage of these heroic thinkers is demonstrable. Because they fiercely "struggled for autonomy and individualism" in the "quiescent days of the 1950s," they were able to provide "rays of Enlightenment" in "dark times." These progressive intellectuals were able to weave the binaries of darkness and light into "before and after" stories that narrate how temporally located social action could transform institutional space. Planting the intellectual seeds for radical transformation, "they helped inspire the emergence of new political energy," "prepar[ing] the way for a new wave of radicalism [in] the sixties."

As they interpret their empirical material, Eyerman and Jameson

108

develop the culture structures that animate intellectual performance, imposing a model of meaning-making that allows intellectual drama to be made. What I want to suggest here is that these culture structures go well beyond the specifics of this American case. They are universal. To be dramatic, the performances of every powerful intellectual must be patterned in similar ways.

Intellectual Heroes of the European Left (1): Live Performance

Intellectuals clarify their times by creating tense moral binaries and narrating these qualities as social struggles between sacred heroes and diabolical enemies. Even as they crystallize dark fears, their theories create the alchemy for transcending them, all at the same time.

- In the chaotic and wrenching admixture of early industrial society, Karl Marx developed an apocalyptic story about good and evil, suffering and salvation.[16] There were just two, fiercely competitive social forces, proletariat and bourgeoisie. Capitalism was to blame, class struggle was the result, and communism the resolution.[17]
- Amidst the suicidal anxieties of fin-de-siècle Vienna[18] and interwar Europe, Sigmund Freud portrayed the struggle between id and superego, the former terrifyingly primitive, the latter superciliously civilized. Id and superego engaged in titanic battle, not only in the course of an individual life but over the course of social evolution. Modernity was built upon massive repression, producing guilt feelings temporarily relieved by outbursts of deadly aggression.[19] Only the heroic interventions of psychoanalysis could save the day. Where id was, ego shall be.[20]
- John Maynard Keynes came to public acclaim as a prophet of doom after what was euphemistically called The Great War. In his caustic, fuming scythe of an essay, *The Economic Consequences of the Peace*,[21] the Cambridge educated and Bloomsbury cultivated Clytemnestra denounced the war's victors as villains and portrayed the war's aggressors as victims.

The Economic Consequences of the Peace ... was no mere technical treatise. The torrid *mise-en-scène* at Paris is vividly recreated; the failings of Clemenceau, Wilson, and Lloyd George are displayed with cruel precision. The writing is angry, scornful and ... passionate. [Keynes's] denunciations of bungling and lying [and] his moral indignation ... ring ... loud and clear. Giving shape to the whole is a brooding sense of menace; a sense of the travails of a civilization *in extremis*; of the mindless mob waiting its turn to usurp the collapsing inheritance; of the futility and frivolity of statesmanship. The result is a personal statement unique in twentieth-century literature. Keynes was staking the claim of the economist to be Prince. All other forms of rule were bankrupt. The economist's vision of welfare, conjoined to a new standard of technical excellence, were the last barriers to chaos, madness, and retrogression.[22]

In the two decades that followed, the sky darkened as Keynes had predicted. The economist who was increasingly regarded as a political hero created an intellectual opus that promised to save the day, the *General Theory*.[23] Capitalism was not organic and self-regulating, but dystonic, disequilibrated, and chaotic, possibly in a fateful way. The animal spirits of business owners made rational evaluation of risk impossible, with boom and bust the inevitable result. Keynes's general theory not only explained this dark reality, but offered salvation.[24] Keynesian economists could provide a new social ego. Where greedy impulse and destructive austerity once were, state planning and counter-cyclical spending could be.

- Jean-Paul Sartre came of age during the ashes of World War II, which Keynes had earlier prophesized, in a country prostrate in military and moral defeat. When Sartre rocketed to intellectual dominance in 1944 and 1945, it was not only because of the subtleties of *Being and Nothingness*,[25] his new phenomenology, but rather because of the promise of existential and national salvation that the work implicitly promised to provide.[26] Social actors live in a condition of freedom, and if they are enchained it is their own doing. At every moment we have a choice. If we take responsibility for our thoughts and actions, we act in good faith, with social liberty the result.[27] If we refuse to take responsibility, denying our ability to choose, we act in bad faith, and possibilities for civil repair disappear.[28] These broad brush ideas provided a morally compelling explanation for France's decrepitude and the promise that, if responsibility were taken, national salvation could still be achieved.

Intellectual ideas can be understood as performance-oriented scripts. Yet, while they represent extraordinarily creative ideation, they are neither *de novo* nor *sui generis*. Drawing from background representations, they constitute new *paroles*, new kinds of speech acts inside already existing *langues*. Only in this manner is it possible for radically innovative intellectual ideas to make themselves understood.

110

Insofar as they succeed in becoming dramatically powerful, they will become a new metalanguage themselves. Marx was a German Hegelian, French socialist, and British political economist before he became "Marx," the communist theorist of capitalism. Freud was a psycho-physiologist and a hypnotherapist before he became "Freud," the psychoanalyst. Keynes was a probability theorist and neo-Marshallian before he became "Keynes," the master economist of the twentieth century. Sartre was the devotee of Husserl and Heidegger before he became "Sartre," the founder of existentialism.

Intellectual Heroes of the European Left (2): Post-Life Performance

Meaning-making is at the center of dramatic intellectual action, but it is not all there is. Materiality is critical, as is power. Performances need to deploy actors who can dramatically speak and act intellectual scripts; the actors need access to the means of symbolic production, to stages, props, media of communication, and other mass-projection techniques; and, even when such elements are at hand, performances need producers and directors who can put them together into *mises-en-scène*. Salvation can be promised intellectually, but it must be dramatically enacted to be felt and practical enough to be seen. And there is one more requirement for fused performance: a broad audience must be deeply engaged. To be dramatic, intellectuals must project their ideas far beyond their immediate networks and professional milieus, beyond disciplines and universities into the wider world. Will efforts to fuse with a broader audience be successful? Nobody can say. The element of surprise is integral to every great performance. It is what makes drama dramatic. Performances are electrifying because they are filled with risk.

- Marx needed the organization of the First and then the Second International for "Marxism" to become intellectually dramatic. Marxism needed mass political parties to act as producers of its social performances,[29] and skilled directors such as Rosa Luxemburg, Vladimir Lenin, and Mao Zedong to develop techniques for so powerfully fusing with worker and peasant audiences that revolutionary action would result.[30]
- Along with his powerful written scripts, Freud developed techniques of therapeutic practice that fused psychoanalytic ideas with suffering patient-audiences. He assembled a priestly core group

111

whose members became the central cast for globally projecting the psychoanalytic way.[31] Their dramatic struggles to remake the modern psyche were empowered by organizations and journals, fueled by world congresses, and punctuated by moments of integrative triumph and splitting despair.

- Keynes would have been able neither to create nor to project *The Economic Consequences of the Peace* if he were not an insider at the postwar peace talks in Versailles. He could not have become an influential member of the British delegation to the peace talks if he had not been educated at King's College, nurtured by Cambridge Apostles and Bloomsbury bohemians, and sheltered at the highest levels of the Treasury for the duration of World War I. Keynes's access and centrality are not sufficient to explain his essay's dramatic power, but they were necessary for its preparation. So was the fact that his audience was ready and primed. Within a year of publication, *Economic Consequences* had sold more than 100,000 copies and was translated into a dozen languages. The script's instant worldwide fame depended on more than Keynes's apocalyptic style and technical arguments: "It captured a mood. It said with great authority, flashing advocacy and moral indignation what 'educated' opinion wanted said."[32]

- Sartre had access to the means of symbolic production only because, in the wake of French humiliation and defeat, much more established and powerful intellectual performers had been accused of collaboration and forced off the stage.[33] His essays on war guilt and existentialism became powerful because they appeared at the epiphanic moment of liberation, when the French nation was trying to salvage self-respect and forge a way forward domestically and on the international scene. Sartre appeared as a hero at mass rallies, wrote columns for newspapers, and spoke eloquently on radio. In *Les Temps modernes*, he organized a core group of existential actors to connect with other intellectuals as well as activists on the local and international scene.[34]

Thus far, my analysis of intellectual performance has been relatively schematic. Assuming familiarity with the ideas and influence of these world-historical thinkers, my aim has been to reframe this common knowledge theoretically, to suggest how the ideas can be understood as meaning-constructions and how their influence can be seen as performative effect. In the second part of this chapter, I investigate two cases in more detail. The intellectual careers and afterlives of Ayn Rand and Frantz Fanon are not nearly as widely known as the canonical thinkers, and their ideas have exerted less performative power. Both intellectuals, however, have achieved remarkable dramatic effect. Exploring the sources of such power, the sociological reasons for its efflorescence and delimitation, can shed further light on how social performance explains practical intellectual success.

Heroine of the American Right

Among political theorists and cultural historians, Ayn Rand and her ideas have rarely been seriously considered. She was an ideological outlier, a radical conservative who celebrated capitalism, particularly what she regarded as the unsung virtues of its wealthiest elite. More theoretically revealing is that Rand was not herself a genial thinker. Mixing free market theory with Nietzsche, rationalism, and natural rights theory, she certainly stirred vinegar into the familiar bromides of bourgeois life. Still, her case violates the first criterion for intellectual power: she was not the creator of a consequential new idea. Rand does, however, meet the second requirement: Her ideas made social things happen. This highlights the paradox that performative success unfolds relatively independently of intrinsic intellectual merit.

In contrast with the regimes of social democracy, communism, and welfare states, twentieth-century capitalism has had few significant intellectual champions. Such philosophers as Michael Oakeshott emphasized the extra-economic dimensions of conservatism; such thinkers as Friedrich Hayek and Ludwig von Mises, whose anti-socialist polemics were highly influential, were narrowly economic in their aims. Since the middle of the twentieth century, no conservative, pro-capitalist intellectual has manifest anywhere near Rand's performative power, characterized by one liberal academic as "the most significant American ideological development of the last 35 years."[35] Even as Rand's thought has barely touched the academic disciplines, corporate leaders and buccaneering entrepreneurs have heralded it as secular theology. "I really felt like an Ayn Rand hero," one Silicon Valley entrepreneur recounted, adding "I didn't just feel like one, I was one. I was building the products. I was thinking independently. I was being rational. I was taking pride in what I did. Those are Ayn Rand hero characteristics."[36] Yet, Rand did not pander to capitalist class-consciousness. She projected her *Weltanschauung* not only to business people, but also to the middle class and to workers, to rebellious youth and pop stars alike.

Rand came of age during the early years of the Russian revolution.

The nascent Soviet state not once but several times confiscated her father's small business, her once wealthy family experiencing not only massive status deprivation but also real poverty. This family trauma, triggered by revolutionary socialism, proved the defining emotional element in Rand's life, propelling her intellectual search for meaning.[37]

Rand clarified the chaos and anxiety of her life and times, organizing the social world into binary codes and working the binaries into compelling stories. Private property is sacred, public property profane; the individual is inviolate, the state corrupt; money and commercial contracts are pure, bureaucracy and organization evil; accumulating wealth is admirable, redistributing it the work of the devil. Transforming these binaries into a narrative form, Rand painted capitalist protagonists as fallen heroes suffering at the hands of oppressive, corrupt government, and ungrateful masses feeding from the public trough. In response to a comment that money is "the root of all evil," one of the protagonists in *Atlas Shrugged* proclaims: "Until and unless you discover that money is the root of all good, you ask for your own destruction. When money ceases to be the tool by which men deal with one another, then men must become the tools of men. Blood, whips and guns – or dollars."[38] Rand prophesied salvation would emerge from capitalist social movements. Not only massive conservative protest, but the organized withdrawal of capitalist labor power – a "property strike" – were necessary if liberty and prosperity were to be restored.

Rand considered herself an intellectual, insisting that ideas were the only things that truly mattered, yet her most influential efforts at coding and narrating were neither abstract theorizing nor empirical analysis. Romantic fiction, not social science or philosophy, provided her most persuasive outlet for intellectual expression, the medium not the message that made her ideas dramatically great.[39] A student of Russian film and photography, Rand fled Petrograd for Hollywood in 1921, becoming a highly remunerated screenwriter and publicist before turning her aesthetic skills to novels. *The Fountainhead* (1943) and *Atlas Shrugged* (1957) – the first 700 pages, the second more than 1,000 – were the epochal results.

With her gift for agonistic plotting and sharply etched, larger than life character, Rand was able to make the script of capitalist ideology walk and talk. From the mundane realities of money, markets, and self-interest, she made mythos, creating gods and goddesses who stalked the earth and held the fate of humanity in their hand. The mysterious hero John Galt haunted the first 700 pages of *Atlas Shrugged*

114

before actually entering the plot. The epitome of rugged individualist, Galt had discovered a revolutionary electric motor, but, hounded by perfidious bureaucrats and ignorant masses, he refused to bring it to the market. Instead, he dropped out of sight, secretly organizing a utopian market society of self-exiled capitalists, Galt's Gulch, in the deep crevices of the Colorado Rockies. Galt's sixty-page-long speech became the stuff of movies and urban legends:

> All the men who have vanished, the men you hated, yet dreaded to lose, it is I who have taken them away from you ... Do not cry that it is our duty to serve you. We do not recognize such duty. Do not cry that you need us. We do not consider need a claim ... We are on strike against self-immolation. We are on strike against the creed of unearned rewards and unrewarded duties. We are on strike against the dogma that the pursuit of one's happiness is evil ... I swear – by my life and my love of it – that I will never live for the sake of another man, nor ask another man to live for mine.[40]

"Where is John Galt?" became the catchword of ideological insiders. When CNN founder Ted Turner was a little known media executive, he paid with his personal funds for 248 billboards across the American South; they read simply "Where is John Galt?"[41]

Rand's novels were catnip for ideological iconoclasts in the 1930s and 40s, but only during the perilous life-and-death atmosphere of the early Cold War did the texts take off, hotly fusing with a wider, ever more fervid audience. "For many *The Fountainhead* had the power of revelation," writes Rand biographer Jennifer Burns: "One reader told Rand ... 'It is like being awake for the first time.' This metaphor of awakening was among the most common devices readers used to describe the impact of Rand's writing."[42] "Rand" became the node of a nationwide network of ideologically excited readers, and coteries of organic intellectuals created organizations spreading popular distillations of her word. The *lingua franca* of these circles were the literary metaphors that clothed Rand's intellectual binaries – "looters," "moochers," and "second-handers" on one side; "producers," "traders," and "creators" on the other. One of the principal protagonists of *The Fountainhead*, Howard Roark, attacked altruism as "the doctrine which demands that man live for others and place others above self," asserting that "the second-hander has used altruism as a weapon of exploitation and reversed the case of mankind's moral principles." Roark declares: "Men have been taught every precept that destroys the creator. Men have been taught dependence as a virtue."[43]

Rand insisted that "each man must be an end in himself and follow his own rational self-interest," but her biography demonstrates a performative contradiction, the theoretical tenet refuted by her exploding symbolic power. A cult of fanatically devoted followers formed around her person, christening itself "The Collective," among whose charter members was Alan Greenspan, a lifelong devotee who went on to become the longest serving and most influential Federal Reserve Board chairman in US history.[44] Rand herself directed the expanding performance of her intellectual power, casting herself as a leading persona, appearing at densely crowded live events and on widely networked television shows, costumed in a flowing black cape adorned with gold dollar sign insignia and flaunting an elongated cigarette holder.

In the1960s, Rand was hailed as an intellectual beacon by right-wing Republican presidential candidate Barry Goldwater, and taken as totem by Young Americans for Freedom (YAF), the radical, newly styled "libertarian" organization that mirrored the New Left, planting the seeds of late twentieth-century neoconservatism.

> For libertarian YAFers it was, above all, Ayn Rand who was most significant. Many libertarians say Rand taught them how to conceptualize, to put ideas in a larger framework. Sharon Presley says she was "totally apolitical" until at nineteen a friend recommended she read Rand's *Atlas Shrugged*. "It was like, 'Oh, my God, what a revelation!' ... I read the book; it came along at just the right time ... What she did for me was get me thinking about ... things in those kinds of philosophical terms that I never had ... That was a major, major influence on my life."[45]

Later, political figures brought this new conservative ideology into the White House. In 1987, five years after Rand's death, *New York Times* Washington correspondent Maureen Dowd described Rand as the "novelist laureate" of the Reagan administration: "Many Reaganites favor the novels of Miss Rand, the goddess of enlightened selfishness and soaring free enterprise."[46] Twenty-five years later, such presidential aspirants as Speaker of the US House of Representatives Paul Ryan and Senators Marco Rubio, Ted Cruz, and Rand Paul proudly claim to have cut their political eye teeth on Rand's work. In Orange County, California, ground zero for America's postwar far right politics, the Ayn Rand Institute is funded by a $10 million annual budget, supports a 35-person research and outreach staff, distributes gratis hundreds of thousands of Rand novels annually to high schools and colleges, and offers $100,000 a year in prizes for essay contests that have involved hundreds of thousands of students.[47] In the late 1990s, *Atlas Shrugged* ranked just after the Bible in a poll asking Book of the Month Club subscribers what book had most influenced American readers' lives.[48]

Hero of the Third World

In contrast with Ayn Rand, Frantz Fanon did create new ideas. Before the publication of *The Wretched of the Earth*, in 1961, no thinker had translated the exploding postwar struggles against colonialism into a coherent social theory. Fanon conceptualized a revolutionary struggle, triggered not by class but by cultural, emotional, and physical domination, and, perhaps most singularly, by global processes of racial stigmatization. Fanon theorized colonialism broadly, as the worst of "Europe's crimes," something "heinous ... which has been committed at the very heart of man." Citing "the immense scale" of the injury, Fanon indicted "racial hatred, slavery, exploitation and, above all, the bloodless genocide whereby one and a half billion men have been written off." Repairing social injury on this scale, he argued, would require an equally massive response, a worldwide revolutionary struggle. "The Third World must start over a new history of man," Fanon declared; "for Europe, for ourselves and for humanity, comrades, we must make a new start, develop a new way of thinking, and endeavor to create a new man."[49] Such an anti-colonial insurrection movement would have to deploy violence against European colonizers as ruthlessly as the Europeans had employed violence to sustain their imperial domination.

While new, this theory about colonialism and its overthrow did not emerge de novo. Fanon's revolutionary ideas drew from Marxist humanism and militant Bolshevism, but the intellectual representations he reconstructed went far beyond such traditional sources of twentieth-century radical thought. Fanon forged his early intellectual identity in the Martinique *lycée* where he studied with Aimé Césaire, the literary and political figure that helped create *négritude*, the celebration of Afro-Caribbean cultural qualities as distinctive and valuable in themselves, independent from European colonial culture. When Fanon studied for his postwar medical degree in Lyon, after fighting with the Free French in North Africa, he took on board ideas from the institutional psychotherapy movement, a radical intervention in psychiatric thinking initiated by François Tosquelle.[50] Fanon absorbed, as well, the left-phenomenology pulsating through the pores of postwar French intellectual life, with its fusion of Heidegger's "lived experience" and Hegelian dialectics.[51] And throughout his *Bildung*, but much more intensely after he began practicing psychiatry in North Africa, Fanon imbibed the ideology of anti-colonialism.

Yet, while the later Fanon certainly created a new theoretical compound from this mixture,[52] the intellectual influence of his ideas derived less from their originality than from their performativity. Throughout the last decade of his life, Fanon's ideas about the anti-colonial were no secret. His articles were published in political, psychiatric, and intellectual journals, and he delivered widely reported public speeches as an official representative of the FLN, the National Liberation Front.[53] Only as he became mortally ill, however, did Fanon condense these ideas into his tensely wrought manifesto, *Wretched of the Earth*, published just days before his death. On the day Fanon died, police in Paris, citing national security, confiscated the book's stock from the city's bookstores.

As the revolutionary's soul rose from his body, Fanon's intellectual transmogrification began. He became an icon, his life a religious parable, his writings a holy text. His biographer David Macey described him as "the most famous spokesman of ... Third Worldism,"[54] and Stuart Hall, the Anglo-Caribbean doyen of the Birmingham School, hailed *Wretched of the Earth* as "the bible of decolonization."[55] In making these claims to Fanon's fame, Macey and Hall implicitly reference the performative status of Fanon's ideas. In a camouflaged manner, so did Fanon himself, explaining to the editor of *Black Skin, White Masks*, "I am trying to touch my reader affectively ... irrationally, almost sensually."[56] Critics have gestured to Fanon's "poetic prose,"[57] to "the inherently dramatic idiom of French left-Existentialism,"[58] and even to the "immensely complex and compelling force" with which "Fanon's texts speak to us when we read their contents as speech acts in the moving body of a dramatic narrative."[59] None of these interpretations, however, have opened the black box to explore the culture structures that actually animated Fanon's text.

In *Black Skin, White Masks*, Fanon represented himself as a primal, redemptive figure: "I came into this world anxious to uncover the meaning of things, my soul desirous to be at the origin of the world."[60] With *Wretched of the Earth*, he sifted the meaning of meanings into an anti-colonial shape. Transforming what Sartre called the "age of conflagration,"[61] Fanon evoked a mythical confrontation between good and evil redeemed by an eschatological struggle for social salvation. An intensely dramatic text, *Wretched of the Earth* was less about empirical description and theoretical generalization

118

than about the sacred and profane. Fanon declared, "de-colonialism is the encounter between two congenitally antagonistic forces."[62] He insisted: "Challenging the colonial world is not a rational confrontation of viewpoints," not a "discourse on the universal," but rather "the impassioned claim by the colonized that their world is fundamentally different." In this "Manichean world," the "colonist is not content with physically limiting the space of the colonized, i.e., with the help of his agents of law and order," but "turns the colonized into a kind of quintessence of evil."[63] Colonizers see themselves as autonomous, active, rational, strong, caring, and fair-minded, and define the colonized as dependent, irrational, impulsive, impotent, aggressive, and filled with shame. Under colonialism, these sacred and profane symbolic qualities become isomorphic with vertically ordered social positions, not only metaphorically connected with economic, political, and cultural hierarchies, but metonymically aligned with skin color and spatial location, with whiteness and blackness, metropolis and periphery.

Fanon's theory of anti-colonial struggle challenged neither these signifiers nor their Manichean split; it upended, rather, the social signifieds with which they were aligned. If colonizers were on top at Time 1, at Time 2, after the revolution, it would be the once colonized peoples who would be independent and strong, cosmopolitan and proud, and the old European world left behind, exhausted, degraded, irrational, and humiliated.

To conceptualize this inversion, Fanon created a narrative that temporalized his morally weighted binaries. The abstract qualities of sacred and profane were given flesh and blood, becoming protagonists and antagonists in an apocalyptic confrontation, for "time must no longer be that of the moment or the next harvest but rather of the rest of the world."[64] For Fanon, decolonization "focuses on and fundamentally alters being, and transforms the spectator crushed to a nonessential state into a privileged actor, captured in a virtually grandiose fashion by the spotlight of History." Ostensibly secular, Fanon's narrative is deeply rooted in a Judeo-Christian structure. When he offers to "describe it accurately,"[65] he draws from Matthew 19:30, suggesting that the anti-colonial struggle can "be summed up in the well-known words: 'The last shall be first'."

The vehicle that energizes this revolutionary plot, the event that prepares its narrative resolution, is righteous violence. Describing the "bare reality" of decolonization, Fanon exclaims, it "reeks of red-hot cannonballs and bloody knives," explaining "the last can be the first only after a murderous and decisive confrontation."[66] To "blow the colonial world to smithereens" is more than simply an effective tactic, however. It is also a "clear image within the grasp and imagination of every colonized subject," not only physical but mythical violence.[67] "This violent praxis is totalizing," Fanon suggests, evoking the transformation of seriality into fusion from Sartre's *Critique of Dialectical Reason*. It is because "each individual represents a violent link in the great chain" that "the armed struggle mobilizes the people, i.e., it pitches them in a single direction, from which there is no turning back."[68] Violence provides the emotional catharsis upon which narrative resolution depends, forcing a new moral understanding from the experience of pity and suffering: "Violence is a cleansing force. It rids the colonized of their inferiority complex, of their passive and despairing attitude. It emboldens them and restores their self-confidence."[69]

But if deconstructing the code and narrative animating Fanon's text is necessary, it still is not sufficient to explain his theory's dramatic power. No matter how original and animated, an intellectual text remains just that – a script that can inform social action, but not social action itself. To become performative, social theories must walk and talk. Only if they can be felicitously inserted into social scenes will they be able to fuse with the intellectual ambitions of peers and the existential hunger of lay audiences, an effort that facilitates, but also sometimes thwarts, efforts at critical mediation.

Well-funded and widely networked editorial groups in Paris gave Fanon access to the means of symbolic production, even as they provided intellectual mediation that primed the critical pump. In the 1950s, pieces by and about Fanon appeared in *Esprit*, the leftist Catholic journal, and *Les Temps modernes*.[70] Jean-Paul Sartre, at once the most powerful and also the most polarizing intellectual in France, staged the publication of *Wretched of the Earth*, Fanon's decisive intellectual performance.[71] In Sartre's acclaimed Preface to *Wretched of the Earth*, he represented Fanon as a hero: "He is not afraid of anything," Sartre admiringly declares. Proclaiming "the Third World discovers itself and speaks to itself through this voice,"[72] Sartre writes of Fanon's theory as if it had already fused with colonial readers, and he invites intellectually sophisticated and politically committed readers to do the same: "Fanon speaks loud and clear. We Europeans, we can hear him. The proof is you are holding this book ... Europeans, open this book, look inside."[73] Sartre's Preface had such an extraordinary impact that, for decades following, it seemed to constitute an essential companion to Fanon's work.[74]

Wretched of the Earth became an international bestseller, its author so lionized that he appeared as the figurative protagonist of his own social theory. Macey has it almost right: Fanon emerged as "an all-purpose revolutionary icon" who could "be transported anywhere and invoked in the name of any cause."[75] The observation evokes the reifying generality of Fanon's intellectual power, but Fanon's theory could become performative only in very particular times and places. The atmospherics, audience, and mediating cultural and political powers had to be right. Blinding corruption, stultifying immiseration, and crippling racial humiliation had to be in the air. So did perfervid revolutionary movement and hallucinatory dreams about liberation. Finally, neither discourse nor mobilization, but only violence, could appear to provide the way out.

The presence of such conditions helps explain the extraordinary explosion of Fanon's deeply dramatic text on the 1960s intellectual and political scene, their absence the virtual disappearance of Fanon's intellectual force in the decades after.

Black Panther Party leaders described the encounter with *Wretched of the Earth* as epiphanic. The work "became essential reading for Black revolutionaries in America," Kathleen Cleaver recalled, "and profoundly influenced their thinking."[76] Describing the fusion of text and audience, the black nationalist *Liberation Magazine* declared, "Every brother on a rooftop can quote Fanon."[77] Bobby Seale claimed to have read Fanon's manifesto six times. "I knew Fanon was right and I knew he was running it down," Seale later recalled, "but how do you put ideas like his over?" To answer this question, he introduced the text to Huey Newton.

> One day I went over to [Newton's] house and asked him if he had read Fanon [and] he said no ... So I brought Fanon over one day. That brother got to reading Fanon ... We would sit down with *Wretched of the Earth* and talk, go over another section or chapter of Fanon, and Huey would explain it in depth ... He knew it already. He'd get on the streets. We'd be walking down the street and get in some discussion with somebody, and throughout the process of this discussion and argument, Huey would be citing facts, citing that material, and giving perception to it.[78]

A founding premise of the Black Panther Party was that the United States was host to a conflict, in the words of Eldridge Cleaver, between the "black colony" and "white mother country."[79] Stokely Carmichael referred to black people as "a colony within the US" in a controversial 1967 speech in Havana.[80] As the Student Nonviolent Coordinating Committee (SNCC) moved from civil rights to insurrection, its founder James Forman issued a pamphlet declaring "we are a colonized people in the United States,"[81] and SNCC militants began holding "rap sessions" on Fanon.[82] The Black Panthers' highly public deployment of violence – carrying weapons, organizing military-style defense forces – was linked to Fanon as well. Kelley and Esch[83] note that Fanon's chapter "On Violence," in *Wretched of the Earth*, was "the perpetual favorite among militants." Kathleen Cleaver recalled: "Fanon's analysis seemed to explain and justify the spontaneous violence ravaging Black ghettos across the country and linked the incipient insurrections to the rise of a revolutionary movement."[84] Forman wrote, "Only violence can totally free a colonized people."[85] In his Havana speech, Carmichael announced: "We are preparing groups of urban guerillas for our defense in the cities," proclaiming, "It is going to be a fight to the death."[86]

Fanon's intellectual power reverberated far beyond the American scene. Che Guevera, the Cuban revolutionary who embodied guerilla war as the pathway to insurrection, took an extraordinary personal interest in Fanon. In late 1964, Guevera traveled to Algiers for an interview with Fanon's widow Josie, staying on for two months,[87] and later that year organized a Cuban translation and publication of *Wretched of the Earth*.[88] There was "a remarkable correspondence between Che's writing and Fanon's," Michael Lowy observes, citing "ideas about the importance of violent action by the oppressed, the anti-imperialist unity of the Third World, and the search for a new model of socialism." Indeed, Guevara's "reading of Fanon" may have "inspired his project for participating in the armed struggle in Africa in 1965–1966." [89] Leaders of the Quebec Liberation Front (FLQ) and the Palestinian Liberation Organization (PLO) poured over Fanon.[90] So did the Irish Republican Army (IRA) soldier Bobby Sands, in the H-block of Belfast prison, where he found multiple copies of *Wretched of the Earth* on the shelves.[91]

The social conditions that primed audiences for Fanon's explosive intellectual performance eventually dissipated, more quietly but almost as rapidly as they had earlier appeared. In the developed world, subordinate racial groups turned out to be as much part of the civil sphere as outside it. It was not the Black Panthers, but the nonviolent movement of Martin Luther King that succeeded in expanding the civil, political, and social rights of millions of working-class African Americans, leaving behind a racial underclass bereft of political will and cultural resources to carry on the fight (see Chapter 1). Nor did the decolonizing process outside the West proceed in the manner Fanon had foreseen. Guerilla warfare was not the rule but the exception, most colonies achieving independence relatively peacefully via a political process. Their highly unequal position vis-à-vis their former colonial masters, however, did not significantly change. And the enlightenment universalism for which Fanon hoped, it turned out, could not be sustained after the heady post-emancipation years; instead, ethnic, religious, racial, and nationalistic ideologies permeated the scene.

In the wake of this radically altered social environment, the intellectual zeitgeist shifted from anti- to postcolonial. Even as it became part of the intellectual pantheon, the social impact of *Wretched of the Earth* faded. In the era of multicultural difference and cultural hybridity, academic interest shifted to Fanon's 1952 work on racial stigma, *Black Skin, White Masks.* Despite its more contemporary relevance, it was not nearly as fecund as the work that, a decade later, would make Fanon's anti-colonial fame.

* * *

Intellectuals are always doing things with words, trying to bring something into being, not simply offering descriptions of things already known. Intellectuals are, then, always performative in Austin's philosophical sense.[92] Only rarely, however, do they become performative sociologically as well. To become performative, intellectuals must create not only smart ideas, but highly dramatic ones, ideas that allow dark times to be understood in a manner that signposts a journey from the darkness to the light. There must also be intellectual life after death. Ideas need to be carried by disciples and inserted into the practicalities of the social scene. Power and materiality are necessary but not sufficient, for, in the end, it is the audience that decides. Reception does not define the quality of ideas, but it decides their effect. Cultural pragmatics determines intellectual power.

— 5 —

SOCIAL THEORY AND THE
THEATRICAL AVANT-GARDE

This was the joke. [You] got out a metro Boston phone book and tore a
White Pages page out at random and thumbtacked it to the wall and ...
throw a dart at it from across the room ... And the name it hit becomes
the subject of the Found Drama. And whatever happens to the protagonist with the name you hit with the dart for like the next hour and a half
is the Drama ... You do whatever you want during the Drama. You're
not there. Nobody knows what the name in the book's doing ... The
joke's theory was there's no audience and no director and no stage or set
because ... in Reality there are none of these things. And the protagonist
doesn't know he's the protagonist in a Found Drama because in Reality
nobody thinks they're in any sort of Drama.[1]

Hans-Thies Lehmann has recently conceptualized a movement to the
"postdramatic" that eerily resembles the joke about "Found Drama"
that David Foster Wallace spins in *Infinite Jest*. Examining a stream
of contemporary avant-garde theatrical productions for evidence
of dramatic practice and theory, Lehmann announces the end of
theater as we know it.[2] The Aristotelian format of drama has been
displaced, he declares, and theater has moved on to the next evolu-
tionary phase. We are now in the era of postdramatic happenings,
staged projects with no discernible plots or written texts, peopled by
characters devoid of internal emotional life. Drama now consists of
simple projections of bodily movements; stages filled with isolated
and opaque iconic objects; temporally sequenced actions without
meaningful connection; and theatrical scenes that unfold simultaneously and cacophonously, whose presentation is shot through by such
nontheatrical art forms as music, sculpture, or painting.

Rather than dramatic representations, written texts, theatrical
lineage, and social languages that make staged performance intel-

ligible, in contemporary theater, Lehmann claims, "the moment of speaking becomes everything." Rather than a "temporal, dynamic formation" generating suspense, theater becomes simply serial "occurrences." Rather than audiences sharing interpretations and forging common feelings into emergent "community," there is now mere "heterogeneity." Rather than a "warming" contact between actor and audience, the interface has become "cold." Not only is contemporary theater "detached from all religious and cultic reference" – a separation that defined modern drama for centuries – but "the whole spectrum of movements and processes that have no referent" at all. Instead of meaningfully organized *mises-en-scène*, the scenes of postdramatic theater possess simply "heightened precision."[3]

Lehmann sees convergence between the postdramatic in theater and performance art. Performance art not only joins postwar aesthetics in challenging the equation of art with the beautiful or sublime; it rejects the very notion of a fixed, final, and material product. Presenting itself as an alternative to "pictorial or object-like presentations of reality through the addition of the dimension of time," performance art, like postdramatic theater, emphasizes "duration, momentariness, simultaneity, and unrepeatability." Rather than appealing to the restrained eye of the connoisseur, performance art seeks to mobilize a mass audience by drawing them, sometimes wittingly but more often not, into the performative process itself.[4]

On the basis of these putative developments in contemporary aesthetic practice, Lehmann believes he has discovered a new aesthetic foundation for critical social theory. The postdramatic in art, he claims, crystallizes a dangerous shift in real social life: there has been a "dwindling of the dramatic space of imagination in the consciousness of society." The "form of experience" has become so degraded that "drama and society cannot come together." In contemporary society, "the most conflictual situations will no longer appear as drama." In the "de-dramatized reality" of contemporary society, "real issues are only decided as power blocs." We are left with the society of the spectacle, the world Guy Debord and the Situationists described in the 1960s and Jean Baudrillard elaborated as simulacra for decades after. "All human experiences (life, eroticism, happiness, recognition) are tied to commodities," Lehmann laments, and the "citizen spectator" can "only look on" without any feeling of connection to the world around her.[5] Sharing neither meaning, ethic, nor experience with the powers who stage social performances, citizens of the spectacle society are impotent to affect them.[6]

In this chapter, I take issue with this idea of the postdramatic, not only as it applies to the theater, but also to social life. My claim is neither that such "Found Drama" is nonexistent, nor that such social spectacles never appear. My contention is more systemic, more theoretical. I argue that instead of seeing dramatic declension, we must see dramatic variation. Instead of being viewed as the newest phase in aesthetic evolution, the postdramatic, in both aesthetic and social theory, should be conceptualized in terms of the variables that establish conditions for performative failure – and success. Postdramatic experience is powerful, sometimes dangerous, and occasionally liberating. It is not, however, endemic to contemporary theatrical and social life; we are not experiencing an infinite regress, or progress, to the postdramatic. As societies have grown more institutionally differentiated, culturally reflexive, and fragmented, theatricality has changed, as have the performative processes that extend beyond the stage into real social life. Lehmann is right to correlate the two, but he has connected them in exactly the wrong way. Over the course of historical time, the elements that make up performance have gradually become separated and specialized, both in theater and in society. With this defusion, the possibility that dramatic efforts might fail to communicate meaning has increased. Postdrama describes a condition of deflation, one in which dramatic performance fails to make strong meaning for either a part of an audience or its entirety; sometimes this failure to make meaning even extends to those who are creating the drama. However, deflationary symbols can be dramatically reinflated; cultural differentiation causes severe strains, but it must not be conflated with devolution.

I develop this alternative perspective on drama and society by examining critical turning points in the emergence of Western theater. My evidence is drawn from avant-garde playwrights, actors, directors, and designers who have shifted the shape of drama's currents, and the critics, philosophers, and contemporary theater theorists who have commented upon this shape-shifting in turn. In this regard, I take a particularly close look at recent developments in performance studies.

Defusion and the Two Avant-Gardes

In the course of the last three centuries, theatrical practice and theory have been defined by anxieties about performative defusion.[7] Lehmann's embrace of the postdramatic is one recent response to this anxiety, but hardly the first. In the early decades of the twentieth century, Bertolt Brecht conceptualized an "alienation effect"

126

(*Verfremdungseffekt*) as an antidote to Aristotelian drama, which he regarded not only as increasingly burdensome to sustain, but politically oppressive as well. It is too "difficult and taxing," Brecht complained, for the actor "to conjure up particular inner moods or emotions night after night." As an alternative, the left-wing German playwright and director suggested that stage actors cultivate not naturalness but artificiality. If actors would merely "exhibit the outer signs ... which accompany emotions," rather than trying to project inner feelings themselves, then the "automatic transfer of emotions to the spectator" will be blocked and the audience "hindered from simply identifying itself with the characters in the play." With Aristotelian catharsis thus prevented, the viewer's "acceptance or rejection" of theatrical "actions and utterances" could now "take place on a conscious plane, instead of, as hitherto, in the audience's subconscious." Even if such an experience of alienation failed in its aim of freeing workers from bourgeois ideology, Brecht believed, "acting like this is healthier and ... less unworthy of a thinking being."[8] Three decades later, the revolutionary Brazilian dramatist Augusto Boal responded to theatrical and social complexity in the same way. Boal attacked Aristotelian drama as a "powerful system of intimidation," a "coercive system" that "functions to diminish, placate, satisfy [and] eliminate all that is not commonly acceptable."[9]

Lehmann's postdramatic manifesto, then, is actually nothing new. It differs from his predecessors' programs only in its rejection of the possibility of socialist salvation. The call for moving beyond the dramatic constitutes one line of the modern theatrical avant-garde, but there is another stream that has continued to embrace an eschatological hope for drama's revitalization. It is this other line that I will reconstruct here, framing it inside the *longue durée* of theatrical history and connecting with social theorizing about the modern condition.

The postdramatic pushes defusion to its limit condition, trying to get beyond meaning and telos by thoroughly shattering any linkage among the elements of performance. The other avant-garde response points away from this post-condition to the (re)dramatic, confronting the conditions of defusion with never-before-conceived-of efforts to overcome them. The (re)dramatic seeks to reforge links among performative elements, conceptualizing and practicing theater in a manner that opens it back up to the telos of myth and the seamlessness of ritual. "In the anguished, catastrophic period we live in," Antonin Artaud announced, "we feel an urgent need for a theatre which events do not exceed, whose resonance is deep within us, dominating the instability of our times." Rather than striving for alienation and spectacle, Artaud declares, "I cannot conceive of a work of art as distinct from life." He calls for "a theatre that wakes us up: nerves and heart," a theatre that "inspires us with the fiery magnetism of its image and acts upon us like a spiritual therapeutics whose touch can never be forgotten."[10] Jacques Copeau[11] may employ the term "spectacle," but he meant it to suggest fullness and fusion, not emptiness and defusion; spectacle allows us to envision a theatrical "audience brought together by need, desire, aspiration, for experiencing together human emotions by means of spectacle more fully realized than life itself."[12]

The (re)dramatic and re-fusing avant-garde of the early twentieth century limed Nietzsche's call for restoring ritual to drama, a call that looked not only to Wagner's project of opera as total art form, but earlier still to the wellsprings of Romanticism itself. Such (re)dramatic currents pulse through the contemporary theatrical avant-garde in numerous permutations, including Jerzy Grotowski's widely reverberating call for the creation of a "sacred," "pure," and "holy" theatre of "trance" and "transillumination," where "the body vanishes and burns" and "the spectator sees only a series of visible impulses";[13] in Peter Brook's living theater, where audiences "have seen the face of the invisible through an experience on the stage that transcended their experience in life";[14] and in such other experimental theater projects as Joseph Chaikin's open theater.[15]

Refusion and Performance Studies

Four decades ago, in the person of The Performance Group dramatist Richard Schechner, this (re)dramatic, re-fusing theatrical avant-garde connected with social theory in the person of cultural anthropologist Victor Turner.[16] The upshot was the new discipline that may be conceived as fundamentally challenging the idea of the postdramatic. Schechner aimed not to deflate theatricality but to reinflate and extend it. He demonstrated how theatrical homologues – "performances" – also permeate nontheatrical, but dramatic, social life. Drawing the relationship between social ritual and theatrical drama as an intertwined figure of eight, Schechner actually made use of avant-garde theater theory to colonize social life.[17] Generations of theater scholars after Schechner have deepened his investigations of dramatic effect, creating a body of richly suggestive if also deeply contradictory studies. Peggy Phelan believes, for example, that only live

128

performances are real and affecting, while Shalom Auslander attacks liveness as a false and misleading ideal.[18] Diana Taylor separates written, formal "archives" from acted out "repertoires," highlighting the importance of "scenarios" that may be cultural structures but are not texts.[19] Joseph Roach extols the symbolic vitality of "it-ness," breaking down the barrier between profane commodity and sacred symbol in performances stretching from fashion to cinema.[20] Jill Dolan reinstates the division, insisting that "mesmerizing moments are what those of us addicted to performance live for. Her analytic interests focus on performances whereby "suddenly and unexpectedly we are lifted from our normal detached contemplation into another place, where time stops, and our breath catches."[21]

As the new discipline of performance studies came into its own two decades ago, it came under harsh attack from William Worthen, a textually-minded theater theorist. Worthen accused performance studies of a "romantic sentimentality" that constructed false dichotomies, of "urgently" contrasting the "supposedly liberating 'textuality' of performance" – "transgressive, multiform, [and] revisionist" – with the "domain of the text" conceived as "dominant, repressive, conventional, and canonical."[22] Declaring this a false choice, Worthen suggested that the model of theatrical text as unified, intentional, and didactic had been thoroughly rejected by twentieth-century literary theory from the New Criticism to Deconstruction.

The letter of Worthen's attack on the romantic binarism of performance studies is largely correct.[23] Performance studies scholars tend to confound the analytical and the normative, romantically championing the vigor of drama against a tired, thin, dried-out theatrical text. Not only is their writing frequently moralistic, but their concepts are often metaphorical, more suggestive of poetics than social theory. Coming to praise performance, not to bury it, scholars in this new discipline have resisted the variability of performance in the age of defusion; as a result, they have failed to theorize the conditions that explain it.

Yet, Worthen missed the forest for the trees.[24] The intellectual achievement of performance studies has been to "secularize" the (re)dramatic avant-garde, to "think" it rather than do it, and their decades of reflexivity has created a signal opening for social theory. If we bring this new discipline to bear on the earlier conceptual innovations of Kenneth Burke, Erving Goffman, and Clifford Geertz, and synthesize them with contemporary cultural sociology, it becomes possible to develop a meaning-oriented but "culturally pragmatic" theory of social performances.[25] Stimulated by the analytics of

129

performance theory, culturally oriented social theory has found new ways to think about symbolic action, cultural structure and contingency, social conflict and solidarity, social criticism, and political responsibility. As a result, we better understand how the relative autonomy of culture allows social actors not only to imagine, but to dramatize hopes for a better life. The dangers of modernity cannot be blamed on the instrumental reason of postdramatic and commodified spectacles.[26] On the contrary, cultural-cum-emotional movements of immense performative power have driven social evils. In modern, modernizing, and postmodern societies, for better and for worse, social dramas are here to stay. It is not only that social life cannot get beyond the dramatic, but that it should not try. Four decades ago, Raymond Williams insisted that societies still need the dramatization of consciousness:

> We live in a society which is at once more mobile and more complex, and therefore, in some crucial respects, relatively more unknowable, relatively more opaque than most societies of the past, and yet which is also more insistently pressing [and] penetrating ... The clear public order of much traditional drama has not, for many generations, been available to us[,] [but] presentation, representation, signification have never been more important. Drama broke from fixed signs, established its permanent distance from myth and ritual and from the hierarchical figures and processions of state ... But drama, which separated, did not separate out altogether ... Beyond what many people can see as the theatricality of our image-conscious public world, there is a more serious, more effective, more deeply rooted drama: the dramatization of consciousness itself.[27]

How Resistance to Defusion Generates the Elements of Theatrical Performance

The emergence of text

While Aristotle ostensibly addresses drama, he is actually explaining the construction of poetic text. "Our subject being poetry, I propose to speak of the structure of plot required for a good poem," he explains, and "of the number and nature of the constitutive parts of a poem."[28] With this intratextual focus, Aristotle illuminates such narrative structures as tragedy and comedy, making use of them to predict dramatic effects.[29] The closest he comes to the pragmatics of performance, however, is advising poets to put themselves imaginatively into the place of the audience:

> At the time when he is constructing his Plots, and engaged in the Diction in which they are worked out, the poet should remember (1) to put the actual scenes as far as possible before his eyes. In this way, seeing everything with the vividness of an eyewitness as it were, he will devise what is appropriate, and be least likely to overlook incongruities ... (2) As far as may be, too, the poet should even act his theory out with the very gestures of his personages ... Distress and anger, for instance, are portrayed most truthfully by one who is feeling them at the moment.[30]

Two thousand years later, when theater had once again emerged from religious ritual, one finds the same intratextual focus in Pierre Corneille's introductions to his collected plays, undergirded by similar faith that theatrical success is guaranteed by the written coherence of a play.[31] Stressing how drama unites action, time, and place, the classical French playwright insists that, properly constructed, the text of a play so subordinates the other elements of theatrical performance that any possible contingency in presentation or interpretation is suppressed. "There must be only one complete action," Corneille advises, "which leaves the mind of the spectator serene." Acknowledging "that action can be complete only through several others," and that these others may be "less than perfect," he asserts, nonetheless, that if such peripheral actions can be made to appear "as preparation" for the central one, then they will succeed in "keep[ing] the spectator in a pleasant suspense." Maintaining the appearance of smooth and flowing continuity is everything, the realities of character and the contingencies of action unimportant. "It is not necessary that we know exactly what the actors are doing in the intervals which separate the acts," Corneille explains; only "that they contribute to the action when they appear on stage." [32]

> A poet is not required to show all the particular actions which bring about the particular one; he must choose to show those which are the most advantageous whether by the beauty of the spectacle or by the brilliance or violence of the passions they produce ... and to hide the others behind the scene while informing the spectator of them by a narration or some other artistic device ... He should involve himself as little as possible with things which have happened before the action he is presenting. Such narrations are annoying, usually because they are not expected, and they disturb the mind of the spectators.[33]

The independent audience

However, even as Corneille penned these intratextual reassurances, private theaters began displacing both public and aristocratic performance spaces. With the decline of theatrical patronage, the rise of drama markets, and the explosion of revolutionary social conflict, the serene confidence of playwrights in the illocutionary effect of their rhetorical wiles faded. Fictional stage world and audience were becoming more clearly distinct.[34] Stalls replaced pits, and footlights – first installed in private theaters in the seventeenth century – placed a newly material barrier between audience and stage. Theatrical texts now confronted audiences in a literal way, and it became ever more difficult to ensure that the newly enfranchised masses, both working and middle class, were stimulated and pleased. In the early decades of the nineteenth century, audiences were raucous. By mid-century, they had become more staid. "Behavior improved," Booth suggests, "and complaints were eventually made not of uproar in the pit and gallery, but of stolid indifference in the stalls."[35] Now less attentive, the audience came to be conceptualized as theater's "fourth wall," not only concretely but metaphorically removed from the supposed-to-be meaningful and affecting text enacted upon the stage. Trying desperately to become a playwright, but failing, Henry James laid the blame squarely on the shoulders of the audience, ignoring the awkwardness of his own dramatic technique. His voice dripping with sarcasm, the American novelist lambasted "the essentially brutal nature of the modern audience":

> The *omnium gatherum* of the population of a big commercial city at the hour of the day when their taste is at its lowest, flocking out of hideous hotels and restaurants, gorged with food, stultified with buying and selling and with all the other sordid preoccupations of the age, squeezed together in a sweltering mass, disappointed in their sets, timing the author, wishing to get their money back on the spot – all before eleven o'clock! Fancy putting the exquisite before such a tribunal as that! ... The dramatist ... has to make the basest concessions. One of his principal canons is that he must enable his spectators to catch the suburban trains, which stop at 11:30. [36]

As brilliantly as James mastered the novelistic text, he could not translate it into a script that could walk and talk upon the stage.

With the audience emerging as an independent, contingently responsive element of theater, Brecht's later political admonitions can be seen not only as normative, but as analytical, his aesthetic techniques thematizing the social withdrawal of identification and affect from the stage. But French philosopher Jacques Derrida understood that "alienation only consecrates, with didactic insistence and systematic heaviness, the non-participation of spectators ... in the creative

132

act, in the irruptive [sic] forces fissuring the space of the stage."[37] As
Sinfield suggests, every "artistic form depends upon some readiness
in the receiver to cooperate with its aims and conventions."[38] But if
the audience was always already there, only relatively recently has it
been conceptualized in such a way that it becomes orthogonal to the
performance, an autonomous element. Still, even the most politically
radical theater depends on the readiness of an audience to subscribe.
"Even in Brecht," Bert States points out, "everything seeks its own
illusory level," his dramatic success relying on the audience's "willingness to vibrate in tune with ... whatever the work may be up to."[39]
Just as Boal follows Brecht in the fight with Aristotle, so he, too,
insists, in spite of himself, that the fourth wall, "built by the ruling
classes," can and must be torn down. "Spectator is a bad word,"
Boal complains, for it makes the viewer into "less than a man [sic]."
Calling for a new theater of the oppressed, this self-avowed critic of
catharsis hoped that drama would inspire hopes for political triumph
and restore the proletariat's "capacity as an actor."[40]

In literary criticism, reader-response theory addressed the split
between text and audience more analytically. Stanley Fish goes so
far as to suggest that "interpretive communities" – audiences, in theatrical terms – actually create their own texts in the act of reading.[41]
Avant-garde dramatists devoted themselves to exploring ways of
breaking through the fourth wall, creating the theory and practice of
internally emotive acting, entraining scripts, iconic props, and mag-
netic directing. Sometimes they even try to overcome the audience
by addressing it directly.[42] If they shock and offend viewers (so the
argument goes), perhaps they can fuse them with their own texts at
the same time. This line of reasoning informs Peter Handke's 1966
introductory diatribe in *Offending the Audience*:

> Here you won't receive your due. Your curiosity is not satisfied. No
> spark will leap across from us to you. You will not be electrified ...
> This world is no different from yours. You are no longer eavesdroppers.
> You are the subject matter [and] this is no mirage. You won't see walls
> that tremble ... This stage represents nothing ... You don't see a dark-
> ness that pretends to be another darkness. You don't see a brightness
> that pretends to be another brightness ... You don't hear any noise that
> pretends to be another noise. You don't see a room that pretends to be
> another room. Here you are not experiencing a time that pretends to be
> another time ... The front of the stage is not a line of demarcation ... It
> is no demarcation line as long as we are speaking to you ... There is no
> radiation belt between you and us.[43]

Dramatically inclined democratic theorists have turned to the independence of the audience to rescue rationality from theatrical artifice. In his paean to the "emancipated spectator," French philosopher Jacques Rancière praises the one who "observes, selects, compares, interprets," who "links what she sees to a host of other things that she has seen on other stages, in other kinds of place," who "composes her own poem with the elements of the poem before her" and "participates in the performance by refashioning it in her own way."[44] In such efforts to do away with the contingency of theatrical life, political philosophy echoes the aesthetic ambitions of the theatrical avant-garde.

From the dawning nineteenth-century revelation of the fateful gap between dramatic text and audience, everything else flowed. Between the hammer of text and the anvil of audience there emerged every subsequent theatrical and conceptual innovation, each conceived as a crucible for forging a new performative fusion.

The actor steps out

The transformation of acting presents the most widely reflected-upon of the innovations I have in mind. In the late eighteenth century, French philosopher Denis Diderot praised the actor as an "unmoved and disinterested onlooker," all "penetration and no sensibility," who had "mastered the art of mimicking everything." For the Enlightenment, in other words, text was still king. Asking "What, then, is truth on stage?," Diderot answers: "It is the conformity of action, diction, face, voice, movement, and gesture, to an ideal model imagined by the poet."[45] By the beginning of the twentieth century, by contrast, the British wunderkind Gordon Craig denounced the very idea of the actor as merely a "photo-machine," issuing a clarion call for the emancipation of actors as independent sources of creativity in their own right: "Today they impersonate and interpret; tomorrow they must represent and interpret; and on the third day they must create."[46]

It was, indeed, only at the beginning of the twentieth century that actor training became a self-conscious craft.[47] The point of this new discipline was to wake up the dead text, to make it stand tall, to walk and talk. David Krasner describes what happened in the 1920s when Constantin Stanislavski's ideas about actor training migrated to the United States.[48] In the hands of such teachers as Lee Strasberg, Stella Adler, and Sanford Meisner, the so-called "method" transformed acting on stage and screen. Acting moved from being "outside in" – from text to actor – to being "inside out," allowing the actor to

134

have an independent effect on the understanding of the text. Instead of merely "indicating" emotions, actors now tried actually to experience them. Instead of mannerism, actors were instructed to project an "unassuming natural presence." Instead of grand theatricality, performances should look like "real behavior." During rehearsals, actors were pushed to get away from texts entirely, to engage in improvisation, to speak gibberish, to paraphrase, and to engage in mindlessly repetitive expression, exercises designed to trigger actors' personal interpretations so that their emotions could become independent of the playwright's printed words. Strasberg encouraged the "Personal Moment" in rehearsals. Recalling and acting out excruciating or exhilarating moments from the actors' personal pasts, Strasberg suggests, is a technique that "releases the actor from any obligations to a text or … to an audience." Method acting was hardly designed to appear methodical. Theater can become dramatic, according to Krasner, only if actors "accomplish the experience of real feelings," working "moment-to-moment on impulse, talking and listening as if the events on stage are actually happening in the immediate present."[49]

In the postwar period, Grotowski carried forward the practical tradition of making acting the center of theatrical success. "The personal and scenic techniques of the actor," he proclaimed, are "at the core of theatre art."[50] The text by itself is useless, he insists: "In the development of theatrical art, the text was one of the last elements to be added." Indeed, compared with the significance of acting, the other elements of performance are virtually useless as well. "By gradually eliminating whatever proved superfluous, we found that theater can exist without make-up, without autonomic costume and scenography, without a separate performance area (stage), without lighting and sound effects." What theater "cannot exist" without is "the actor–spectator relationship of perceptual, direct, 'live' communion."[51] Schechner once asked the Polish director what he meant by the admonition, "Don't play the text." Grotowski responded:

> If the actor wants to play the text, he is doing what's easiest. The text has been written [and] he frees himself from the obligation of doing anything himself. But if … he unmasks this lack of personal action and reaction, [t]hen the actor is obliged to refer to himself within his own context and to find his own line of impulses … The problem is always the same: stop the cheating, find the authentic impulses. The goal is to find a meeting between the text and the actor.[52]

As States explains, there is no "privileged voice" in theatre.[53] In contrast with the opportunities for authorial intervention in prose and poetry, in theater there can be only the "objective presence of an illusion," and such an "aura" can be created only by "an actor's awareness of his own self-sufficiency." Chaikin's "Open Theatre" famously organized an ensemble that created theatrical texts through their own collaborative performance. He wrote *The Presence of the Actor* to explain its success: "All the history of theatre refers to actors who possess this presence."[54] Roach explores it-ness to examine the same thing – "the quality that makes you feel as though you're standing right next to the actor, no matter where you're sitting in the theatre."[55]

Producers, directors, and props emerge

It was in response to the same kinds of performative challenges that producing and directing emerged as specialized roles. Creators of theater needed to focus on seducing the audience. When powerful playwrights became producers, they hired actors, organized complex productions and promotional campaigns, and gauged the affective power of performances through trial runs and later by means of surveys and focus groups. Armed with this information, they demanded that playwrights rewrite again and again, hoping to narrow the gap between text and audience by opening night. Preparing for the opening of *Fool for Love*, Sam Shepard had the theater's walls wired for reverberation and speakers placed under the theater's seats.[56]

The same challenges triggered the emergence of directing, which allowed a new focus on what came to be called *mise-en-scène*. Until the late nineteenth century, the tasks of acting, producing, and staging had been bundled together in the role of theatrical entrepreneur, a figure typically of large personality who sometimes actually wrote the text as well. Directing became an independent theatrical role in the course of bitter struggles against producers, financiers, and actors. Bernard Dort's historical reconstruction describes how the stage manager accepted elements of performance as set in stone, seeking to maintain the pre-existing theatrical order. When the director emerged, his conception could not have been more different. The director "doesn't accept these elements as they are [but] sets to work before the elements of production have been determined." Seeing himself as the real "author of the performance," the director "wants to be recognized as its creator."[57] It was a long struggle. As late as the 1930s and 1940s, Artaud was bemoaning that directors played "second fiddle to the author," proclaiming "it is essential to put an end to the subjugation of the theatre to the text." Artaud felt com-

136

pelled to dispute the idea of the director as "slave," as "merely an artisan, adaptor, a kind of translator eternally devoted to making a dramatic work pass from one language to another." If "the language of literature" is to be revived, the director must be allowed to "create in complete autonomy," for his "domain is closer to life than the author's."[58]

By mid-century, the director's controlling authority was more firmly in place. "What makes movies a great popular art form," Pauline Kael wrote in her homage to Orson Welles, "is that certain artists can, at moments in their lives, reach out and unify the audience – educated and uneducated – in a shared response."[59] The distinctive intellectual contribution of French New Wave auteur theory placed directors, not star actors, at the core of cinematic power. It was to protest this newly pre-eminent element of performance that, in the early 1980s, the German theater theorist Bernard Dort turned Artaud on his head. He accused directors of being "dictators," of making the other elements of performance "helpless and impotent," of having "reduced them almost to slavery." Like other avant-garde manifestos for other kinds of theatrical freedom, Dort called for "the progressive emancipation of the elements of theatrical performance."[60]

Having examined the emancipation of audience, actor, producer, and director from written text, I now turn to an element of theatrical performance that seems among the least dramatic. Every performance depends on material "means of symbolic production," and in per-formances of a contemporary theatrical kind this means not only a stage, but the props and lighting that help create more dramatic scenes. Earlier I mentioned the performative effect of footlights, how their introduction underscored the growing sense of a chasm between audience and drama. What the footlights illuminated was, in fact, an only recently darkened stage. It was the producer André Antoine who first thought to extinguish overhanging houselights in his 1888 pro-duction of *La Mort du Duc d'Enghien*. Jean Chothia calls Antoine's "darkening of the house lights" a "significant gesture in the creation of illusionist theatre."[61] What lighting illuminates, by creating the illu-sion of reality, is not just actors but props, an element of great interest in recent theater scholarship. Theatrologist Marvin Carlson wrote an influential essay about "the thing-ness of the theater."[62] Andrew Sofer devoted an entire book to "transformational props" that "appear to signify independently of the actor who handles them."[63] Scenic objects seem to exemplify icons in the Peircean sense, material objects that literally resemble the things they are intended to represent. It is this purportedly iconic quality of drama that interests States who, drawing attention to "the theater's special openness to the world of objects," asserts that theater is "a language whose words consist … of things that are what they seem to be."[64] Asking "What semiotic competence is really necessary in theatre?," Jean Alter answers: "There is only one," the "competence in the use of an iconic code whereby all signs on the stage refer to their mirror image in the imaginary story space outside [the] stage."[65]

But these new appreciations for the independence of materiality are too literal. It is actually the not-like-the-referent quality of material things that makes them ideal stage props. Icons have seductively familiar material surfaces, but their sensual shapes are anchored in invisible meanings derived as much from discursive cultural structures as from plastic form.[66] Props are not only material but symbolic, not so much reflections of ordinary things as translations of dramatic meanings into material forms. Sofer is careful to explain that it is because transformational props can "absorb dramatic meaning and become complex symbols" that they are able to "motivate the stage action."[67] When Peter Handke writes about "a brightness that pretends to be another brightness," a "light that pretends to be another light,"[68] he is getting at just such intertwining of material surface and textual depth.

The independence of scenario-script

If the elements of performance have become liberated, then the text performed on stage is not the one printed on the page. Contemporary theater has moved far away from intratextuality. The audience has been sharply separated, and actor, director, producer, and means of symbolic production have emerged as efforts to more effectively organize the *mise-en-scène* on stage. In this context of differentiation, the written play provides a set of background collective representations, the specific meanings of which are worked out on the stage. What is foregrounded on stage are scripts. Goffman was the first social theorist to speak of scripts, but failing to differentiate them from background meanings, he conceived scripts as rigid, noncontingent texts. Influenced by the contexts of defusion that define modern performance studies, Robin Bernstein has approached the concept more flexibly: "The word script captures the moment when the dramatic narrative and movement through space are in the act of becoming each other."[69] Bernstein references Taylor's influential distinction between repertoire and archive (see above), but it is the latter's concept of "scenario" that actually fits best with script. Scenarios are not written, but they are by no means entirely invented, either. Taylor sees them as "meaning-making paradigms that structure social environments, behaviors, and potential outcomes."[70] Relatively, not absolutely, independent of written archives, scenarios conjure physical location, cultural codes, and embodiment all at the same time. They allow actors to be culturally pragmatic.

The playwright responds

These powerful movements of dramaturgical innovation were, as I have reconstructed them, first and foremost uprisings against textual power, even as they also aimed at becoming separated from each other. However, as the era of defusion deepened, writers of theatrical texts did not simply stand pat. They, too, were mightily anxious about the growing gap between audience and stage. In response, they created new forms of theatrical writing, radically revisionist styles that revived dramatic impact and addressed directly fears about fragmentation, isolation, and meaningless in the modern age. The late nineteenth-century Scandinavian playwrights Henrik Ibsen and August Strindberg, no matter how melodramatic their realism and how antipathetic their personal relations, were the first self-consciously "modern" stage writers to embark on this quest. In his introduction to the publication of *Miss Julie*, Strindberg decried "the serious theatre crisis now prevailing throughout Europe, especially in those bastions of culture that produced the greatest thinkers of the age, England and Germany," and he announced that "the art of drama, like most of the other fine arts, is dead." Criticizing the efforts of his contemporaries as merely filling "old forms with new contents," Strindberg announces he has "modernized" the theatrical form "in accordance with [the] demands I think contemporary audiences make upon this art."[71] Social realism in 1930s theater – for example, the work of Clifford Odets – elaborated this modernizing response on a more politically engaged, working-class oriented form.

Samuel Beckett's transformation of theatrical style challenged such efforts at dramatic realism, reinvigorating textual engagement with the postwar, post-mass-murder world. Doing away with plot and even character, the starkness of Beckett's scenes and the bleak poetry of his dialogue powerfully articulated the spirit of the audiences of his time. "I can't go on!" Vladimir exclaims in *Waiting for Godot*, but he immediately reconsiders. "What have I said?" he asks, and at play's end he has decided to continue to wait. Yet, while extraordinarily innovative with text, Beckett displayed marked rigidity vis-à-vis the other elements of performance, trying to re-fuse roles that had become emancipated, putting the writer back into control. Beckett rarely assented to requests for licensed performance of his plays. When he did so, he exercised total authority over the staffing and *mise-en-scène*, frequently from on site.[72] Here is another demonstration of a paradox we have continually encountered: even as the distinctive elements of performance have sought independence for themselves, they have often tried to subordinate the others.

Film and other Arts

There are several related themes I have not taken up here. One is filmic drama, whether in cinema, TV, video, or online, and its powerful contribution to the (re)dramatic movement it has been the point of this chapter to describe. The French film theorist and *Cahiers du Cinema* founder André Bazin[73] rightly insists that, compared with writing and theater, the ontology of film is realism. Virtually every cinematic innovation – from montage to animation and 3D, from close-ups to long shots and panning, from hand-held video cameras to cinema verité, from short to long form TV – has sought to deepen audience conviction that what they are seeing and feeling is vivid and true, if obviously dramatically different from actual social life.

Another theme moves beyond the theatrical to the fate of the modern dramatic in other arts. Over roughly the same period I have considered here, painting and sculpture moved from narrative representation to abstraction as their dominant modality, with music shifting from harmony to atonality. Did the transition from concreteness and realism push these arts to postdrama? Such a case has often been made, but it seems a poor one to me. Pre- and post-Impressionism, Fauvism, Constructivism, Cubism, Surrealism, Abstract Expressionism, Minimalism, Pop art, conceptual art: all these radical innovations of the painterly avant-garde may be seen not as efforts to create alienation from contemporary art, but as techniques for recreating its aura and mystery, for providing more intensive engagements with the aesthetic.[74]

What's at Stake?

There are social, not only theoretical issues at stake in this argument about postdrama. If avant-garde theater may be conceptualized as postdramatic, then contemporary society may be theorized merely as spectacle, and the story David Foster Wallace tells about "Found Drama" would not be a joke at all, but something true. My argument suggests, on the contrary, that Wallace was exactly right to frame his Found Drama story in an ironic tone. If the elements that compose theatrical performance have become separated over the course of the last three centuries, the rationale has been to reclaim dramatic power. For each theatrical innovation, the argument has been that, by liberating this particular and distinctive form of dramatic power, it would become possible to re-fuse the elements of performance.

If theories about theatrical and social dramas are mutually reflective, they are also substantively intertwined. As I have shown throughout this book, tools of aesthetic artifice enter deeply into the institutions and lifeworlds of contemporary society, into struggles for power and its vertical operation, and into efforts to cut power down to size. Democratic movements to control power cannot afford to be postdramatic. Not empty spectacle, but the invigorating experience of myth is the goal for which both aesthetic and social performances strive.

Converting cosmos into text, drama projects powerful narratives in which protagonists and antagonists fight against one another's vision of the good and the right. Identifying with these characters, audiences connect with meanings outside themselves and reflectively work through their moral implications; they learn about heroes and enemies, make epiphanies out of historical events, and experience solidarity with others by sharing catharsis.[75] Theater crystallizes and concentrates these processes in a reflexively aesthetic idiom, but the dramatic form permeates the entirety of modern social life.[76] Without drama, collective and personal meanings could not be sustained, evil could not be identified, and justice would be impossible to obtain.

NOTES

INTRODUCTION: A NEW THEORY OF MODERNITY FROM RITUAL TO PERFORMANCE

1 Delillo, D. (1985) *White Noise*. Viking, New York, p. 150, italics added.
2 Kleinfeld, N. R., Oppel, Jr. R. A., & Eddy M. (2016) Moment in Convention Glare Stirs Parents' American Life. *New York Times*, August 6, p. A12, italics added.
3 Alexander, J. C. (1996) Cultural Sociology or Sociology of Culture? *Culture* 10(3/4), pp. 1–4; Alexander, J. C. & Smith, P. (2010) The Strong Program in Cultural Theory: Elements of a Structural Hermeneutics. In J. Turner (ed.), *Handbook of Sociological Theory*. Kluwer Academic, New York, pp. 135–150; Alexander, J. C. & Smith, P. (2010) The Strong Program: Origins, Achievements and Prospects. In J. Hall, et al. (eds.), *Handbook of Cultural Sociology*. Routledge, London.
4 Durkheim, E. (1995/1911) *The Elementary Forms of Religious Life*. Free Press, New York.
5 Cf. Alexander, J. C. (1982) *Theoretical Logic in Sociology*. Vol 2: *The Antinomies of Classical Thought*. University of California Press, Berkeley.
6 Goffman, E. (1956) *The Presentation of Self in Everyday Life*. Doubleday, New York.
7 Shils, E. A. (1975) *Center and Periphery: Essays in Macrosociology*. University of Chicago Press, Chicago; Bellah, R. N. (1970) *Beyond Belief: Essays on Religion in a Post-Traditional World*. Harper and Row, New York; Collins, R. (2004) *Interaction Ritual Chains*. Princeton University Press, Princeton.
8 Schechner, R. (1976) From Ritual to Theatre and Back. In R. Schechner and M. Schechner (eds.), *Ritual, Play, and Performance: Readings in the Social Sciences/Theatre*. Seabury Press, New York, pp. 196–202.
9 Schechner, R. (2002) *Performance Studies: An Introduction*. Routledge: New York.
10 Turner, V. (1982) *From Ritual to Theatre: The Human Seriousness of Play*. PAJ Press, Baltimore.
11 Alexander, J. C. (2011) *Performance and Power*. Polity, Cambridge, UK. Cf., Alexander, J. C., Giesen, B., & Mast, J. (eds.) (2006) *Social Performance*:

Symbolic Action, Cultural Pragmatics, and Ritual. Cambridge University Press, New York.

12 Alexander J. C. & Colomy, P. (eds.) (1990) *Differentiation Theory and Social Change*. Columbia University Press, New York.

13 Goody, J. (1986) *The Logic of Writing and the Organization of Society*. Cambridge University Press, Cambridge, UK.

14 Eisenstadt, S. N. (1982) The Axial Age: The Emergence of Transcendental Visions and the Rise of Clerics. *European Journal of Sociology* 23, pp. 294–314.

15 Bellah, R. N. (2011) *Religion in Human Evolution: From the Paleolithic to the Axial Age*. Harvard University Press, Cambridge, MA.

16 McCoy, R. C. (2013) *Faith in Shakespeare*. Oxford University Press, New York, pp. ix, 6.

17 Alexander, J. C. (2010) *The Performance of Politics: Obama's Victory and the Democratic Struggle for Power*. Oxford, New York; Alexander J. C. & Jaworsky, B. (2014) *Obama Power*. Polity, Cambridge, UK; Mast, J. (2012) *The Performative Presidency: Crisis and Resurrection during the Clinton Years*. Cambridge University Press, New York.

CHAPTER 1 SEIZING THE STAGE: MAO, MLK, AND BLACK LIVES MATTER TODAY

1 Cf. Eyerman, R. (2006) Performing Opposition or, How Do Social Movements Move? In J. C. Alexander, B. Giesen, & J. Mast (eds.), *Social Performance: Symbolic Action, Cultural Pragmatics, and Ritual*. Cambridge University Press, New York, pp. 193–217.

2 Alexander, J. C. (2004) Cultural Pragmatics: Social Performance between Ritual and Strategy. *Sociological Theory* 22(4), pp. 527–573.

3 Lenin, V. (1966/1902) *What Is to Be Done?* Bantam Books, New York.

4 Gramsci, A. (1959) *The Modern Prince and Other Writings*. International Publishers, Moscow.

5 Gramsci, *The Modern Prince and Other Writings*.

6 Apter, D. E. & Saich, T. (1994) *Revolutionary Discourse in Mao's Republic*. Harvard University Press, Cambridge, MA, p. 75.

7 Apter & Saich, *Revolutionary Discourse*, pp. xi, 298.

8 Apter & Saich, *Revolutionary Discourse*, pp. xv, 75.

9 Apter & Saich, *Revolutionary Discourse*, p. 85.

10 Apter & Saich, *Revolutionary Discourse*, p. 301.

11 Apter & Saich, *Revolutionary Discourse*, p. 69.

12 Apter & Saich, *Revolutionary Discourse*, p. 99.

13 Apter & Saich, *Revolutionary Discourse*, p. 182.

14 Apter & Saich, *Revolutionary Discourse*, p. 182.

15 Apter & Saich, *Revolutionary Discourse*, p. xv.

16 Apter & Saich, *Revolutionary Discourse*, p. 224.

17 Apter & Saich, *Revolutionary Discourse*, pp. 130–131, 388 n.31.

18 Perry, E. J. (2012) *Anyuan: Mining China's Revolutionary Tradition*. University of California Press, Berkeley, pp. 4–5. Cf., Denise Y. Ho (2015) "The Power of Culture." *The PRC History Review* 1 (2): 5–6. Despite these clear signals, neither Perry nor the other scholars whose work I employ in this section draw their arguments from the performative turn. In *Anyuan*,

Perry presents her principal theoretical term, "cultural positioning," as indicating Chinese revolutionary efforts to instantiate Marxist ideology inside more traditional forms of Chinese culture, and in an earlier, also widely noted effort, she deployed the acultural sociological concept of "emotion work" to describe an historical intervention that was equally performative in its framing (Perry, E. J. (2002) Moving the Masses: Emotion Work in the Chinese Revolution, *Mobilization: An International Quarterly* 7(2), pp. 111–128). In the same manner, both Yung-fa Chen and Feiyu Sun – whose writings I employ below to further elaborate a performative approach – describe their own contributions as "show[ing] the importance of the psychological dimensions in CCP policy" (Chen, Y. (1986) *Making Revolution: The Communist Movement in Eastern and Central China, 1937–1945*. University of California Press, Berkeley, p. 100) and in terms of "the traditions of both classical psychoanalysis and phenomenology – Sigmund Freud, Herbert Marcuse, Hannah Arendt, Michel Foucault, and Paul Ricoeur" (Sun, F. (2013) *Social Suffering and Political Confession: Suku in Modern China*. Peking University Series on Sociology and Anthropology, vol. 1. World Scientific, Beijing). The theoretical movement I am here tracing from poststructural to performatively oriented cultural analysis, in other words, is my own interpretation of the framework that has informed these recent studies, not those of the authors' cited.

19 Perry, *Anyuan*, pp. 48–51.
20 Two decades later, in Mao's *Talks at the Yenan Forum on Literature and Art*, he may have been recalling this wardrobe shift when he insisted that, in order to "ensure that literature and art fit well into the whole revolutionary machine," CCP artists needed to be more responsive to "the problem of audience" (Zedong, M. (1942) *Talks at the Yenan Forum on Literature and Art*. May 2. Accessed July 17, 2016: https://www.marxists.org/reference/archive/mao/selected-works/volume-3/mswv3_08.htm). "Since the audience for our literature and art consists of workers, peasants and soldiers and of their cadres," Mao suggested, "the problem arises of understanding them and knowing them well" (Zedong, *Talks*). Addressing the disconnect between cultural elites and masses, Mao asserted that "the thoughts and feelings of our writers and artists should be *fused* with those of the masses," advising that "to achieve this fusion, they should conscientiously learn the language of the masses" (Zedong, *Talks*, italics added). But "if you want the masses to understand you," Mao warned, you must "undergo a long process of tempering." "Here I might mention the experience of how my own feelings changed. I began life as a student [and] felt that intellectuals were the only clean people [and] workers and peasants were dirty. [W]earing the clothes of other intellectuals [,] I would not put on clothes belonging to a worker ... But after I became a revolutionary and lived with workers [I] fundamentally changed" (Zedong, *Talks*).
21 Perry, *Anyuan*, p. 61.
22 Perry, *Anyuan*.
23 Perry, *Anyuan*.
24 Perry, *Anyuan*, pp. 59–60.
25 Perry, *Anyuan*, p. 60.
26 Perry, *Anyuan*, p. 95.
27 Perry, *Anyuan*, p. 95.

28 Perry, *Anyuan*, p. 95–96.
29 Perry, *Anyuan*, p. 96.
30 Perry, *Anyuan*.
31 Perry, *Anyuan*, pp. 96–97.
32 Snow, E. (2007 [1938]) *Red Star Over China*. Random House, New York, pp. 123–124.
33 Chen, *Making Revolution*, p. 173.
34 Sun's ability to document the CCP's culturally pragmatic strategy depends on access to unpublished, intra-party documents, which are much more open about performative efforts and obstacles than the rah-rah documents the CCP issued for public consumption. Chen (*Making Revolution*, p. xix) contrasts the internal and external documents explicitly. Perry also relies primarily on previously unpublished sources.
35 Sun, *Social Suffering and Political Confession*, pp. 35ff.
36 Sun, *Social Suffering and Political Confession*, p. 36.
37 Sun, *Social Suffering and Political Confession*, p. 37.
38 Chen, *Making Revolution*, p. 331.
39 Sun, *Social Suffering and Political Confession*, p. 2.
40 Sun, *Social Suffering and Political Confession*, p. 46.
41 Hinton, W. (2008/1966) *Fanshen: A Documentary of Revolution in a Chinese Village*. Monthly Review Press, New York, pp. 112–114.
42 Hinton, *Fanshen*, p. 55.
43 Sun, *Social Suffering and Political Confession*, p. 46.
44 Hinton, *Fanshen*, pp. 57–60
45 Hinton, *Fanshen*, p. 46.
46 Sun, *Social Suffering and Political Confession*, pp. 46–47.
47 Wu, G. (2014) Recalling Bitterness: Historiography, Memory, and Myth in Maoist China. *Twentieth-Century China* 399(3), pp. 245–268, at p. 247.
48 During the cultural revolution, the "revolutionary operas" scripted and produced by Jiang Qing, the celebrity actress and political activist who became Mao's wife in Yan'an in 1939, replaced traditional opera and played a significant propaganda role. Despite her outsized political power during these years, however, there is little evidence that Qing's theatrical expertise contributed to the performativity of Chinese revolutionary politics more broadly conceived in the decades before (Terrill, R. (1984) *The White Boned Demon: A Biography of Madame Mao Zedong*. William Morrow, New York). Staging theatrical drama is one thing; staging social performances quite another, though they often historically intertwine. Mao Zedong had a performative gift for politics, though he never wrote or performed for theater.
49 Wu, Recalling Bitterness, p. 247.
50 Wu, Recalling Bitterness, p. 263.
51 Burke, E. (1990/1757) *A Philosophical Enquiry*. Oxford University Press, Oxford.
52 Morris, A. D. (2007) Naked Power and The Civil Sphere. *The Sociological Quarterly* 48(4), pp. 615–628.
53 McAdam, D. (1982) *Political Process and the Development of Black Insurgency, 1930–70*. University of Chicago Press, Chicago; Payne, C. M. (1995) *I've Got the Light of Freedom: The Organizing Tradition and the Mississippi Freedom Struggle*. University of California Press, Berkeley.
54 First, of course, there had to *be* a movement. King's performances had to

successfully mobilize black masses in the south. It was not only King – as director and star – but the cast of black foot soldiers who created the dramatic performances that could be projected to white audiences in the North.

55 Garrow, D. (1957) Nonviolence and Racial Justice. *Christian Century* 74, February 6, pp. 165–167. There were, of course, some southern whites who did support the black movement (Sokol, J. (2006) *There Goes My Everything: White Southerners in the Age of Civil Rights, 1945–1975.* Vintage, New York), and while most did so passively, a few were active supporters: for example, clergy (Campbell, W. D. (1997) *And Also with You: Duncan Gray and the American Dilemma.* Providence House Publishers. Franklin); rabbis (Bauman, M. K. & Kalin, B. (eds.) (2014) *The Quiet Voices: Southern Rabbis and Black Civil Rights, 1880s to 1990s.* University of Alabama Press, Tuscaloosa); women (Little, K. K. (2009) *You Must Be from the North: Southern White Women in the Memphis Civil Rights Movement.* University of Mississippi Press, Jackson; Moody, A. (2011); *Coming of Age in Mississippi: White Sympathizers and Supporters of the Civil Rights Movement.* Random House, New York; Murphy, S. A. (1997) *Breaking the Silence: The Little Rock Women's Emergency Committee to Open Our Schools, 1958–1963.* University of Arkansas Press, Fayetteville); students (Michel, G. L. (2004) *Inside Agitators: White Southerners in the Civil Rights Movement.* Palgrave Macmillan, New York); editors (Roberts, G. & Klibanoff, H. (2007) *The Race Beat: The Press, The Civil Rights Struggle, and the Awakening of a Nation.* Vintage, New York); and business people (Robinson, A. L. & Sullivan, P. (eds.) (1991) *New Directions in Civil Rights Studies.* University of Virginia Press, Charlotte). While Chappell argues that "covert moral support from local white people" was "immensely encouraging to black protestors," the point is that such support rarely became overt (Chappell, D. (1994) *Inside Agitators: White Southerners in the Civil Rights Movement.* Johns Hopkins University Press, Baltimore, p. xvi). A handful of southern whites may indeed have functioned as "inside agitators," but they were effectively invisible to the audience observing from the outside. White southerners experiencing empathy and displaying sympathy could not be publicly placed on the performative scene. In the national civil rights drama, the "role" of white southerner was reserved for figures who represented racist masses and repressive elites.

56 Branch, T. (1988) *Parting the Waters: America in the King Years, 1954–63.* Simon and Schuster, New York.

57 Cf., Meier, A. (1965) On the Role of Martin Luther King. *New Politics* 4(1) pp. 52–59.

58 Quoted in Lentz, R. (1990) *Symbols, the News Magazines, and Martin Luther King.* Louisiana State University Press, Baton Rouge, p. 26.

59 Quoted in Lentz, *Symbols*, p. 34.

60 Eskew, G. T. (1997) *But for Birmingham: The Local and National Movements in the Civil Rights Struggle.* University of North Carolina Press, Chapel Hill; Garrow, D. (1978) *Protest at Selma: Martin Luther King, Jr., and the Voting Rights Act of 1965.* Yale University Press, New Haven.

61 Garrow, *Protest at Selma*, p. 321.

62 Alexander, J. C. (2006) *The Civil Sphere.* Oxford University Press, New York.

63 Alexander, J. C. (2013) The Arc of Civil Liberation: Obama–Tahrir–Occupy. *Philosophy and Social Criticism* 39(4–5), pp. 341–347. The iterative performances that constituted the Chinese Revolution, before and after the Communist regime change in 1949, created a similarly powerful narrative arc that reverberated on the global stage for decades after. Without the Maoist script, it is hard to imagine the strands of anti-colonialism in the 1950s (e.g., Franz Fanon and Fidel Castro) and 1960s (Che Guevara) that promoted violent agrarian revolution and, quite often, exemplary violence as a vanguard trigger (Alexander, J. C. (2016) Dramatic Intellectuals: Elements of Performance. *European Journal of Social Theory*), much less the revolutionary performances of such Western leftist groups as the Weathermen and the Black Panthers, who drew upon interpretations of Mao, Fanon, and Che for their scripts. However, Maoism and its iterations were revolutionary, not civil society movements. By contrast, the US civil rights movement was oriented toward radical reform, not revolution, and its embrace of nonviolence was critical for such performance. This difference is what allowed it to become a central inspiration, a transforming script, for the radical civil society movements that emerged after the socialist utopia faded.

64 Duneier, M. (2016) *Ghetto: The Invention of a Place, the History of an Idea*. FSG, New York; Landry, B. (1988) *The New Black Middle Class*. University of California Press, Berkeley.

65 Anderson, E. (2012) The Iconic Ghetto. In E. Anderson et al. (eds.), *Bringing Fieldwork Back In: Contemporary Urban Ethnographic Research, The Annals of the American Academy of Political and Social Science*, vol. 642, Sage Publications; Anderson, E. (2015) The White Space. *Sociology of Race and Ethnicity* 1(1), pp. 10–21.

66 Wilson, W. J. (1987) *The Truly Disadvantaged: The Inner City, the Underclass, and Public Policy*. University of Chicago Press, Chicago; Patterson, O. (1998) *Rituals of Blood*. Civitas, Washington, DC; Massey, D. S. & Denton, N. A. (1993) *American Apartheid: Segregation and the Making of the Underclass*. Harvard University Press, Cambridge, MA; Alexander, M. (2012) *The New Jim Crow: Mass Incarceration in the Age of Colorblindness*. New Press, New York.

67 Morris, A. D. (1984) *The Origins of the Civil Rights Movement: Black Communities Organizing for Change*. Free Press, New York.

68 Kuttner, P. (2015) Black Symbols Matter. *Cultural Organizing*. August 10. Accessed July 17, 2016 (original italics): http://culturalorganizing.org/black-symbols-matter/

69 McLaughlin, M. (2016) The Dynamic History of #BlackLivesMatter Explained: This Is How a Hashtag Transformed into a Movement. *The Huffington Post*, February 29. Accessed July 17, 2016: http://www.huffingtonpost.com/entry/history-black-lives-matter_us_56d0a3b0e4b0871f60eb4af5.

70 Kang, J. C. (2015) "Our Demand Is Simple: Stop Killing Us." *New York Times Magazine*, May 4.

71 Pew Research Center (2015) Across Racial Lines, More Say Nation Needs to Achieve Racial Equality. August 5. Accessed 7 July 17, 2016: http://www.people-press.org/2015/08/05/across-racial-lines-more-say-nation-needs-to-make-changes-to-achieve-racial-equality/.

72 Pew Research Center, Across Racial Lines.

73 Shear, M. (2012) Obama Speaks Out on Trayvon Killing. *New York Times*, March 23. Accessed July 17, 2016: http://thecaucus.blogs.nytimes.com/2012/03/23/obama-makes-first-comments-on-trayvon-martin-shooting/.

74 Miller, J. T. (2012) "Million Hoodie March" in New York Rallies Support for Trayvon Martin. *Time*, March 22.

75 Healy, J., Stolberg, S. G., & Yee, V. (2015) Ferguson Report Puts 'Hands Up' to Reality Test. *The New York Times*, March 6, p. A1.

76 Associated Press. (2014) Thousands protest nationally after Ferguson grand jury decision, more protests planned. November 24. Accessed July 17, 2016: http://www.nola.com/crime/index.ssf/2014/11/national_ferguson_protest_mike.html.

77 Zillgit, J. & Strauss, C. (2014) Protests Greet Prince William and Kate at Cavaliers-Nets. *USA Today*. December 9.

78 Healy, Stolberg, & Yee, Ferguson Report Puts "Hands Up" to Reality Test.

79 "Clearly there is some degree of overlap between #Blacklivesmatter and Black Lives Matter: organization members (along with many others) use the hashtag, which in turn almost certainly leads prospective members to the organization. At the same time, the two terms are sometimes used to refer to a third idea: the sum of all organizations, individuals, protests, and digital spaces dedicated to raising awareness about and ultimately ending police brutality against Black people" (Freelon, D., McIlwain, C. D., & Clark, M. D. (2016) *Beyond the Hashtags: #Ferguson, #Blacklivesmatter, and the Online Struggle for Offline Justice*. Center for Media and Social Impact, School of Communication, American University. Washington DC. February 29. Accessed July 17, 2016: http://www.cmsimpact.org/sites/default/files/beyond_the_hashtags_2016.pdf.).

80 Freelon, McIlwain, & Clark, *Beyond the Hashtags*.

81 teleSUR. (2014) 2014 Freedom Ride Arrives in Ferguson Today. August 29. Accessed July 17, 2016: http://www.telesurtv.net/english/news/2014-Freedom-Ride-Arrives-in-Ferguson-Today-20140829-0032.html.

82 Cobb, J. (2016) The Matter of Black Lives. *The New Yorker*, March 14, pp. 33–40, at p. 36.

83 Cobb, The Matter of Black Lives, p. 35.

84 Cobb, The Matter of Black Lives, p. 26.

85 http://patrissecullors.com/bio/.

86 Kang, "Our Demand Is Simple: Stop Killing Us."

87 Kang, "Our Demand Is Simple."

88 Cobb, The Matter of Black Lives.

89 Kang, "Our Demand Is Simple."

90 Kang, "Our Demand Is Simple."

91 Kang, "Our Demand Is Simple."

92 Rauer, V. (2006) Symbols in Action: Willy Brandt's Kneefall at the Warsaw Memorial. In J. C. Alexander, B. Giesen, & J. Mast (eds.), *Social Performances: Symbolic Action, Cultural Pragmatics, and Ritual*. Cambridge University Press, New York, pp. 257–282.

93 Kang, "Our Demand Is Simple."

94 Kang, "Our Demand Is Simple."

95 Freelon, McIlwain, & Clark, *Beyond the Hashtags*.

96 Freelon, McIlwain, & Clark, *Beyond the Hashtags*, p. 16; "With a graph density of .003 ... only a tiny fraction of all the links that could exist within

the network actually exist. As a comparison, a random network with the same number of nodes has a density of .02, meaning that the network contains two percent of all possible ties. There is little reciprocity between sites (in 97% of cases, sites linking out to another site don't receive a link in from the latter site). Whether unidirectional or reciprocal, few sites have multiple links to any one site (the average tie weight – the number of times any two sites link to each other – is one, and only 30% of ties have a weight greater than one)."

97 Freelon, McIlwain, & Clark, *Beyond the Hashtags*, p. 17: "59% of the entire Black Lives Matter network are news sites [and] more than 75% of sites with direct connections to BlackLivesMatter.com are news sites. We've pointed out that as a whole, the network is very sparse. However, connections among news sites in the network are extremely dense, meaning that they primarily connect to one another, and much less so to non-news sites."

98 Not the police killings themselves, however. In a twelve-month Pulitzer winning investigation, the *Washington Post* discovered there had been 990 fatal police shootings in 2015 (Kindly, K. et al. (2015) A Year of Reckoning: Police Fatally Shoot Nearly 1000. *Washington Post*, December 26) and 250 in the first 3 months of 2016 (Sullivan, J. et al. (2016) In Fatal Shootings by Police, 1 in 5 Officers' Names Go Undisclosed. *Washington Post*, April 1). Those killed in 2015 were disproportionally minorities, 258 African Americans and 172 Hispanics, for a total of 430 as compared with 494 whites. One-third of the victims were aged 18–29.

99 Howard, G. (2016) DeRay Mckesson Won't Be Elected Mayor of Baltimore. So Why Is He Running? *New York Times Magazine*, April 11.

100 Aron, H. (2015) These Savvy Women Have Made Black Lives Matter the Most Crucial Left-Wing Movement Today. *LA Weekly*, November 9; Ruffin, H. G. 2nd. Black Lives Matter: The Growth of a New Social Justice Movement. *Blackpast.org*. Accessed July 17, 2016: http://www.blackpast.org/perspectives/black-lives-matter-growth-new-social-justice-movement; Stockman, F. (2016) On Crime Bill and the Clintons, Young Blacks Clash with Parents. *New York Times*, April 18, p. A1. Cf. Eligon, J. (2016) Activists Move from Street to Ballot, Emboldened by Protests. *New York Times*, February 7, p. A1.

101 Helsel, P. (2015) "Black Lives Matter" Activists Disrupt Bernie Sanders Speech. *NBC News*. August 9. Accessed July 17, 2016: http://www.nbcnews.com/politics/2016-election/black-lives-matter-activists-disrupt-bernie-sanders-speech-n406546.

102 Moore, D. C. (2015) Black Activists Are Literally Stealing the Stage from 2016 Contenders – And It's Working. *Identities.Mic.*, August 13. Accessed July 17, 2016: http://mic.com/articles/123796/black-activists-called-out-bernie-sanders-jeb-bush-hillary-clinton-and-martin-omalley#.8ktXIiucn.

103 Moore, D. C. (2015) Two Years Later, Black Lives Matter Faces Critiques, But It Won't Be Stopped. *Identities.Mic.*, August 10. Accessed July 17, 2016: http://mic.com/articles/123666/two-years-later-black-lives-matter-faces-critiques-but-it-won-t-be-stopped#.kE68fRkeH.

104 Chozick, A. (2016) Mothers of Black Victims Emerge as a Force for Hillary Clinton. *New York Times*, April 14, p. A1.

105 Chozick, A. (2016) Bill Clinton Says He Regrets Showdown with Black Lives Matters Protesters. *New York Times*, April 9, p. A12.

106 Kang, "Our Demand Is Simple."

107 Bellah, R. N. (1970) Civil Religion in America. In R. N. Bellah (ed.), *Beyond Belief*. Harper and Row, New York, pp. 168–189.

108 Eligon, J. & Stolberg, S. J. (2016) A year After Gray's Arrest, 'Baltimore's Mind-Set Has Changed'. *New York Times*, April 13, p. A18.

109 Sidner, S. & Simon, M. (2015) The Rise of Black Lives Matter: Trying to Break the Cycle of Violence and Silence. *CNN.Com*, December 28. Accessed July 17, 2016: http://edition.cnn.com/2015/12/28/us/black-lives-matter-evolution/.

110 Howard, DeRay Mckesson Won't Be Elected Mayor of Baltimore.

111 It is revealing that, while recounting Mckesson's many accomplishments, the *Times* observed that "he collects celebrity "friends" (Azealia Banks, Jesse Williams, Susan Wojcicki, Susan Sarandon, Rashida Jones, Tracee Ellis Ross) [and] refers to them solely by their first names," explaining this was "because, over the last year and a half, he has been the best known face of the Black Lives Matter movement, traveling the country to protest police violence" (Howard, DeRay Mckesson Won't Be Elected Mayor of Baltimore).

CHAPTER 2 REVOLUTIONARY PERFORMANCE IN EGYPT: THE 2011 UPRISING

1 Mekhennet, S. & Kulish, N. (2011) With Muslim Brotherhood Set to Join Egypt Protests, Religion's Role May Grow. *New York Times*, January 28, p. A10.

2 Blow, C. M. (2011) The Kindling of Change. *New York Times*, February 5, p. A17.

3 Hennion, C. (2011) Un Mouvement de contestation gagne l'Egypte. *Le Monde*, January 27, p. 5.

4 Egypt: Rage Against the Mubaraks. Editorial. (2011) *Guardian*, January 27, p. 36. See also Levinson, C. & Dagher, S. (2011) Rallies Fan Out as Regime Closes Ranks. *Wall Street Journal*. February 9. Accessed June 20, 2011: http://online.wsj.com/article/SB10001424052748704858404576133630107794342.html.

5 Mason, P. (2011) Twenty Reasons Why It's Kicking Off Everywhere. *Idle Scrawl Blog*, BBC, February 5. Accessed June 10, 2011: http://www.bbc.co.uk/blogs/newsnight/paulmason/2011/02/twenty_reasons_why_its_kicking.html.

6 Slackman, M. (2011) In Mideast Activism, a New Tilt Away from Ideology. *New York Times*, January 23, p. 10; El Naggar, M., & Slackman, M. (2011) Egypt's Leader Used Old Tricks to Defy New Demands. *New York Times*, January 28, p. A11.

7 Montefiore, S. S. (2011) Every Revolution Is Revolutionary in Its Own Way. *New York Times*, March 27, p. WK11.

8 Todd, E. (2011) Interview by Lara Ricci. *Il Sole 24 Ore*, February 26. Accessed June 12, 2011. http://lararicci.blog.ilsole24ore.com. These remarks referenced the interviewee's earlier work (Todd, E. (2007) *Le Rendez-vous des civilizations*. Seuil, Paris), which laid out the case for demographic shifts transforming the Arab world, equated modernization with eventual democratization, and presented political ideology and culture as reflections of underlying population shifts.

9 William Sewell's early responses to Theda Skocpol remain the most interesting theoretical-cum-empirical statements of a more cultural approach to revolution. Writing in the context of conflict theory, the Marxist revival, and newly institutionalist readings of Weber, Skocpol set out the basic premises of a materialist emphasis on political economy and state violence (Skocpol (1979) *States and Social Revolutions*. Cambridge University Press, New York), modifying her position only to acknowledge ideology as an intentional manipulation of ideas in response to the religious revolution in Iran (Skocpol (1982) Rentier State and Shi'a Islam in the Iranian Revolution. *Theory and Society* 11, pp. 265–303). Influenced by Geertz and the semiotic turn in French historiography, William Sewell polemically challenged Skocpol's perspective, describing the French revolution as an "act of epoch-making cultural creativity" and "a momentous ... act of signification" (Sewell, W. (1996) Historical Events as Transformations of Structures: Inventing Revolution at the Bastille. *Theory and Society* 25(6), pp. 841–888, at pp. 852, 861; see also Sewell, W. (1985) Ideologies and Social Revolutions: Reflections on the French Case. *Journal of Modern History* 57(1), pp. 57–85). In the decades since, with the marked diminution of academic interest in revolution, the sociological literature has been pulled between abstract theoretical affirmations of cultural causation (e.g., Goldstone, J. A. (1991) Ideology, Cultural Frameworks, and the Process of Revolution. *Theory and Society* 20(4), pp. 405–453; Emirbayer, M. & Goodwin, J. (1996) Symbols, Positions, Objects: Toward a New Theory of Revolutions and Collective Action. *History and Theory* 35(3), pp. 358–374) and concrete, historical examples of cultural effects (e.g., Moaddel, M. (1992) Ideology as Episodic Discourse: The Case of the Iranian Revolution. *American Sociological Review* 57(3), pp. 353–370; Reed, J. (2002) Culture in Action: Nicaragua's Revolutionary Identities Reconsidered. *New Political Science* 24(2), pp. 235–263). But see Anne Kane's ambitious new work (Kane, A. (2011) *Constructing Irish Nationalist Identity: Ritual and Discourse during the Irish Land War, 1879–1882*. Palgrave Macmillan, New York), which renews and elaborates a cultural sociological approach.

10 For codes and narratives as the key concepts for understanding the power of relatively autonomous culture structures; for the centrality of meaning in social explanation and causation; and for a critique of the exaggerated role that noncultural factors such as demography play in more traditional social scientific explanations, see Alexander, J. C. (2003) *The Meanings of Social Life: A Cultural Sociology*. Oxford University Press, New York; and Alexander, J. C. (2010) *The Performance of Politics: Obama's Victory and the Democratic Struggle for Power*. Oxford University Press, New York. For a recent cultural sociological approach to social suffering and its cultural narration, see Alexander, J. C. & Breese, E. B. (2011) Introduction: On Social Suffering. In R. Eyerman, J. C. Alexander, & E. B. Breese (eds.), *Narrating Trauma*. Paradigm Press, Boulder.

11 In the same month that Khaled Said was tortured and murdered – June 2010 – the anti-regime protest movement established the 'We Are All Khaled Said' (WAAKS) Facebook page to honor Said as a martyr and to inspire protests in his name. It contained two pages, one in English, and one in Arabic, both of whose administrators maintained anonymity for security reasons. In the final days of that struggle, the Arab language administrator

revealed his identity. Appearing on a popular satellite television program in Cairo after being released from twelve days of captivity, Wael Ghonim acknowledged that he had initiated and led the Facebook project. In the final days of the struggle, the Egyptian became a heroic figure, not only inside the nation but outside as well. For example, *Time* magazine placed him at the head of its annual list of the hundred most important people of the year. Ghonim could perform as WAAKS (Arabic) administrator only until the day of his arrest, which was on or about January 27, 2011; after this date, another administrator or administrators took over, and remained anonymous. After Ghonim's release from prison, he was offered posts on WAAKS (Arabic), but probably did not resume the full-time administrator role.

Both WAAKS pages played central roles in the days leading up to the revolution and throughout the eighteen days of protest that marked the event itself, from January 18 to February 11, 2011. The English and Arabic pages differed substantially from one another, not only in substance but in tone. While the two administrators carefully followed one another's language postings, they did not work together and neither claimed to know the other's identity. The Arabic language page more often adopted religious idioms and its substance was more directed to immediate events, such as timing of demonstrations, advice about protective clothing, and directions about where to meet. The English page was directed less to Egypt and the Arab region and more to the putative global audience, as I will elaborate in the final section of this chapter. In my quotations from these WAAKS pages, grammar, spelling, and punctuation have been left as they were written, in the heat of the moment and often amidst great commotion, stress, and upheaval. The times and dates noted in the Facebook pages are those of Egypt.

12 Slackman, In Mideast Activism.

13 Alexander, J. C. (2006) *The Civil Sphere*. Oxford University Press, New York.

14 Slackman, In Mideast Activism.

15 Kirkpatrick, D. D. & Sanger, D. E. (2011) A Tunisian-Egyptian Link that Shook Arab History. *New York Times*, February 14, p. A1.

16 WAAKS (Arabic), January 27, 2011, 3:46 p.m.

17 WAAKS (English), February 1, 2011, 12:54 a.m.; WAAKS (English), February 6, 2011, 2:14 p.m.

18 Hill, E. (2011) Egypt's Rooftop Revolutionaries. Al Jazeera (English), February 6. Accessed March 7, 2011: http://english.aljazeera.net/news/mid dleeast/2011/02/201126194730350605.html.

19 Hussein, M. (2011) Après la Tunisie, l'Egypte cherche sa liberté. *Le Monde*, January 27, p. 18.

20 Barthe, B. & Hennion, C. (2011) La Révolte Egyptienne; "On s'est remis à respirer normalement, la peur a disparu." *Le Monde*, February 3, p. 6.

21 Barthe & Hennion, La Révolte Egyptienne.

22 Al Aswany, A. (2011) Comment: Police Alone Can't Keep Rulers in Power. Egypt's Battle Is On. *Guardian*, January 28, p. 38; *La Repubblica* (2011) Scontri e Morti in Tutto l'Egitto. Il Presidente in TV: "E" Complotto. *La Repubblica*, January 29. Accessed April 22, 2011: http://www.repub blica.it/esteri/2011/01/29/news/scontri_e_morti_in_tutto_l_egitto_il_presi

dente_in_tv_e_complotto-11795852; Shadid, A. (2011) Street Battle Over the Arab Future. *New York Times*, February 3, p. 1.

23 Prail, B. (2011) In the Mideast, Days of Tumult, [Letter to the Editor]. *New York Times*, January 29, p. A22.

24 Slackman, In Mideast Activism.

25 Fahim, K. & El-Naggar, M. (2011) Violent Clashes Mark Protests Against Mubarak's Rule. *New York Times*, January 26, p. A1.

26 Kirkpatrick, D. D. (2011) Egyptians Defiant as Military Does Little to Quash Protests. *New York Times*, January 30, p. 1.

27 Alderman, L. (2011) Arab Executives Predict Regime Change in Egypt. *New York Times*, January 29. Accessed June 12, 2011: http://www.nytimes.com/2011/01/30/business/global/30davos.html.

28 Kirkpatrick, D. D. (2011) Mubarak Orders Crackdown, With Revolt Sweeping Egypt. *New York Times*, January 29, p. A1.

29 Fahim, K. (2011) Hopes of Egyptians, Poor and Wealthy, Converge in Fight for Cairo Bridge. *New York Times*, January 29, p. A12.

30 Fahim, Hopes of Egyptians.

31 Shadid, A. (2011) Seizing Control of Their Lives and Wondering What's Next. *New York Times*, January 30, p. A1.

32 Kirkpatrick D. D. & El-Naggar, M. (2011) Rich, Poor and a Rift Exposed by Unrest. *New York Times*, January 31, p. A6.

33 Kirkpatrick, D. D. (2011) Mubarak's Grip Is Shaken as Millions Are Called to Protest. *New York Times*, February 1, p. A1.

34 Shadid, Seizing Control of Their Lives.

35 Shadid, Seizing Control of Their Lives.

36 Al Jazeera (2011) Egypt Protestors Clash with Police. 25 January 25. Accessed March 7, 2011: http://english.aljazeera.net/news/middleeast/2011/01/201112511362207742.html.

37 Ambrust, W. (2011) Tahrir: Shock and Awe Mubarak Style. Al Jazeera (English), February 3. Accessed March 7, 2011: http://english.aljazeera.net/indepth/opinion/2011/02/20112310224495606.html.

38 Shenker, J. (2011) Egypt Awaits Nationwide 'Day of Revolution'. *Guardian*, January 25, p. 22.

39 Soueif, A. (2011) Fittingly, It's the Young of the Country Who Are Leading Us. *Guardian*, January 28, p. 1.

40 Rampoldi, G. (2011) La Rivolta che Cambia la Storia Araba. *La Repubblica*, January 29. Accessed April 22, 2011: http://www.repubblica.it/esteri/2011/01/29/news/la_rivolta_che_cambia_la_storia_araba-11796023.

41 WAAKS (Arabic), January 27, 2011, 9:23 p.m.

42 WAAKS (Arabic), January 26, 2011.

43 Al Jazeera (Arabic), January 25, 2011, 7:43 a.m. Accessed June 12, 2011: http://www.aljazeera.net/NR/exeres/B0C28F6C-8BFB-4786-B183-FFFB488C956E.htm.

44 Al Jazeera (Arabic), January 25, 2011, 7:43 a.m. Accessed June 12, 2011: http://www.aljazeera.net/NR/exeres/B0C28F6C-8BFB-4786-B183-FFFB488C956E.htm.

45 Ghannoushi, S. (2011) Comment: A Quagmire of Tyranny: Arabs Are Rebelling Not Just against Decrepit Autocrats but the Foreign Backers Who Kept Them in Power. *Guardian*, January 29, p. 32.

46 Friedman, T. (2011) Speakers' Corner on the Nile. *New York Times*, February 8, p. A27.

47 Dowd, M. (2011) Stars and Sewers. *New York Times*, February 20, Week in Review, p. 11.

48 At the heart of the institutions and interactions of a civil society – even one in *status nascendi* – is a binary discourse that contrasts a sacred, purifying discourse justifying liberty with a profane, polluting discourse justifying repression. For a detailed analysis of this binary cultural structure, and its necessary if ambiguous relation to democratic aspirations, see Alexander, *The Civil Sphere*. While the specification of this cultural structure differs according to historical time and geographical place (for references to varie-gated historical and national studies, see Alexander, *The Civil Sphere*, pp. 573–574), its fundamentals are universal, insofar as they identify the kinds of motives, relations, and institutions required to sustain a self-governing democratic order. That the same discourse so clearly propelled the move-ment of revolutionaries in an Arab, primarily Muslim, setting provides further evidence of this universal status.

49 Slackman, M. (2011) Compact Between Egypt and Its Leader Erodes. *New York Times*, January 29, p. 11.

50 Creswell, R. (2011) Egypt: The Cultural Revolution. *New York Times*, February 20, Book Review, p. 27.

51 Creswell, Egypt: The Cultural Revolution.

52 Slackman, Compact Between Egypt and Its Leader Erodes.

53 The quoted phrases about the sacred and profane character of the Mubarak regime and its opponents are drawn from the regime's official press releases, from its speeches, and from anonymous, off-the-record statements to jour-nalists. For the polluting quotations, see Slackman, In Mideast Activism; Fahim & El-Naggar, Violent Clashes Mark Protests Against Mubarak's Rule; Youssef, M. I. (2011) Quotation of the Day. *New York Times*, January 27, p. A2; Mekhennet & Kulish, With Muslim Brotherhood Set to Join Egypt Protests; Fahim K. & Stack, L. (2011) Opposition in Egypt Gears Up for Major Friday Protest. *New York Times*, January 28, Section A; Kirkpatrick, D. D. (2011) As Egypt Protest Swells, US Sends Specifics Demands. *New York Times*, February 9, p. A1; Shadid, A. & Kirkpatrick, D. D. (2011) Mubarak Won't Quit, Stoking Revolt's Fury and Resolve. *New York Times*, February 11, p. A1. For the quotes sacralizing the regime, see Fahim & Stack, Opposition in Egypt Gears Up for Major Friday Protest; El-Naggar & Slackman, Egypt's Leader Used Old Tricks; Kirkpatrick, Mubarak Orders Crackdown; Cooper, H. & Mazzetti, M. (2011) Prideful and Prizing Status Quo, Mubarak Resists Pressure. *New York Times*, February 7, p. A10; Shadid, A. (2011) In the Euphoria of the Crowd, No Party or Leader Unifies the Opposition. *New York Times*, February 1, p. A11. While drawn from quotations in the *New York Times*, these characterizations were widely reported in the other media as well, including Al Jazeera (e.g., Al Jazeera (Arabic), January 25, 2011, 7:43 a.m. Accessed June 12, 2011: http://www.aljazeera.net/NR/exeres/B0C28F6C-8BFB-4786-B183-FFFB488C956E.htm.

54 Tisdall, S. (2011) World Briefing: New Wave of Protest Takes Mubarak Out of Comfort Zone. *Guardian*, January 26, p. 22.

55 For these statements by the revolutionaries about themselves, see, e.g.

Kirkpatrick, D. D. & Slackman, M. (2011) In New Role, Egypt Youths Drive Revolt. *New York Times*, January 27, p. A1; Fahim & Stack, Opposition in Egypt Gears Up for Major Friday Protest; Fahim, Hopes of Egyptians. For their statements about the regime and Mubarak, see, e.g. Fahim, K. & Stack, L. (2001) Egypt Intensifies Effort to Crush Wave of Protests, Detaining Hundreds. *New York Times*, January 27, p. A10; Mekhennet & Kulish, With Muslim Brotherhood Set to Join Egypt Protests; Fahim & Stack, Opposition in Egypt Gears Up for Major Friday Protest; Landler, M. & Lehrer, A. W. (2011) State's Secrets; Cables Show US Tack on Egypt: Public Support, Private, Pressure. *New York Times*, January 28, p. A1; Kirkpatrick, Mubarak Orders Crackdown; Fahim, Hopes of Egyptians; Kirkpatrick, D. (2011) In Protests, a Nobelist Has an Unfamiliar Role. *New York Times*, January 29, p. A11; MacFarqhar, N. (2011) Egypt's Respected Military Is Seen as Pivotal in What Happens Next. *New York Times*, January 29, p. A13. Again, while these translated quotations are drawn from the *New York Times*, the same characterizations are widely reported not only in American and European media, but in Al Jazeera (Arabic) as well (e.g. Al Jazeera (Arabic), January 25, 2011, 7:43 a.m. Accessed June 12, 2011: http://www.aljazeera.net/NR/exeres/B0C28F6C-8BFB-4786-B183-FFFB488C956E.htm.

56 The intertwining of disillusionment with the postcolonial project and support for renewing civil society was represented in fictional form in the early 1980s by the great Egyptian novelist Naguib Mahfouz in his moral allegory, *Before the Throne: Dialogs with Egypt's Great from Menes to Anwar Sadat* ((2009/1983) The American University in Cairo Press, Cairo). In the mythical Hall of Justice, Osiris, god of the afterlife, holds court in a trial of Egyptian rulers to determine who deserves to take a seat among the Immortals in the Hall of Sacred Justice or, instead, be consigned to hell or purgatory. When Abdel Nasser appears before the tribunal, he is confronted by one of his famous predecessors, Saad Zaghloul. Nasser came to power in a 1952 military coup and championed state socialism, pan-Arabism, anti-Zionism, and radical postcolonial ideology. Zaghloul, Egypt's most revered revolutionary leader from the early twentieth century, was founder of the politically and economically liberal Wafd party. Warning that "leadership is a divine gift," Zaghloul admonishes Nasser that "it was in your power to build … an enlightened, democratic form of government." Nasser replies, "true democracy to me … meant the liberation of the Egyptians from colonialism, exploitation, and poverty." To this, Zaghloul's successor as Wafd leader, Mustafa al-Nahhas, angrily replies: "You were heedless of liberty and human rights [and] while I don't deny that you kept faith with the poor, you were a curse upon political writers and intellectuals … You cracked down on them with arrest and imprisonment, with hanging and killing" (Mahfouz, *Before the Throne*, pp. 135–136).

57 Gerecht, R. M. (2011) How Democracy Became Halal. *New York Times*, February 7, p. A23.

58 It is not an exaggeration to say that Western intellectual history has betrayed a deep skepticism about the very possibility of Arab democracy, from Greek tropes about Persian barbarism to Marx's Asiatic mode of production, Weber's sultanism and warrior religion, and the civilizational claims of such contemporary conservatives as Samuel Huntington. Over the last three

decades, this "Orientalism" has been called out, not only by Edward Said's sweeping Foucaultian critique (Said, E. (1979) *Orientalism.* Vintage, New York) but by painstaking works of historical-cum-philosophical scholarship, such as Patricia Springborg (1986) Politics, Primordialism, and Orientalism: Marx, Aristotle, and the Myth of the Gemeinschaft. *American Political Science Review*, 80(1), pp. 185–211, and (1992) *Western Republicanism and the Oriental Prince.* Polity, Cambridge). It was during this same period that important currents in Arab intellectual life initiated a far-reaching break with "Occidentalism," the defensive mirror image of Orientalism that, especially with the rise of the anti-colonial movement, denigrates various elements of Western modernity, especially those having to do with civil society and democracy. As state communism crumbled abroad and pan-Arab socialism foundered at home, Islamicism certainly continued to provide for some in North Africa and the Middle East an Occidentalist alternative. There also emerged, however, a new openness, a new grappling with Western intellectual traditions and, most remarkably, with the idea of civil society. Almost two decades ago, al-Azmeh ((1994) *Democracy without Democrats: The Renewal of Politics in the Arab World.* I. B. Tauris, London) already observed that "the ubiquity of Arab discourse on democracy in recent years," how "together with ... the notion of civil society [it] is addressed in the Arab world in a myriad of political, academic, journalist and other writings," and how it "is the subject of inveterate commentary in casual conversation." Two years after that, in *Democracy and Civil Society in Arab Political Thought: Transcultural Possibilities* ((2006) Syracuse University Press, Syracuse), Browers documented that among Arabic intellectuals "in the latter part of the 1980s, a literally new term entered on the scene – civil society (*al-mujtama' al-madani*)," and along with it "a constellation of concepts that radically altered the available tools of political discourse, opening up unforeseen possibilities for political thought and action." Browers demonstrated that what civil society means is highly contested among Arab intellectuals, yet, as she also pointed out, the term has been highly contested from the very beginnings of Western intellectual life as well. In the Arab world, for example, more communal Islamic approaches have been contrasted, favorably and unfavorably, with definitions that emphasize more individualistic and pluralistic understandings of civil society, whether liberal or socialist. Browers concludes, nonetheless, that "the polarization between advocates of secularism and advocates of Islamicization belies an underlying consensus about at least some of the ideational constellations that construct a liberal public sphere (democracy, civil society, citizenship)" and that "despite the variation among particular conceptions of civil society there is broad agreement that enlarging a democratically engaged public sphere must be a priority for the development of the Arab region" (*Democracy and Civil Society in Arab Political Thought*, p. 209). In the most recently published book-length examination of contemporary Egypt, Tarek Osman finds such intellectual developments paralleled by trends in the nation's popular culture: "Formulating their own definition of Egyptianism" and "depressed by the devastating decline of Egyptian culture, values, attitudes and behavior," young Egyptians "leapt over the past fifty years (seeing only troubles and failures), and embraced Egypt's liberal experiment of the 1920s, 1930s and 1940s" (Osman, T. (2010) *Egypt on the Brink: From Nasser to*

Mubarak. Yale University Press, New Haven, p. 210). Osman reports that "the 2000s saw a plethora of films, TV series and novels glorifying and extolling the liberal experiment, especially its tolerant values, and its relaxed modus vivendi," and he notes also the "rise of private universities, business-men associations, chambers of commerce, consumer protection groups and the multitude of independent press and [satellite] TV channels" (*Egypt on the Brink*, p. 220).

It represented a remarkable lapse in the mass media reporting on the Arab Spring in general, and on the Egyptian revolution in particular, that scarcely any mention was made of the Arab intellectual revolution of the preceding decades. This neglect reflects the broader failures of Western commentary to highlight the cultural nature of the Egyptian revolution and of Western social scientists to put meaning at the center of their analysis of revolutions. For singular academic efforts demonstrating the decisive role shifting intellectual traditions play in revolutions, see Bailyn, B. (1967) *The Ideological Origins of the American Revolution*. Harvard University Press, Cambridge, MA, and Baker, K. M. (1990) *Inventing the French Revolution: Essays in French Political Culture in the 18th Century*. Cambridge University Press, Cambridge, UK.

59 *USA Today*. (2011) Anti-Mubarak Protest Brings Moment of Truth for US. *USA Today*, January 31, p. 8A.

60 Rampoldi, La Rivolta che Cambia la Storia Araba.

61 Rampoldi, La Rivolta che Cambia la Storia Araba.

62 El-Errian, E. (2011) What the Muslim Brothers Want. *New York Times*, February 10, p. A25. El-Errian is identified by the *New York Times* as a member of the Muslim Brotherhood's "guidance council" in Egypt.

63 Al Jazeera (Arabic), January 25, 2011, 7:43 a.m. Accessed June 12, 2011: http://www.aljazeera.net/NR/exeres/B0C28F6C-8BFB-4786-B183-FFFB488C956E.htm.

64 Dorell, O. & Fordham, A. Fury Grows in Egypt. *USA Today*, February 11, p. 1A.

65 Friedman, T. L. (2011) Up with Egypt. *New York Times*, February 9, p. A27; Kirkpatrick & Slackman, In New Role, Egypt Youths Drive Revolt; Fahim, Hopes of Egyptians.

66 El-Naggar and Slackman, Egypt's Leader Used Old Tricks to Defy New Demands.

67 Shadid, Seizing Control of Their Lives.

68 Al-Bushra. F. (2011) Egyptian Revolution. Al Jazeera. January 29. Accessed June 2, 2011: https://www.youtube.com/watch?v=JYuxjgU6yeE.

69 Friedman, Speakers' Corner on the Nile.

70 Hendawi, H. (2011) Egyptian Protesters Denounce Mubarak; Clash with Riot Police. Associated Press, January 25. Accessed March 7, 2011: http://www.aolnews.com/2011/01/25/egyptians-denouncemubarak-clash-with-riot-police.

71 ElBaradei, M. (2011) The Next Step for Egypt's Opposition. *New York Times*, February 11, p. A27.

72 El-Naggar and Slackman, Egypt's Leader Used Old Tricks to Defy New Demands.

73 Shadid, Seizing Control of Their Lives.

74 Shenker, J. (2011) Mubarak Regime in Crisis as Biggest Anti-government

Demonstrations in a Generation Sweep across Egypt. *Guardian*, January 26.

75 WAAKS (Arabic), January 27, 2011, 12:42 a.m.

76 Al Jazeera (Arabic), February 5, 2011, Accessed June 12, 2011: http://www.youtube.com/watch?v=wkvzYY_Kp7c&feature=relmfu&safety_mode=true&persist_safety_mode=1.

77 Slackman, M. (2011) A Brittle Leader, Appearing Strong. *New York Times*, February 12, p. A1; Mekhennet & Kulish, With Muslim Brotherhood Set to Join Egypt Protests; Kirkpatrick, D. D. (2011) Egypt Protests Continue as Government Resigns. *New York Times*, 29 January. Accessed 20 June 2011: http://warsclerotic.wordpress.com/2011/01/29/egypt-protests-continue-as-government-resigns-nytimes-com.

78 Slackman, In Mideast Activism; Kirkpatrick & Slackman, In New Role, Egypt Youths Drive Revolt; Friedman, T. L. (2011) Pharaoh Without a Mummy. *New York Times*, February 16, p. A25; Slackman, In Mideast Activism.

79 Ibrahim, S. E. (2011) Mubarak's Interests Are Not America's; The Dictator Can't Be Trusted. *Wall Street Journal*. February 8. Accessed June 20, 2011: http://online.wsj.com/article/SB100014240527487048584045761284505116119 70.html.

80 Champion, M. (2011) In a Flash, Alexandria Erupts in Mass Jubilee. *Wall Street Journal*. February 11. Accessed June 20, 2011: http://online.wsj.com/article/SB10001424052748704329104576138353660891850.html; Valli, B. (2011) Egitto, Nella Piazza che Grida 'Da qui non ce ne andiamo'. *La Repubblica*, February 5. Accessed 22 April 2011: http://www.repubblica.it/esteri/2011/02/05/news/egitto_nella_piazza_che_grida_da_qui_non_ce_ne_andiamo-12081033; Valli, B. (2011) La Beffa Finale del Faraone di Plastic. *La Repubblica*, February 11. Accessed April 22, 2011. http://www.repubblica.it/esteri/2011/02/11/news/beffa_faraone-12321773.

81 Al Jazeera (Arabic), January 25, 2011, 7:43 a.m. Accessed June 12, 2011: http://www.aljazeera.net/NR/exeres/B0C28F6C-8BFB-4786-B183-FFFB488C956E.htm.

82 Beaumont, P. & Shenker, J. (2011) A Day of Fury: Cairo in Flames as Cities Become Battlegrounds. *Guardian*. January 29, p. 2.

83 Fahim & El-Naggar, Violent Clashes Mark Protests Against Mubarak's Rule.

84 Hennion, C. (2011) Egypte: Moubarak sous pression. *Le Monde*, January 29, p. 1.

85 Scuto, F. (2011) El Baradei, l'Uomo del Destino 'Oggi Nasce un Paese Nuovo'. *La Repubblica*, February 1. Accessed 15 April 2011: http://www.repubblica.it/esteri/2011/02/01/news/baradei_uomo_destino-11904735.

86 This distinction can be made only if the civil sphere and the nation-state are made analytically distinct. A common error of "nationalism studies" is to explain cultural identities entirely in terms of varieties of nationalism. But the civil sphere is a relatively independent world of culture and social organization, which has its own discourse and modes of incorporation, even as enforcement is related to state functions. To suggest that Egyptians were embracing civic as compared to primordial nationalism points to their aspiration to construct a civil sphere that was relatively independent, not only from state coercion but from religious qualifications, ethnicity, regional, and economic statuses as well.

87 Here and in later sections, the extracts that have quotation marks are statements by participants; the remainder are quotations from media observations.

88 Shadid, Seizing Control of Their Lives.

89 Kirkpatrick, D. D. & Sanger, D. E. (2011) Egypt Officials Seek to Nudge Mubarak Out. *New York Times*, February 5, 2011, p. A1.

90 Fahim, K. (2011) Birthplace of Uprising Welcomes Its Success. *New York Times*, February 12, p. A9.

91 Barthe & Hennion, La Révolte Egyptienne.

92 Al Jazeera (2011) Fresh Anti-government Protests in Egypt. January 26. Accessed March 7, 2011: http://english.aljazeera.net/news/middleeast/2011/01/201112663450547321.html.

93 Mohamed, Z. et al. (2011) The Word on the Street: The Protests This Week Egypt Against the Mubarak Regime Have Gripped the Country. *Guardian*, January 28, G2, p. 6.

94 Soueif, A. (2011) Protesters Reclaim the Spirit of Egypt. *BBC News*, February 13. Accessed April 22, 2011: http://www.bbc.co.uk/news/world-middle-east-12393795.

95 Fahim, K. & El-Naggar, M. (2011) Emotions of a Reluctant Hero Inject New Life into the Protest Movement. *New York Times*, February 9, p. A14.

96 Behind these near-term collective representations, the political culture of the movement's secular and religious leaders – in Gramsci's terms, the movement's "organic" and "high" intellectuals – remains to be further explored. If one looked more deeply into shifting Islamic themes about freedom, justice, and community, one would undoubtedly find hyphenations between the religious and the secular, recalling the kinds of amalgamations that were made, centuries ago, between Christianity and secular political ideologies during the English and American revolutions. For the American case, see Bloch, R. (1985) *Visionary Republic: Millennial Themes in American Thought, 1756–1800*. Cambridge University Press, New York, and Hatch, N. C. (1997) *The Sacred Cause of Liberty*. Yale University Press, New Haven; for the British, see Walzer, M. (1965) *The Revolution of the Saints*. Harvard University Press, Cambridge, MA.

97 See Eyerman, R. & Jameson, A. (1991) *Social Movements: A Cognitive Approach*. Polity, Cambridge, and Eyerman, R. (2006) Performing Opposition or, How Social Movements Move. In J. C. Alexander, B. Giesen, & J. Mast (eds.), *Social Performance: Symbolic Action, Cultural Pragmatics, and Ritual*. Cambridge University Press, New York, pp. 193–216.

98 Kirkpatrick, D. D. (2011) Protest's Old Guard Falls in Behind the Young. *New York Times*, January 31, p. A1.

99 Kirkpatrick, Protest's Old Guard Falls in Behind the Young.

100 Black, I. (2011) Middle East: Protest Plans: Leaflets Being Circulated in Cairo Give Blueprint for Mass Action. *Guardian*, 28 January, p. 26.

101 Fahim, Hopes of Egyptians.

102 Kirkpatrick, D. D. (2011) Wired, Educated and Shrewd, Young Egyptians Guide Revolt. *New York Times*, February 10, p. 1.

103 For the long political-cum-conceptual history of new class ideas, see King, L. P. & Szelenyi, I. (2004) *Theories of the New Class: Intellectuals and Power*. University of Minnesota Press, Minneapolis.

104 For the idea that a "culture of critical discourse" is specific to the new class,

see Gouldner, A. W. (1979) *The Future of Intellectuals and the Rise of the New Class.* Seabury, New York.

105 In analyses of the Arab Spring as it was unfolding, Farhad Khosrokhavar employed the new class trope in a less economistic manner; see Khosrokhavar, F. (2011) Fin des dictatures au Proche et Moyen-Orient? *Le Monde,* January 17. Accessed June 12, 2100: http://www.lemonde.fr/idees/article/2011/01/17/fin-des-dictatures-au-proche-et-moyen-orient_1466683_3232.html; Khosrokhavar, F. (2011) Les Neuf Piliers de la révolution Arabe. *Le Nouvel Observateur,* February 10–16, pp. 94–95. Writing of "the emergence of the new middle classes" as providing "political and moral direction," Khosrokhavar's usage is close to the concept of carrier group deployed here. Understanding revolutionary leadership as a carrier group, rather than as a representative of a class, clarifies that the leadership represents not only its own interest, or even interests per se, but broader cultural and political aspirations that are not only specific to a particular time and place, but extend to groups other than their own. For an enduring study of the relation between Puritan clergy and English gentry, which together constituted the carrier group for the English Revolution, see Walzer, *The Revolution of the Saints.*

106 Kirkpatrick & Sanger, A Tunisian-Egyptian Link that Shook Arab History.

107 While speaking of the organizers as a group, one should not reify the network that linked people who comprised the revolutionary leadership. At various times from 2005 onward, there were a number of associations with overlapping memberships, and shifting coalitions emerged even during the eighteen days of the revolution itself. In his field notes, for example, Atef Said notes that on "the 30th of January or so, one of the main coalitions was formed" and that "this include[d] many youth organizations who called for the protests on January 25th." It was the Coalition for the Youth of the Revolution, and included "justice and freedom (leftist), the 6th of April (liberally oriented), el Baradie supporters (liberally oriented), Muslim Brotherhood (moderate political Islamist), the youth of the Democratic Front Party (liberally oriented) … The Coalition had a Facebook page and its press releases were circulated widely" (Said, A. (2011) On the Communication During the Internet Blackout in Egypt and Generally During the 18 Days of the Egyptian Revolution. Ethnographic Field Notes, unpublished manuscript, April 22). See also Ishani, M. (2011) The Hopeful Network. In M. Lynch, S. B. Glasser, & B. Hounshell (eds.), *Revolution in the Arab World.* Foreign Policy, Washington, DC. Yet, if the carrier group was more network than central committee, in the days after the Jasmine revolution in Tunisia a fairly well-organized directing group did form in Egypt, providing the strategic and tactical organization for the January 25 Revolution. In the years to come, debates will undoubtedly flourish about the history and sociology of the groups and interests constituting this revolutionary leadership and their ideologies. Hossam El-Hammalawy and Atef Said, for example, emphasize antecedent political events going back to 2000, and claim that labor activism and "anti-imperialist" (anti-Israeli occupation, anti-American) ideology played significant, even foundational roles (El-Hammalawy, H. (2011) Egypt's Revolution Has Been Ten Years in the Making. *Guardian,* March 2. Accessed June 10, 2011: http://www.guardian.co.uk/commentisfree/2011/mar/02/egypt-revolution-mubarak-

wall-of-fear; Said, A. (2011) Uprising in Egypt: America in the Egyptian Revolution. *The Immanent Frame* [blog], April 4. Accessed June 15, 2011: http://blogs.ssrc.org/tif/2011/04/11/america-in-the-egyptian-revolution). In this chapter, I place more weight on developments that were discontinuous with earlier forms of Egyptian and Middle Eastern protest: the broadly cross-class, civil-society character of the January 25 movement; the transforming effects of the intellectual revolution in Arab society; the incorporation of nonviolence as a tactic; and, more broadly, the emergent properties of civil solidarity as a performative accomplishment.

108 For the relation between young Egyptian organizers and the nonviolent movement in Serbia that Otpor initiated, and an analysis of the international outreach of CANVAS, the Center for Applied Non-Violent Action and Strategy, which Otpor's founders created in 2003 in Belgrade, see Rosenberg, T. (2011), Revolution U, in M. Lynch, S. B. Glasser, & B. Hounshell (eds.), *Revolution in the Arab World*. Foreign Policy, Washington, DC.

109 Nixon, R. (2011) US Groups Helped Nurture Arab Opposition. *New York Times*, April 15, p. A1.

110 Words with meanings are merely locutionary, in Austin's terms (Austin, J. L. (1962) *How to Do Things with Words,* 2nd ed. Harvard University Press, Cambridge, MA), but actually doing things with words indicates that speech acts go "beyond" meaning to having illocutionary or even perlocutionary effect. Illocutionary suggests the audience takes on a deep understanding of the implications of the speech, perlocutionary that the hearer takes action in response to this understanding. There are, of course, gradients. In China today, free speech is relatively protected inside private spheres and certain institutional spaces, such as elite universities, but it is increasingly restricted in public spaces. The effect is to allow locutionary but not illocutionary or perlocutionary action – in my terms, to allow scripts to be written but to prevent them from being performed.

111 Holt, D. B. (2004) *How Brands Become Icons: The Principles of Cultural Branding*. Harvard Business School, Boston.

112 Kirkpatrick & Sanger, A Tunisian-Egyptian Link that Shook Arab History.

113 Kirkpatrick & Sanger, A Tunisian-Egyptian Link that Shook Arab History.

114 Kirkpatrick, Wired, Educated and Shrewd.

115 Kirkpatrick & Sanger, A Tunisian-Egyptian Link that Shook Arab History.

116 Fahim, K. & El-Naggar, M. (2011) Across Egypt, Protests Direct Fury at Leader. *New York Times*, January 26, p. A1.

117 Soueif, Fittingly, It's the Young of the Country Who Are Leading Us.

118 Slackman, In Mideast Activism, a New Tilt Away from Ideology.

119 Kaplan, R. D. (2011) One Small Revolution. *New York Times*, January 23, Week in Review, p. 11. Kaplan made his name as a neoconservative political intellectual; he was an enthusiastic supporter of the Bush administration's invasion and occupation of Iraq.

120 Fahim & El-Naggar, Across Egypt, Protests Direct Fury at Leader.

121 Shenker, J. (2011) Revolt Spreads to Egypt, Violent Clashes on Streets of Cairo. *Guardian*, January 26, p. 1.

122 Slackman, Compact Between Egypt and Its Leader Erodes.

123 Shadid, A. & Kirkpatrick, D. D. (2011) In Egypt, Opposition Unifies Around Government Critic. *New York Times*, January 31, p. 1.

124 Mohamed, The Word on the Street.

125 Shadid, In the Euphoria of the Crowd, No Party or Leader Unifies the Opposition.

126 Michaels, J. (2011) "Tech-savvy Youths Led the Way in Egypt Protests; And They Want Seat at the Table in Negotiations. *USA Today*, February 7, p. 2A.

127 Fahim & El-Naggar, Across Egypt, Protests Direct Fury at Leader.

128 Mekhennet & Kulish, With Muslim Brotherhood Set to Join Egypt Protests, Religion's Role May Grow.

129 Worth, R. F. (2011) On Al Jazeera, a Revolution Televised Despite Hurdles. *New York Times*, January 29, p. A11.

130 Shenker, Revolt Spreads to Egypt.

131 *La Repubblica* (2011) 'Mubarak Vattene. Basta Dittatura,' La Protesta degli Egiziani a Roma. *La Repubblica*, January 31. Accessed April 15, 2011: http://roma.repubblica.it/cronaca/2011/01/31/news/mubarak_vattene_basta_dit tatura_la_protesta_degli_egiziani_a_roma-11893136. This message was written on the signs of Egyptian protestors in Rome.

132 *Guardian* (2011) Front: Egypt: How the Events Unfolded. *Guardian*, January 29, p. 2.

133 Beaumont, P. & Shenker, J. (2011) Front: Egypt: A Day of Fury: Cairo in Flames as Cities Become Battlegrounds. *Guardian*, January 29, p. 2.

134 Sherwood, H. A. et al. (2011) Fall of Mubarak: Hope and Fear, How the Arab World Reacted. *Guardian*, February 12, p. 4; Seib, G. (2011) Now Dawning: The Next Era of Middle East History. *Wall Street Journal*, January 31. Accessed June 20, 2011: http://online.wsj.com/article/SB10001 4240527487042543045761161101105 96324.html; Bussey, J. (2011) How to Handle Employee Activism: Google Tiptoes Around Cairo's Hero. *Wall Street Journal*, February 10. Accessed 2 June 20, 2011: http://online.wsj.com/article/SB10001424052748704132204576136323073589858.html.

135 Dorell & Fordham, Fury Grows in Egypt.

136 Shadid, Seizing Control of Their Lives and Wondering What's Next.

137 Levinson & Dagher, Rallies Fan Out as Regime Closes Ranks; cf., *Guardian*, Front: Egypt: How the Events Unfolded.

138 Tait, R. (2011) Front: Egypt: 28 Hours in the Dark Heart of Egypt's Torture Machine. *Guardian*, February 10, p. 4.

139 Ajami, F. (2011) Egypt's '"Heroes with no Names"; We Must Remember that Mohamed Atta and Ayman Zawahiri Were Bred in the Tyranny of Hosni Mubarak. *Wall Street Journal*. February 12. Accessed June 20, 2011: http://online.wsj.com/article/SB10001424052748704132204576136442019920256.html.

140 *New York Times*, February 4, 2011, A12.

141 Kirkpatrick, Egyptians Defiant as Military Does Little to Quash Protests.

142 Mohamed, The Word on the Street.

143 Fahim & El-Naggar, Across Egypt, Protests Direct Fury at Leader.

144 El-Naggar & Slackman, Egypt's Leader Used Old Tricks to Defy New Demands.

145 Landler, M. (2011) Obama Cautions Embattled Egyptian Ally Against Violent Repression. *New York Times*, January 29, p. A1.

146 MacFarquhar, N. (2011) Egypt's Respected Military Is Seen as Pivotal in What Happens Next. *New York Times*, January 29, p. A13.

147 Kulish, N. & Mekhennet, S. (2011) In Alexandria, Protesters Win After a Day of Fierce Fighting with Riot Police. *New York Times*, January 29, p. A12.

148 Rampoldi, La Rivolta che Cambia la Storia Araba.
149 Slackman, M. (2011) Omar Suleiman: A Choice Likely to Please the Military, not the Crowds. *New York Times*, January 30, p. A10. The quotation is from Mahmoud Shokry, former ambassador to Syria and personal friend of Omar Suleiman, on Mr. Suleiman's appointment as vice-president.
150 Shadid, Seizing Control of Their Lives and Wondering What's Next.
151 Shadid, Seizing Control of Their Lives and Wondering What's Next.
152 Soueif, A. (2011) Egypt: 'For Everyone Here, There's No Turning Back'. *Guardian*, February 2, p. 1.
153 Yaffa, J. (2011) Downloading the Uprising; Can Technology's Tools Liberate Those Living Under Political Repression? *Wall Street Journal*, February 4. Accessed June 20, 2011: http://online.wsj.com/article/SB100014240527487 04150104576122751785029870.html.
154 Shadid, A. (2011) Discontented Within Egypt Face Power of Old Elites. *New York Times*, February 5, p. A7.
155 Dorell, O. (2011) Protests Have Economic Ripple Effects; Movement Gets Mixed Reviews from Those Who Aren't Taking Part as Tourism has Disappeared. *USA Today*, February 7, p. 4A.
156 Black, I. (2011) Egypt: Analysis. Constitution at the Heart of Change in Egypt. *Guardian*, February 8, p. 22.
157 Shadid, A. (2011) Egypt's Leaders Seek to Project Air of Normalcy. *New York Times*, February 8, p. A1.
158 Bradley, M., Rhoads, C. & El Gazzar (2011) Cairo Demonstrators Dig In. *Wall Street Journal*, February 8. Accessed June 20, 2011: http://online.wsj.com/article/SB10001424052748704364004576131560748488384.html.
159 *New York Times* (2011) Mr. Suleiman's Empty Promises. February 9, p. A26.
160 Shenker, J. (2011) Teargas and Baton Charges Sweep Protesters Off Cairo's Streets. *Guardian*, January 26, p. 22.
161 Kirkpatrick, Mubarak's Grip Is Shaken as Millions Are Called to Protest.
162 *New York Times* (2011) Beyond Mubarak. February 2, p. A22.
163 Shenker, J. et al. (2011) Egypt: Power to the People: Mubarak Finally Bows to the Inevitable. *Guardian*, February 2, p. 1.
164 Fahim, K. & El-Naggar, M. (2011) Some Fear a Street Movement's Leaderless Status May Become a Liability. *New York Times*, February 4, p. A7.
165 *Le Monde* (2011) Le Régime Moubarak Contre-attaque. February 4, p. 1.
166 Valli, Egitto, Nella Piazza che Grida "Da qui non ce ne andiamo."
167 Stanley, A. (2011) As Crisis Plays Out Live on TV, Commentators Hurl Brickbats at One Another. *New York Times*, February 5, p. A7.
168 *La Repubblica* (2011) Manifestanti Ancora in Piazza al Cairo Usa Premono per Cambiamento. February 5. Accessed April 22, 2011: http://www.repubblica.it/esteri/2011/02/05/news/sostituiti_vertici_partito_mubarak_lascia-12100571.
169 Sanger, D. (2011) As Mubarak Digs In, Complications for US Policy. *New York Times*, February 6, p. A12.
170 Shadid, Egypt's Leaders Seek to Project Air of Normalcy.
171 Kirkpatrick, As Egypt Protest Swells.
172 Valli, Egitto, Nella Piazza che Grida "Da qui non ce ne andiamo."

173 El-Naggar, M. (2011) The Legacy of 18 Days in Tahrir Square. *New York Times*, February 20, Week in Review, p. 4.

174 Al Jazeera (English) (2011) Egypt Protesters Clash with Police. January 25. Accessed March 7, 2011: http://english.aljazeera.net/news/middle east/2011/01/201112511362207742.html.

175 Friedman, Speakers' Corner on the Nile.

176 Shadid, A. (2011) Yearning for Respect, Arabs Find a Voice. *New York Times*, January 30, p. A10.

177 Machiavelli, N. (2007/1531) *The Discourses*, in *The Essential Writings of Niccolò Machiavelli*, translated and edited by Peter Constantine. Modern Library, New York. Bk I, p. 25.

178 Shadid, A. (2011) Egypt Officials Widen Crackdown; US in Talks for Mubarak to Quit. *New York Times*, February 4, p. A1.

179 Shadid & Kirkpatrick, In Egypt, Opposition Unifies Around Government Critic.

180 Shadid & Kirkpatrick, In Egypt, Opposition Unifies Around Government Critic.

181 Dorell, Protests Have Economic Ripple Effects.

182 Barthe, B. (2011) A Zamalek, la Bourgeoisie du Caire Défend ses Biens et Prend ses Distance avec le Régime. *Le Monde*, February 1, p. 6.

183 Shadid & Kirkpatrick, In Egypt, Opposition Unifies Around Government Critic.

184 Shadid & Kirkpatrick, In Egypt, Opposition Unifies Around Government Critic.

185 Dorell, Protests Have Economic Ripple Effects.

186 Shadid & Kirkpatrick, In Egypt, Opposition Unifies Around Government Critic.

187 Shadid & Kirkpatrick, In Egypt, Opposition Unifies Around Government Critic.

188 Shadid & Kirkpatrick, In Egypt, Opposition Unifies Around Government Critic. The director's first name is misspelled in the *New York Times* article. It should be Selma al-Tarzi, not Salma.

189 Hobbes, T. (1996/1651) *Leviathan, or The Matter, Forme, & Power a Common-wealth Ecclesiastical and Civill*, edited by Richard Tuck (2nd ed.). Cambridge University Press, Cambridge, UK, p. 84.

190 *La Repubblica*, Scontri e Morti in Tutto l'Egitto.

191 Al Jazeera (English) (2011) Timeline: Egypt's Revolution, February 14. Accessed June 12, 2011: http://english.aljazeera.net/news/middleeast/2011 /01/201112515334871490.html.

192 Kirkpatrick, Mubarak Orders Crackdown.

193 Kirkpatrick, Egyptians Defiant as Military Does Little to Quash Protests.

194 Kirkpatrick, Mubarak Orders Crackdown.

195 Turner, V. (1969) *The Ritual Process*. Aldine, Chicago. Jill Dolan connects Turner's ideas to contemporary performance theory and to the radical political imagination in her book, Dolan, J. (2005) *Utopian Performances: Finding Hope at the Theater*. University of Michigan Press, Ann Arbor.

196 ElBaradei, Mohamed (2011) Quotation of the Day. *New York Times*, January 31, p. A2.

197 Barthe & Hennion, La Révolte Egyptienne.

198 Barthe & Hennion, La Révolte Egyptienne.

199 Mohamed, The Word on the Street.
200 Beaumont & Shenker, Front: Egypt: A Day of Fury.
201 Rampoldi, La Rivolta che Cambia la Storia Araba.
202 Shadid, Seizing Control of Their Lives and Wondering What's Next.
203 Shadid, Seizing Control of Their Lives and Wondering What's Next.
204 Shadid, Yearning for Respect, Arabs Find a Voice.
205 *USA Today*, Anti-Mubarak Protest.
206 *Guardian* (2011) Egypt: Beyond Mubarak. February 2, p. 32.
207 Shadid, In the Euphoria of the Crowd.
208 *New York Times* (2011) From Sadat to Mubarak: A Reminiscence, and a Prayer. February 3. Accessed June 12, 2011: http://www.nytimes.com/2011/02/03/opinion/lweb03cairo.html.
209 Hennion, C. (2011) La Révolte Egyptienne; Venus en famille, les manifestants ont donné à la place Tahrir un air de Kermesse. *Le Monde*, February 3, p. 5.
210 Feith, D. (2011) Democracy's Tribune on the Arab Awakening. *Wall Street Journal*, February 4. Accessed June 20, 2011: http://online.wsj.com/article/SB10001424052748704150104576122882240386172.html.
211 Shenker, J. & Khalili, M. (2011) Day of No Departure: Cairo's Biggest Turnout Yet, but Mubarak Clings On. *Guardian*, February 5, p. 1.
212 Shadid, A. (2011) At Night in Tahrir Square, Cairo Protest Gives Way to Poetry and Performances. *New York Times*, February 7, p. A9.
213 Friedman, Speakers' Corner on the Nile.
214 Hall, M. & Johnson, K. (2011) White House Pushes for 'Genuine Transition'; 'Fast-Changing Situation' in Egypt Difficult to Track. *USA Today*, February 11, p. 1A.
215 *New York Times* (2011) Egypt's Moment. February 12, p. A20.
216 Shadid, A. (2011) After Tahrir, Uncharted Ground. *New York Times*, February 12, p. A1.
217 Kristoff, N. D. (2011) Exhilarated by the Hope in Cairo. *New York Times*, February 1, p. A27.
218 Shadid, At Night in Tahrir Square.
219 Barthe & Hennion, La Révolte Egyptienne.
220 Shadid, At Night in Tahrir Square.
221 Bradley, M. (2011) Rioters Jolt Egyptian Regime. *Wall Street Journal*, January 25. Accessed June 20, 2011: http://online.wsj.com/article/SB10001424052748704698004576104112320465414.html.
222 Soueif, Fittingly, It's the Young of the Country Who Are Leading Us.
223 Shadid, At Night in Tahrir Square.
224 Barthe & Hennion, La Révolte Egyptienne.
225 Al Jazeera (English) (2011) Tahir: The Epicenter of the Revolution. February 7. Accessed March 7, 2011: http://www.youtube.com/watch?v=SeTzu9aK3xs.
226 Carlstrom, G. (2011) Community Amid Egypt's Chaos. Al Jazeera (English), February 7. Accessed March 7, 2011: http://english.aljazeera.net/news/middleeast/2011/02/201127162644461244.html.
227 Hennion, C. (2011) Sur la place Tahrir, epicentre de la révolte Egyptienne. *Le Monde*, February 1, p. 6.
228 Shadid & Kirkpatrick, In Egypt, Opposition Unifies Around Government Critic.

229 Shadid, In the Euphoria of the Crowd.
230 El-Naggar, The Legacy of 18 Days in Tahrir Square. El-Naggar refers here to an encounter two weeks earlier.
231 Shadid, A. (2011) Mubarak Won't Run Again, But Stays; Obama urges a Faster Shift of Power. *New York Times*, February 2, p. A1.
232 Shadid, Discontented Within Egypt Face Power of Old Elites.
233 Friedman, Speakers' Corner on the Nile.
234 The violence was concentrated on February 2 but carried into the next day (Shadid, Street Battle Over the Arab Future).
235 McGreal, C. (2011) Front: Egypt in Crisis: "Mubarak is Still Here, But There's Been a Revolution in Our Minds." *Guardian*, February 6, p. 4.
236 May, T. (2011) Protesters Stand Fast in Cairo's Tahrir Square. *USA Today*, February 8, p. 4A.
237 Shadid, Egypt Officials Widen Crackdown.
238 Assaf, R. (2011) Thugs Confront Egyptian Protesters. Al Jazeera (Arabic) (Read by Hatem Ghandir), 4 February 4. Accessed June 10, 2011: http://www.youtube.com/watch?v=5zX8IlGBDZ4&feature=relmfu.
239 Shadid, Egypt's Leaders Seek to Project Air of Normalcy.
240 Kirkpatrick, As Egypt Protest Swells, US Sends Specifics Demands.
241 WAAKS, February 8, 2011. Kirkpatrick, D. D. (2011) Google Executive Who Was Jailed Said He Was Part of Online Campaign in Egypt. *New York Times*, February 8, p. A10. Translated from the Arabic by the *New York Times*.
242 Fahim and El-Naggar, Emotions of a Reluctant Hero Inject New Life into the Protest Movement.
243 Kirkpatrick, Google Executive Who Was Jailed.
244 Fahim and El-Naggar, Emotions of a Reluctant Hero Inject New Life into the Protest Movement.
245 Mubarak, H. (2011) I Will Not … Accept to Hear Foreign Dictations. *Washington Post*, February 10. Accessed June 10, 2011: http://www.washingtonpost.com/wp-dyn/content/article/2011/02/10/AR2011021005290.html.
246 Shadid & Kirkpatrick, Mubarak Won't Quit.
247 Kirkpatrick, D. D. (2011) Egypt Erupts in Jubilation as Mubarak Steps Down. *New York Times*, February 11, p. 1.
248 Ajami, Egypt's "Heroes with no Names."
249 Soueif, A. (2011) Fall of Mubarak: "Look at the streets of Egypt … this is what hope looks like." *Guardian*, February 12, p. 2.
250 Shadid, After Tahrir, Uncharted Ground.
251 Fahim, op. cit., n. 105.
252 *Wall Street Journal* (2011) Celebrations Follow Resignation in Egypt. *Wall Street Journal*, 12 February. Accessed 20 June 2011: http://blogs.wsj.com/photojournal/2011/02/11/celebrations-follow-resignation-in-egypt/.
253 Shadid, Birthplace of Uprising Welcomes Its Success.
254 Kirkpatrick & Sanger, A Tunisian-Egyptian Link that Shook Arab History.
255 Worth, On Al Jazeera, a Revolution Televised Despite Hurdles.
256 Al-Bushra, Egyptian Revolution.
257 Worth, On Al Jazeera, a Revolution Televised Despite Hurdles.
258 Worth, On Al Jazeera, a Revolution Televised Despite Hurdles. Lynch, M. (2003) Beyond the Arab Street: Iraq and the Arab Public Sphere. *Politics*

and Society 31(1), pp. 55–91. Of course, mass media of communication are not the only means for dissenting discourse and drama to be displayed and distributed. Under Nazi and Communist totalitarianism, underground ("*samizdat*") mimeographed and printed material circulated secretly alongside word of mouth "whispering" campaigns. In ethnographic field notes from his stay in Cairo during the latter days of the revolution, Atef Said reports that word-of-mouth communication was a significant response to the government's efforts at blocking digital communication: "Activists who left for their homes talked to their neighbors. Also, activists used land lines during this period, at night, to call their friends and make sure things are ok or send messages about what to do tomorrow." Said's notes also mention that, although talking to taxi drivers "is an old method," they "knew stories and they tell others stories" (Said, On the Communication During the Internet Blackout in Egypt).

259 Said's field notes make clear that even when the regime's effort to blackout digital communication was at its most intense level (during the two-day period January 28–29) the attempt was never more than partially successful: "During these days both Facebook and Twitter were not working properly [but] bloggers and activists in Twitter distributed information about opening Facebook by proxy or twitter ... On 29th [January] cell-phones were back to work ... On January 30th, Google provided voice your tweet service to Egypt ... On Feb. 2nd, internet was back. During all this time, [while] Al Jazeera Arabic was often subjected to disarraying [*sic*] ... Egyptians [with] a particular satellite could watch [or follow it] via the internet" (Said, On the Communication During the Internet Blackout in Egypt).

260 Stelter, B. (2011) From Afar, News about Egypt. *New York Times*, February 14, p. B4.

261 Preston, J. (2011) While Facebook Plays a Star Role in the Revolts, Its Executives Stay Offstage. *New York Times*, February 15, p. 10.

262 Preston, While Facebook Plays a Star Role in the Revolts.

263 Hauser, C. (2011) New Service Lets Voices from Egypt Be Heard. *New York Times*, February 2, p. A14.

264 Ez-Eldin, M. (2011) Date with a Revolution. *New York Times*, January 31, p. A19.

265 Keying on the word "Mubarak," a Stanford computer studies graduate student, Rio Akasaka, constructed a real-time "vimeo" (shared video) of worldwide social network activity from February 7 to February 14, 2011. Among the 455,840 tweets whose motion he mapped, by far the highest concentration was in North America and Europe, with significant activity as well in the Middle East (see http://vimeo.com/20233225). A similar pattern of global social networking activity is revealed in Akasaka's vimeo collection of 123,000 tweets during the final minutes of Mubarak's February 10 speech, when he announced he would not resign (see http://vimeo.com/19824159). As this tweet networking map indicates, the transnational surround of Egypt's revolution very much included a regional force of more immediately contiguous countries, often referred to as the Arab public sphere (Lynch, Beyond the Arab Street). Culturally and politically, events in Egypt have for centuries been intertwined with such a broader Arab connection, and they are ever more closely connected in the digitalized social media world of today. The narrative of national decline and resurrection,

for example, was directed as much to the restoration of Egypt's once leading place in the Arab world as it was to Egypt's place in "civilization" as such. And vice versa: Egypt's cultural and political institutions have been matters of great import to the Arab public sphere. Al Jazeera's dense and enthusiastic coverage of the Egyptian revolution was energized by these regional bonds even as it was regulated by the standards of independent journalism and global civil society.

266 The ideal of a global civil sphere captures something terribly significant about contemporary social realities, but it also fundamentally distorts them in a wish-fulfilling way (Alexander, J. C. (2007) Globalization as Collective Representation: The New Dream of a Cosmopolitan Civil Sphere. In I. Rossi (ed.), *Frontiers of Globalization Research: Theoretical and Methodological Approaches.* Springer, New York, pp. 371–382). Some strands of public opinion do circulate globally, from popular and high culture to moral opinions about current events, but this collective will formation hardly possesses the wide reach of public opinion inside the civil spheres of democratic nation-states. Nor can global public opinion, even in its necessarily fragmented form, be implemented by political power acting in its name. The global community has no state, no electoral process, no political party competition, and no monopoly on violence – all basic institutional prerequisites for regulating social processes on behalf of civil power.

267 Clinton, H. R. (2011) Remarks with Spanish Foreign Minister Trinidad Jimenez After Their Meeting. Washington, DC. January 25. Accessed June 10, 2011: http://www.state.gov/secretary/rm/2011/01/155280.htm.

268 If China's economic rise is eventually accompanied by commensurate military power – as modern Japan and Germany's postwar economic revivals were not – it may aggressively challenge Western civil definitions of "global." If China itself undergoes a democratic transition, binding its state to domestic civil power, it could have quite the opposite effect, allowing the civil definition of "global" to become more truly global in a substantive sense. This would be especially true if a new China were aligned with democracies in Japan and Korea. The glaring weakness of such realist geopolitical treatises as Paul Kennedy's *The Rise and Fall of the Great Powers* (Random House, New York, 1987) or Samuel Huntington's *The Clash of Civilizations* (Simon & Schuster, New York, 1996) is their failure to consider the potential effect on state interest and military power of such civil sphere binding or the lack thereof. This issue was forcefully articulated by an opinion piece in *Le Monde*: "The events in Egypt and Tunisia pose an important question to Western democracies: Should they practice public diplomacy committing themselves to 'universal' values? In sum, should they keep the flag of civil liberties and human rights in their pocket, pull it out halfway or deploy it permanently? ... The demonstrators in Cairo and Tunis send a message to the school of realist diplomacy: they must call a dictator a dictator, and loudly" (*Le Monde* (2011) Editorial; Il faut appeler un dictateur un dictateur. February 2, p. 1). While this is a forceful normative statement, however, the ideals of a global civil sphere are not universally applied and so-called realist considerations often overrule. Not every dictator is called a dictator. Neither is it the case that the internal construction of a civil society will make it behave externally in a peaceful manner. The discourse of civil society is binary and splitting, and it often sustains aggres-

sion outside the nation state even as it promotes pacific democracy at home. A post-dictatorship Egypt could be violently anti-Zionist, for example.

269 For the role of metaphor in politics, see Ringmar, E. (2007) The Power of Metaphor: Consent, Dissent & Revolution. In R. Mole (ed.), *Discursive Constructions of Identity in European Politics*. Palgrave Macmillan, London; for the role of performance in the international relations between states, see Ringmar, E. (2012) Performing International Relations: Two East Asian Alternatives to the Westphalian Order. *International Organization* 66(2).

270 Kristoff, N. D. (2011) Militants, Women and Tahrir Square. *New York Times*, February 6, Week in Review, p. 8.

271 *New York Times*, Beyond Mubarak.

272 Kristoff, Militants, Women and Tahrir Square.

273 Kristoff, Militants, Women and Tahrir Square.

274 Fourest, C. (2011) Sans détour; Le Mur du Caire doit tomber. *Le Monde*, February 5, p. 20.

275 Kaplan, S. L. (2011) De 1789 à L'Intifada Egyptienne, le Pain. *Le Monde*, February 8, p. 19.

276 Caracciolo, L. (2011) L'Occasione che Perderemo. *La Repubblica*, January 31. Accessed April 22, 2011: http://www.repubblica.it/esteri/2011/01/31/news/occasione_egitto-11862368.

277 There was variation in the speed with which media resolved the ambiguity between "1979" and "1989." In the United States, the *New York Times* moved more quickly than more conservative papers such as the *Wall Street Journal* and *USA Today*. In Europe, while the *Guardian* moved much more quickly than either *Le Monde* or *La Reppublica*, this was not because of ideological differences but because of the greater continental fear of North African instability increasing immigration. As for Al Jazeera, the news agency did not manifest ambivalence in the first place.

278 Beehner, L. (2011) In Egypt, 'Islamist' Fears Overblown. *USA Today*, February 1, p. 7A.

279 *USA Today* (2011) Rumblings abroad test American ideals. *USA Today*, January 27, p. 8A.

280 The extraordinary consensus among these otherwise widely divergent media in their reporting of the Egyptian revolution – which aligned itself with the democratic aspirations of the revolutionary protagonists in Egypt – provides an operational definition of "global civil sphere." The definition of "global" is as much normative as real. At the time of this writing, the Chinese government has formally designated the Egyptian Revolution as a "sensitive subject" to which references may not be publicly made.

281 While the tone of Al Jazeera (Arabic) was often more overtly critical than that of the *New York Times*, and frequently more passionate and emotional, it contrasted less with the tone of television coverage in America and Europe. In its Arabic broadcasts, Al Jazeera also often intermingled reportage with overt "editorial" opinion, a practice more typical in European than American newspapers.

282 Al Jazeera (Arabic), January 25, 2011, 11:59 a.m. Accessed 12 June 2001: http://www.aljazeera.net/NR/exeres/35AFA009-4090-41FD-9C73-9A703FB54E12.htm.

283 Shenker, J. (2011) Egypt: Journalist's Detention: Bloody and Bruised in the Back of a Truck, Destination Unknown. *Guardian*, January 27, p. 18.

284 For contemporary accounts of the Egyptian government's efforts to repress journalists during the January 25 Revolution, see Khalil, A., February 3: Sword vs. Pen, in Lynch, Glasser, & Hounshell, *Revolution in the Arab World*, and Miles, H. (2011) The Al Jazeera Effect, in Lynch, Glasser, & Hounshell, *Revolution in the Arab World*.

285 Kirkpatrick, Mubarak's Grip Is Shaken as Millions Are Called to Protest.

286 Beaumont & Shenker, Front: Egypt: A Day of Fury.

287 *Guardian*, Front: Egypt: How the Events Unfolded.

288 Beaumont & Shenker, Front: Egypt: A Day of Fury.

289 Shenker, J. & Black, I. (2011) Egypt: Change is Coming, Says ElBaradei as US Calls for 'orderly transition'. *Guardian*, January 31, p. 1.

290 Soueif, Egypt: "For Everyone Here, There's No Turning Back."

291 Borger, J. & Shenker, J. (2011) Egypt: Day of Rumour and Sky-high Expectations Ends in Anger and Confusion. *Guardian*, February 11, p. 4.

292 Dorell & Fordham, Fury Grows in Egypt.

293 Sanger, D. E. (2011) When Armies Decide. *New York Times*, February 20, Week in Review, p. 1.

294 For example: "To the Editor: While Al Jazeera may have a bias toward the long-suffering downtrodden of the Arab world, its highly professional reporting is a breath of fresh air, representing journalism at its finest. It brings transparency to a part of the world that has been burdened with far more than its share of autocratic regimes living off the backs of the poor" (Miller, T. (2011) In the Mideast, Days of Tumult. *New York Times*, January 29, p. A22). "To the Editor: Why do the people of Egypt have to place themselves in danger of being shot and tear-gassed by the riot police before the United States realizes that it has a 'moral responsibility to stand with those who have the courage to oppose authoritarian rulers'? The United States government has been aware of the nature of President Hosni Mubarak's regime for decades and has sustained it through generous foreign aid, but for whose 'national security concerns'? America's or Israel's? It's time to come down off the fence and stand up for justice. That's what Americans claim they are good at, and now is the time to prove it, across the Middle East" (Hewitt, I. (2011) Sorting Out the Uprising in Egypt. *New York Times*, 1 February, p. A26).

295 Landler, Obama Cautions Embattled Egyptian Ally Against Violent Repression.

296 Landler, M. (2011) Clinton Calls for "Orderly Transition" to Greater Freedom in Egypt. *New York Times*, January 31, p. A6.

297 Dempsey, J. (2011) Key European Leaders Urge Restraint in Cairo. *New York Times*, January 30. Accessed June 12, 2011: http://www.nytimes.com/2011/01/31/world/europe/31europe.html.

298 Landler, M. & Lehren, A. (2011) State's Secrets; Cables Show US Tack on Egypt: Public Support, Private Pressure. *New York Times*, January 28, p. A1.

299 Kirkpatrick & Sanger, A Tunisian-Egyptian Link that Shook Arab History.

300 Kirkpatrick, Egypt Erupts in Jubilation as Mubarak Steps Down.

301 Zimmer, B. (2011) How the War of Words Was Won. *New York Times*, February 13, Week in Review, p. 4.

302 Kirkpatrick, Egyptians Defiant as Military Does Little to Quash Protests.

CHAPTER 3 POLITICAL PERFORMANCE IN THE US: OBAMA'S 2012 RE-ELECTION

1 Alexander, J. C. (2010) *The Performance of Politics: Obama's Victory and the Democratic Struggle for Power*. Oxford University Press, New York; Alexander J. C. (2011) *Performance and Power*. Polity, Cambridge, UK; Alexander, J. C. & Jaworsky, B. (2014) *Obama Power*. Polity, Cambridge, UK.

2 These posts are reproduced here, substantially but not in their entirety, with the permission of the *Huffington Post*.

3 Alexander, J. C. (2012) Obama's Downcast Eyes. *The Huffington Post*, October 4. Accessed October 2, 2016: http://www.huffingtonpost.com/jeffrey-c-alexander/obama-debate-performance_b_1938755.html.

4 Alexander, J. C. (2012) Laughing Man and Choir Boy. *The Huffington Post*, October 11. Accessed October 2, 2016: http://www.huffingtonpost.com/jeffrey-c-alexander/biden-laughing-debate-ryan_b_1960862.html.

5 Alexander, J. C. (2012) Courtroom Drama of Truth and Lies. *The Huffington Post*, October 17. Accessed October 2, 2016: http://www.huffingtonpost.com/jeffrey-c-alexander/obama-benghazi-act-of-terror_b_1972616.html.

6 Williams, R. (1983) Drama in a Dramatized Society. In R. Williams (ed.), *Writing in Society*, Verso, London, pp. 13–18ff.

CHAPTER 4 DRAMATIC INTELLECTUALS

1 Rorty, R. (1979) *Philosophy and the Mirror of Nature*. Princeton University Press, Princeton.

2 Marx, K. & Engels, F. (1962/1848) *The Manifesto of the Communist Party* in *Marx and Engels: Selected Works*. International Publishers, Moscow, p. 46.

3 Marx & Engels, *Manifesto of the Communist Party*, p. 44.

4 Bourdieu, P. (1988) *Homo Academicus*. Stanford University Press, Stanford; Bourdieu, P. (1991) *The Political Ontology of Martin Heidegger*. Stanford University Press, Stanford; Lamont, M. (1987) How to Become a Dominant French Philosopher: The Case of Jacques Derrida. *The American Journal of Sociology* 93(3), pp. 584–622.

5 Cf. Bartmanski, D. (2012) How to Become an Iconic Intellectual: The Intellectual Pursuits of Malinowski and Foucault. *European Journal of Social Theory* 15(4), pp. 426–452.

6 Parsons, T. (1937) *The Structure of Social Action*. Free Press, New York.

7 Gouldner, A. W. (1979) *The Future of the Intellectuals and the Rise of the New Class*. Macmillan, New York.

8 Konrad, G. & Szelenyi. I. (1979) *The Intellectuals on the Road to Class Power: A Sociology of the Intelligentsia in Socialism*. Harcourt, Brace, Jovanovich, New York.

9 Shils, E. A. (1972) *Intellectuals and the Powers and Other Essays*. University of Chicago Press, Chicago.

10 Alexander, J. C. & Smith, P. (2004) The Strong Program in Cultural Sociology: Elements of a Structural Hermeneutics. In J. C. Alexander, *The Meanings of Social Life: A Cultural Sociology*. Oxford University Press, New York, pp. 11–26; cf. Alexander, J. C., Jacobs, R. N., & Smith, P. (eds.)

(2012) *The Oxford Handbook of Cultural Sociology*. Oxford University Press, New York.

11 Alexander, J. C. (2011) Market as Narrative and Character: For a Cultural Sociology of Economic Life. *Journal of Cultural Economy*, 4(4), pp. 477–488.

12 Eisenstadt, S. N. (1982) The Axial Age: The Emergence of Transcendental Visions and the Rise of the Clerics. *European Journal of Sociology* 23(2), pp. 294–314.

13 Bartmanski, How to Become an Iconic Intellectual; cf., Alexander, J. C. (2010) Marxism and the Spirit of Socialism: Cultural Origins of Anti-Capitalism. *Thesis Eleven* 100, pp. 84–105.

14 The culturally oriented Marxist theorist Antonio Gramsci insisted, in developed capitalist societies, that the Communist struggle for material power – economically via control of the state – can succeed only if is complemented by the struggle for cultural hegemony, which he called the struggle for position (Gramsci (1971) *Selections from the Prison Notebooks (1929–1937)*, ed. Q. Hoare & G. N. Smith. International Publishers, New York, pp. 206–76),

15 The quotations following are from Eyerman, R. & Jameson, A. (1995) *Seeds of the Sixties*. University of California Press, Berkeley, pp. 1–7.

16 De Man, H. (1984) *The Psychology of Marxian Socialism*. Transaction Books, New York.

17 Marx & Engels, *Manifesto of the Communist Party*; Marx, K. (1962/1867) *Capital*, vol. 1. International Publishers, Moscow.

18 Schorske, C. E. (1980) *Fin-de-siècle Vienna: Politics and Culture*. Knopf, New York.

19 Freud, S. (1962/1930) *Civilization and Its Discontents*. Trans. James Strachey. W. W. Norton, New York.

20 Freud, S. (1962/1923) *The Ego and the Id*, trans. James Strachey. W. W. Norton, New York. See also Rieff, P. (1959) *Freud: The Mind of the Moralist*. Viking, New York.

21 Keynes, J. M. (1920) *The Economic Consequences of the Peace*. Harcourt, Brace and Howe, New York.

22 Skidelsky, R. (1983) *John Maynard Keynes: Hopes Betrayed 1883–1920*. Macmillan, London, p. 384.

23 Keynes, J. M. (1936) *The General Theory of Employment, Interest, and Money*. Macmillan, London.

24 Note the subtitle of the second volume of Skidelsky's biography of Keynes: *John Maynard Keynes: The Economist as Savior 1920–1937*. Cf., Alexander, Market as Narrative and Character.

25 Sartre, J. P. (1956/1943) *Being and Nothingness*. Philosophical Library, New York.

26 Baert, P. (2015) *The Existentialist Moment: Sartre's Rise as a Public Intellectual*. Polity, Cambridge, UK.

27 Sartre, J. P. (2007/1945) *Existentialism as a Humanism*, trans. George J. Becker. Yale University Press, New Haven.

28 Sartre, J. P. (1995 [1948]) *Anti-Semite and Jew: An Exploration of the Etiology of Hate*, trans. George J. Becker. Schocken, New York.

29 Michels, R. (1962/1911) *Political Parties*, trans Eden Paul and Cedar Paul. Free Press, New York.

30 McLellan, D. (1979) *Marxism after Marx*. Macmillan, London; Apter, D. E. & Saich, T. (1994) *Revolutionary Discourse in Mao's Republic*. Harvard University Press, Cambridge, MA; Sun, F. (2013) *Social Suffering and Political Confession: Suku in Modern China*, Peking University Series on Sociology and Anthropology, vol. 1. World Scientific Publishing, Singapore; Alexander, J. C. (2017) Seizing the Stage: Social Performances from Mao Zedong to Martin Luther King, and Black Lives Matter Today. *TDR: The Drama Review*, 61(1).

31 Roazen, P. (1971) *Freud and his Followers*. Knopf, New York.

32 Skidelsky, *John Maynard Keynes: Hopes Betrayed 1883–1920*, p. 399.

33 Baert, *The Existentialist Moment*.

34 Davies, H. (1987) *Sartre and "Les Temps Modernes."* Cambridge University Press, Cambridge.

35 http://www.rawstory.com/2015/04/ayn-rands-philosophy-of-selfishness-has-a-deep-influence-on-the-mindset-of-the-right/. Accessed October 2, 2016.

36 Adams, C. (2011) Love and Power. *All Watched Over By Machines of Loving Grace*. BBC Production, United Kingdom.

37 Burns, J. (2009) *Goddess of the Market: Ayn Rand and the American Right*. Oxford University Press, New York, pp. 1–19.

38 http://capitalismmagazine.com/2002/08/franciscos-money-speech/. Accessed October 2, 2016.

39 In the wake of the extraordinary impact of her literary work, Rand made an effort to upgrade her ideas into an abstract philosophy she called Objectivism. The move contributed something to Rand's performative power, allowing her to place herself at the head of the pantheon of the great thinkers (see, e.g., https://www.youtube.com/watch?v=U6gV1MUSXMg; accessed November 14, 2016) and providing a glossy patina for her followers. Only a tiny handful of contemporary philosophers, however, regard the upgrading as an intellectual success. In my view, it was the fictional, not the philosophical version of her thinking that propelled Rand's dramatic impact.

40 https://docs.google.com/document/d/1x08QhNX_a1iB5Dt5uEC21q_GMvrM0sbd6zba2UOb6c0/edit. Accessed October 2, 2016.

41 Burns, *Goddess of the Market*, p. 214.

42 Burns, *Goddess of the Market*, p. 91.

43 http://www.workthesystem.com/getting-it/howard-roarks-courtroom-speech/. Accessed October 2, 2016.

44 "Greenspan's attraction to Rand was fairly standard for those drawn into her orbit ... Before meeting Rand, Greenspan was 'intellectually limited ... I was a talented technician, but that was all.' Under Rand's tutelage he began to look beyond a strictly empirical, numbers-based approach to economics, now thinking about 'human beings, their values, how they work, what they do and why they do it, and how they think and why they think' .... Rand pushed him ... to connect his economic ideas to the big questions in life." Burns (*Goddess of the Market*, p. 150) quotes here from Greenspan's 2007 memoir, *The Age of Turbulence: Adventures in a New World*. Penguin, New York.

45 Klatch, R. E. (1999) *A Generation Divided: The New Left, the New Right, and the 1960s*. University of California Press, Berkeley.

46 Dowd, M. (1987) Where Atlas Shrugged is Still Read – Forthrightly. *New York Times*, Week in Review, September 13.

47 https://ari.aynrand.org/blog/2015/04/21/ari-encourages-greater-educator-awareness-of-ayn-rands-ideas. Accessed October 2, 2016; cf., Weiss, G. (2012) *Ayn Rand Nation*. St. Martin's Press, New York, p. 17.

48 Heller, A. C. (2009) *Ayn Rand and the World She Made*. Doubleday, New York, p. 287.

49 Fanon, F. (2004/1961) *The Wretched of the Earth*, trans. Richard Philcox. Grove Press, New York, pp. 238–239.

50 Félix Guattari describes this movement in a way that illuminates its relevance for Fanon: "Its main characteristic is a determination never to isolate the study of mental illness from its social and institutional context, and, by the same token, to analyze institutions on the basis of interpreting the real, symbolic and imagery effects of society upon individuals" (Guattari, F. (1984) *Molecular Revolution: Psychiatry and Politics*, Penguin, Harmondsworth, p. 208).

51 "The Marxism of the early 1950s had nothing to say about the lived experience of the black man. Sartre and Merleau-Ponty were of much more use to Fanon" (Macey, D. (2012) *Frantz Fanon: A Biography*. 2nd ed. Verso, London).

52 The idea of creating a compound from a mixture suggests that, while providing background representations, none of these intellectual influences retained their original form in Fanon's later thought. For example, while Fanon's theory incorporated racial difference, as both independent cause and effect, he engaged in a fundamental critique of *négritude* for what he saw as its tendency to essentialize and romanticize blackness as more emotional and less rational, rather than asserting a fundamental universal humanity.

53 "Less than half of the material included in the book [*Wretched of the Earth*] was actually produced in 1961. The section on 'national culture' is an expanded version of the speech given by Fanon to *Presence africaine*'s Rome congress at Easter 1959. The final section on 'colonial war and mental illness' consists mainly of case-notes made in Blida and Tunis between 1954 and 1959, supplemented by a short essay which takes up and revises both Fanon's 1952 essay on 'The North-African syndrome' and his one brief contribution to *Consciences maghrébines* ... The notorious first chapter on violence first appeared as a long – fifty-page – article published in *Les Temps modernes* in May 1961" (Macey, *Frantz Fanon: A Biography*, pp. 8715–8730)

54 Macey, *Frantz Fanon: A Biography*, p. 373.

55 Hall, S. (1996) Interview with Stuart Hall. In I. Julien (ed.), *Frantz Fanon: Black Skin, White Masks*. Arts Council of England, UK.

56 Hall, Interview with Stuart Hall, p. 3245.

57 Zeilig, L. (2012) Pitfalls and radical mutations: Frantz Fanon's revolutionary life. *International Socialism*, 134.

58 King, R. (1992) *Civil Rights and the Idea of Freedom*. Oxford University Press, Oxford.

59 Sekyi-Otu, A. (1996) *Fanon's Dialectic of Experience*. Harvard University Press, Cambridge, MA, p. 236.

60 Fanon, F. (2008/1952) *Black Skin, White Masks*, trans. Richard Philcox. Grove Press, New York, p. 89.

61 Sartre, J. P. (2004/1963) Preface, in Fanon, *The Wretched of the Earth*, p. liv.

62 Fanon, *The Wretched of the Earth*, p. 2.

63 Quotes from Fanon, *The Wretched of the Earth*, p. 6.

64 Fanon, *The Wretched of the Earth*, p. 135.

65 Fanon, *The Wretched of the Earth*, p. 2.

66 Fanon, *The Wretched of the Earth*, p. 3.

67 Sorel, G. (1915/1908]) *Reflections on Violence*. George Allen and Unwin, London.

68 Sorel, *Reflections on Violence*, p. 50.

69 Fanon, *The Wretched of the Earth*, p. 51. Such a classical Aristotelian view points to the dramaturgical underpinnings of the psychoanalytic concept of catharsis upon which Fanon's theory of violence draws.

70 For *Les Temps modernes*, see the May 1961 publication of the draft of Fanon's critical chapter on violence (see n. 53, above) and, e.g., Maschino, M. (1960) *L'An V de la revolution algérienne* de Frantz Fanon. *Les Temps modernes*, February–March.

71 While the elements of performance are deeply implicated in materiality, the exchange between Sartre and his colleagues with Fanon was much more about gift-giving than utilitarian exchange. Fanon's writing had already affected the views Sartre and his colleagues developed about the anti-colonial struggle, which made them eager to put their networks and influence at Fanon's disposal, in turn. Simone de Beauvoir recounts the three-day long encounter she and Sartre had with Fanon in Rome five months before his death. Sartre and Fanon, she writes, talked virtually nonstop. When the three parted, de Beauvoir shook Fanon's hand, and she recalled "touching the passion that burned within him," averring "he could communicate that fire" (Macey, *Frantz Fanon: A Biography*, p. 8851)

72 Sartre, Preface, pp. xlvii, xlvi.

73 Sartre, Preface, pp xlvii–xlviii.

74 "There was ... the danger that the preface would overshadow the text itself, and many reviews made it do just that ... It was as though Sartre's preface were taking on a life of its own ... Sartre's preface was, after all, a major selling point" (Macey, *Frantz Fanon: A Biography*, pp. 8931, 8954, 8983).

75 Macey, *Frantz Fanon: A Biography*, p. 621.

76 Cleaver, K. (1997) Back to Africa: The Evolution of the International Section of the Black Panther Party (1969–1972). In C. Jones (ed.) *The Black Panther Party Reconsidered*. Black Classic Press, Baltimore, pp. 211–254, at p. 214.

77 Zolberg, A. & Zolberg, V. (1967) The Americanization of Frantz Fanon. *The Public Interest* 9(Fall), p. 50.

78 Seale, B. (1991/1970) *Seize the Time: The Story of the Black Panther Party and Huey P. Newton*. Black Classic Press, Baltimore, pp. 25–26.

79 Cleaver, E. (1969) *Post-Prison Writings and Speeches*. Random House, New York, p. 157.

80 Carmichael, S. (1967) Black Power and the Third World: Address to the Organization of Latin American Solidarity. The Third World Information Service, Thornhill, Ontario.

81 Forman, J. (1971) A Year of Resistance. In J. Gerassi (ed.), *Towards Revolution: Vol. II, The Americas*. Weidenfeld and Nicolson, London, pp. 700–703.

82 Rushdy, A. H. A. (1999) *Neo-slave Narratives: Studies in the Social Logic of a Literary Form*. Oxford University Press, New York, p. 46.
83 Kelley, R. D.G. and Esch, B. (2008) Black Like Mao: Red China and Black Revolution. In F. Ho & B. V. Mullen (eds.), *Afro-Asia: Revolutionary Political and Cultural Connections Between African-Americans and Asian-Americans*. Duke University Press, Durham.
84 Cleaver, *Post-Prison Writings and Speeches*, p. 214.
85 Forman, J. (1997/1972) *The Making of Black Revolutionaries*. University of Washington Press, p. 106.
86 Kauffman, M T. (1968) Stokely Carmichael, Rights Leader Who Coined 'Black Power,' Dies at 57. *New York Times*, November 16.
87 The interview appeared in the December 26 issue of the magazine *Révolution Africaine* (James, D. (2001/1969) *Che Guevara: A Biography*. Cooper Square Press, New York, p. 156).
88 See the section "Che reads *The Wretched of the Earth*," in Young, R. (2003) *Postcolonialism: A Very Short Introduction*. Oxford University Press, Oxford, pp. 121–122.
89 Löwy, M. (2007) *The Marxism of Che Guevara: Philosophy, Economics, Revolutionary Warfare*. Rowan & Littlefield, London, p. 73.
90 Macey, *Frantz Fanon: A Biography*, pp. 738, 773.
91 Bhabha, H. (2004) Foreword: Framing Fanon. In F. Fanon, *The Wretched of the Earth*. Grove Press, New York, pp. vii–xli, at p. xxix.
92 Austin, J. L. (1957) *How to Do Things with Words*. Harvard University Press, Cambridge, MA.

CHAPTER 5 SOCIAL THEORY AND THE THEATRICAL AVANT-GARDE

1 Wallace, D. F. (2009) *Infinite Jest*. Little, Brown, New York, pp. 1027–1028, n. 145.
2 Lehmann, H. (2006/1999) *Postdramatic Theatre*. Routledge, London; see also Lodge D. (2004) *Author, Author*. Viking, New York.
3 Quotes are from Lehmann, *Postdramatic Theatre*, pp. 76, 132–133, 69.
4 Lehmann, *Postdramatic Theatre*, pp. 134–135; cf. Muse, J. H. (2010) Flash mobs and the diffusion of the audience. *Theatre* 40(3), pp. 1–24.
5 Lehmann, *Postdramatic Theatre*, pp. 181–184.
6 For an elaboration of this postdramatic-spectacle perspective in contemporary aesthetic theory, see Kennedy D. (2009) *The Spectator and the Spectacle: Audiences in Modernity and Postmodernity*. Cambridge University Press, New York; for its elaboration in contemporary social theory, see Abercrombie, N. & Longhurst, B (1998) *Audiences: A Sociological Theory of Performance and Imagination*. Sage, London.
7 Alexander, J. C. (2011) *Performance and Power*. Polity, Cambridge, UK.
8 Brecht, B. (2000/1937) Alienation Effects in Chinese Acting. In D. Gerould (ed.), *Theatre/Theory/Theatre: The Major Critical Texts*. Applause Books, New York, pp. 453, 457.
9 Boal, A. (2000/1974) Theatre of the Oppressed. In Gerould, *Theatre/Theory/Theatre*, pp. 470, 471.
10 Artaud, A. (2000/1938) The Theatre and its Double. In Gerould, *Theatre/Theory/Theatre*, pp. 435, 433, 435.

11 Copeau, J. (1955/1923) *Notes sur le Métier de Comédien*. Michel Brient, Paris.
12 Auslander, P. (1997) *From Acting to Performance: Essays in Modernism and Postmodernism*. Routledge, London.
13 Grotowski, J. (2002/1968) *Towards a Poor Theatre*, ed. E. Barba. Routledge, New York, pp. 15–34.
14 Brook, P. (1968) *The Empty Space*. Atheneum, New York, p. 42.
15 Chaikin, J. (1972) *The Presence of the Actor*. Atheneum, New York.
16 Schechner, R. (2002/1982) *Performance Studies: An Introduction*. Routledge, New York.
17 Schechner, *Performance Studies*, p. 68, passim.
18 Phelan, P. (1993) *Unmarked: The Politics of Performance*. Routledge, New York; Auslander, *From Acting to Performance*.
19 Taylor, D. (2003) *The Archive and the Repertoire: Performing Cultural Memory in the Americas*. Duke University Press, Durham.
20 Roach, J. (2007) *It*. Ann Arbor, University of Michigan Press.
21 Dolan, J. (2005) *Utopia in Performance: Finding Hope at the Theatre*. Ann Arbor: University of Michigan Press, p. 8.
22 Worthen, W. B. (1995) Disciplines of the text/sites of performance. *The Drama Review* 39(1), pp. 13–28, at p. 14.
23 Cf. Alexander, J. C. and Mast (2006) Introduction: Symbolic Action in Theory and Practice: The Cultural Pragmatics of Symbolic Action. In J. C. Alexander, B. Giesen, & J. Mast (eds.), *Social Performances*. Cambridge University Press, New York.
24 In what became a contentiously public and disciplinary-defining dispute, leading performance study scholars responded with umbrage to Worthen's critique (Dolan, J. (1995) Responses to W. B. Worthen's "Disciplines of the Text/Sites of Performance." *The Drama Review* 39(1), pp. 28–35; Roach, J. (1995) Responses to W. B. Worthen's "Disciplines of the Text/Sites of Performance." *The Drama Review* 39(1), pp. 35–36; Schechner, R. (1995) Responses to W. B. Worthen's "Disciplines of the Text/Sites of Performance." *The Drama Review* 39(1), pp. 36–38). Worthen subsequently revised and softened his claims (Worthen, W.B. (1998) Drama, performativity, and performance. *PMLA* 113(5), pp. 1093–1107).
25 Alexander, *Performance and Power*.
26 Alexander, J. C. (2013) *The Dark Side of Modernity*. Polity, Cambridge, UK.
27 Williams, R. (1983) Drama in a Dramatized Society. In R. Williams (ed.) *Writing in Society*. Verso, London, pp. 13–18.
28 Aristotle (2000) The Poetics. In Gerould, *Theatre/Theory/Theatre*, p. 59.
29 In commenting upon Sophocles' Oedipus trilogy, Freud articulated the same fusion of textual figuration with audience in psychological terms: 'The poet is at the same time compelling us to recognize our inner minds, in which these same impulses though suppressed are to be found' (in Bennett, S. (1997) *Theatre Audiences: A Theory of Production and Reception*, 2nd ed. Routledge, London, p. 36).
30 Bennett, *Theatre Audiences*, p. 59.
31 Corneille, P. (2000/1660) Of the Three Unities of Action, Time, and Place. In Gerould, *Theatre/Theory/Theatre*.

32 Corneille, Of the Three Unities of Action, Time, and Place, p. 155–156.
33 Corneille, Of the Three Unities of Action, Time, and Place, pp. 156, 158.
34 Bennett, *Theatre Audiences*, pp. 3ff.
35 Bennett, *Theatre Audiences*, p. 3.
36 James, H. (1936/1889) *The Tragic Muse*. Scribner's, New York, pp. 66–67. David Lodge (*Author, Author*) and Colm Tóibín (*The Master*. Scribner's, New York, 2004) provide barely fictionalized reconstructions of the hopes and failures of this illustrative stage of James's writing career.
37 States, B. (1985) *Great Reckonings in Little Rooms: On the Phenomenology of Theatre*. University of California Press, Berkeley, p. 113.
38 Quoted in Bennett, *Theatre Audiences*, p. 4.
39 States, *Great Reckonings in Little Rooms*, p. 94, 104.
40 Boal, Theatre of the Oppressed, p. 471, 473.
41 Fish, S. (1980) *Is There a Text in This Class?* Harvard University Press, Cambridge, MA. Cf. Chaudhuri, U. (1984) The Spectator in Drama/Drama in the Spectator. *Modern Drama* XXVII (3), pp. 281–298.
42 Ridout, N. (2006) *Stage Fright, Animals, and Other Theatrical Problems*. Cambridge University Press, New York, p. 70.
43 Handke, P. (1971) *"Offending the Audience" and "Self-Accusation."* Methuen, London, pp. 15–16.
44 Rancière, J. (2009) *The Emancipated Spectator*. Verso, London, p. 13.
45 Diderot, D. (2000/1773–8) The Paradox of Acting. In Gerould, *Theatre/Theory/Theatre*, pp. 198, 201.
46 Craig, G. (2000/1907) The Actor and Ubermarionette. In Gerould, *Theatre/Theory/Theatre*, p. 394.
47 Hodge, A. (2000) Introduction. In A. Hodge (ed.) *Twentieth Century Actor Training*. Routledge, London.
48 Krasner, D. (2000) Strasberg, Adler and Meisner: Method Acting. In Hodge, *Twentieth Century Actor Training*.
49 Krasner, Strasberg, Adler and Meisner, p. 146.
50 Grotowski, *Towards a Poor Theatre*, p. 15ff.
51 Grotowski, *Towards a Poor Theatre*, p. 19.
52 Schechner, *Performance Studies*, pp. 249–250.
53 States, *Great Reckonings in Little Rooms*, pp. 125, 132.
54 Chaikin, *The Presence of the Actor*, p. 20.
55 Roach, *It*; Chaikin, *The Presence of the Actor*, p. 20.
56 Bennett, *Theatre Audiences*, p. 142.
57 Dort, B. (1982) The Liberated Performance. *Modern Drama* XXI (1), pp. 60–68, at 63–64.
58 Artaud, The Theatre and its Double, p. 442.
59 Kael, P. (1968) Orson Welles: There Ain't No Way. In P. Kael (ed.), *Kiss Kiss Bang Bang*. Little Brown, Boston, p. 196.
60 Dort, The Liberated Performance, pp. 63–64.
61 In Ridout, *Stage Fright, Animals, and Other Theatrical Problems*, p. 49.
62 Carlson, M. (1989) The Iconic Stage. *Journal of Dramatic Theory and Criticism*, 3(2), pp. 3–18, at p. 8.
63 Sofer, A. (2003) *The Stage Life of Props*. University of Michigan Press, Ann Arbor, p. 24.
64 States, *Great Reckonings in Little Rooms*, p. 20.

65 Alter, J. (1990) *A Sociosemiotic Theory of Theatre*. University of Pennsylvania Press, Philadelphia, p. 97.

66 Alexander, J. C. (2008) Iconic Experience in Art and Life: Surface/Depth Beginning with Giacometti's "Standing Woman." *Theory, Culture & Society* 25(5), pp. 1–19.

67 Sofer, *The Stage Life of Props*.

68 In States, *Great Reckonings in Little Rooms*, p. 20.

69 Bernstein, R. (2009) Dances with Things: Material Culture and the Performance of Race. *Social Text* 101(4), pp. 67–94, at p. 89.

70 Taylor, *The Archive and the Repertoire*, p. 28.

71 Strindberg, A. (2000/1888) Preface to *Miss Julie*. In Gerould, *Theatre/Theory/Theatre*, p. 371.

72 Bair, D. (1978) *Samuel Beckett: A Biography*. Harcourt, Brace, Jovanovich, New York.

73 Bazin, A. (1967) *What Is Cinema?* University of California Press, Berkeley.

74 Cf. Lash, S. (2010) *Intensive Culture: Social Theory, Religion, and Contemporary Capitalism*. Sage, London.

75 Baker, S. A. (2010) Imitating Art or Life: The Tragic Hero's Emergence on France's Postcolonial Stage. In K. Wilson (ed.), *Looking at Ourselves: Multiculturalism, Conflict & Belonging*. Inter-Disciplinary Press. Oxford University Press, Oxford.

76 For empirical cultural-sociological studies demonstrating the social dramatic in modern contexts, see Wagner-Pacifici, R. (1986) *The Moro Morality Play: Terrorism as Social Drama*. University of Chicago Press, Chicago; Berezin, M. (1997) *Making the Fascist Self: The Political Culture of Interwar Italy*. Cornell University Press, Ithaca; Edles, L. (1998) *Symbol and Ritual in the New Spain: The Transition to Democracy after Franco*. Cambridge University Press, New York; Cottle, S. (2004) *The Racist Murder of Stephen Lawrence: Media Performance and Public Transformation*. Praeger, London; Reed, I. (2007) Why Salem made Sense: Culture, Gender, and the Puritan Persecution of Witchcraft. *Cultural Sociology* 1(2), pp. 209–234; Smith, P. (2008) *Punishment and Culture*. University of Chicago Press, Chicago; McCormick, L. (2009) Higher, Faster, Louder: Representations of the International Music Competition. *Cultural Sociology* 3(1), pp. 5–30; Goodman, T. (2010) *Staging Solidarity: Truth and Reconciliation in the New South Africa*. Paradigm, Boulder; Eyerman, R. (2011) *The Cultural Sociology of Political Assassination: From MLK and RFK to Fortyn and van Gogh*. Palgrave, New York; Norton, M. (2011) A Structural Hermeneutics of "The O'Reilly Factor." *Theory and Society* 40(3), pp. 315–346; Gao, R. (2011) Revolutionary Trauma and Representation of the War: The Case of China in Mao's Era. In J. C. Alexander, E. Breese, & R. Eyerman (eds.), *Narrating Trauma*. Paradigm, Boulder; Mast, J. (2012) *The Performative Presidency: Crisis and Resurrection During the Clinton Years*. Cambridge University Press, New York; Tognato, C. (2012) *Central Bank Independence: Cultural Codes and Symbolic Performance*. Palgrave, New York; and Ringmar, E. (2013) *Liberal Barbarism and the European Destruction of the Summer Palace*. Palgrave, New York.

INDEX